Social Capital Modeling in Virtual Communities:
Bayesian Belief Network Approaches

Ben Kei Daniel
University of Saskatchewan, Canada

Information Science REFERENCE

INFORMATION SCIENCE REFERENCE

Hershey · New York

Director of Editorial Content:	Kristin Klinger
Senior Managing Editor:	Jamie Snavely
Managing Editor:	Jeff Ash
Assistant Managing Editor:	Carole Coulson
Cover Design:	Lisa Tosheff
Printed at:	Yurchak Printing Inc.

Published in the United States of America by
Information Science Reference (an imprint of IGI Global)
701 E. Chocolate Avenue,
Hershey PA 17033
Tel: 717-533-8845
Fax: 717-533-8661
E-mail: cust@igi-global.com
Web site: http://www.igi-global.com/reference

and in the United Kingdom by
Information Science Reference (an imprint of IGI Global)
3 Henrietta Street
Covent Garden
London WC2E 8LU
Tel: 44 20 7240 0856
Fax: 44 20 7379 0609
Web site: http://www.eurospanbookstore.com

Library of Congress Cataloging-in-Publication Data

Daniel, Ben Kei, 1971-
  Social capital modeling in virtual communities : Bayesian belief network approaches / by Ben Kei Daniel.

      p. cm.

  Includes bibliographical references and index.
  Summary: "In this book researchers have employed different approaches to examine and describe various types of relationships among people in communities by using social capital as a conceptual and theoretical tool" -- Provided by publisher.

  ISBN 978-1-60566-663-1 (hbk.) -- ISBN 978-1-60566-664-8 (ebook) 1. Social capital (Sociology) 2. Community development. 3. Technology--Social aspects. 4. Online social networks. I. Title.
  HM708.D36 2009
  302.30285--dc22
                              2008055724

British Cataloguing in Publication Data
A Cataloguing in Publication record for this book is available from the British Library.

All work contributed to this book is new, previously-unpublished material. The views expressed in this book are those of the authors, but not necessarily of the publisher.

Dedication

To mama Helena Ropi, mama Margaret Kiden, and to loving memory of my father Daniel Motidyang Lokuri-Soma. Respect, patience, persistence, strength, and the value of education and learning; I learned them all from you. You are the best parents and teachers! The journey was long but your patience and encouragement made it shorter! This is the result; this is dedicated to you and this is yours!

Table of Contents

Section I:
Theory and Application of Social Capital

Foreword

As you open this book you might question if this reading weighs against joining social talk. "Small talk" is usually easy-going and promises to lead you efficiently to what others already found out. Well, after reading this book, I can assure you that reading its content is worth your time and efforts. This book builds upon the long roads its author walked before, but also has the guts to write it down bluntly. Its underlying goal is to understand how social networks work both via direct and indirect routes through the presentation of social capital. Neither the connections, nor the social protocols nor decision rules are fixed in any community.

We know that social trust includes sentiments, seasonal affections and pragmatic needs; they all work in parallel in order to overcome fixation and blind corners. This book provides you with clear-cut answers as to why societies rest upon gossip, conspiracies and blind trust. Societal capital, even more than financial trust, rests upon a dynamic process of "induced reputation"; its actors serve as sources and are subject to induced criteria as well. Except in certain stages of Maslow's 'hierarchy of human needs', reputation and trust are not the end goals in themselves; but rather serve as social exchange currency necessary to enable us cope with deep doubts and risks. 'Social capital' can easily be treated as "trust"; it is not only the outcome; it is an input resource as well. This book makes the various and critical components of social capital fundamentally clear, more so than any other book has ever made.

The Bayesian mechanism presented in the book is a wise choice to cope with the capricious and chaotic nature of social structures in any forms of communities. The author makes it clear that there is typically not a priori rational for assuming one model to be more adequate than another. In this sense the Bayesian analysis method is congruent to the evolution itself: The observer embodies a part of the object domain itself. Understanding social capital is instrumental to effective analysis of social issues in virtual communities. For many years researchers and scientists, especially in the Social Sciences and the Humanities have established it without any doubt the power inherent in social relations and in establishing social capital as an important framework for understanding social issues in communities. Today, leveraging social issues to overcome many social and economic dilemmas in communities is becoming increasingly necessary.

For the most important question of the 21st century is not so much *what* you know; more decisive is *who* you know. Even one step further is the acceptance that expertise manifests *between* rather than *inside* persons. The increasing thrust towards Web 2.0 has lead to the emergency of important terms such as "social software", which in turn inspired the coinage of the term "social networking" and subsequently, brought us productive software (Facebook, MySpace, Youtube, LinkedIn etc.) These technologies allow robust and seamless ways of sharing content, engaging groups online and drastically increasing the presence of virtual communities. They strengthen and extend existing social network of trusted contacts to new terrains and enable people to social network with each other, helping them to discover inside connections in virtual communities.

However, the added value of virtual communities to the many faculties of our lives is still underestimated. Virtual (as opposed to local or geographical) communities are increasingly deployed for education, health, job training and creative activities. They are social systems and platforms aimed to go beyond information access and cooperation to more deeper, long lasting social relationships. Steadily the web-based or virtual communities for that matter touch the more delicate aspects of our lives such as existential reorientation, ambiance, mental support etc.

They even widen our apprehension of professionalism or identity. Ego's, temperament and altruism become more tangible and submissive to specialized virtual communities such as gaming and role play.

For the last decade many organizations have been practicing effective interactions and transactions through virtual communities in order to supplement day-to-day activities. Higher education started accepting virtuality and mobility making learning more dynamic and realistic. We may expect that no media attribute will be omitted from the learning arena; the only scruple is that we do not like to admit that our envisioning of learning has stayed far behind.

Learning in its feudal and industrial roles can no longer serve knowledge- and network societies. We may even soon arrive at the point that "learning" loses its exquisite position of 'ultimate survival'. Seen from an evolutionary point of view, the human mind has evolved in order to adapt; not so much to learn from the past. It may be clear that social assets like trust and commitment are much more essential than the typical intellectual values that we typically target in regular education. We may expect that virtual- and vicarious learning will play an essential role to make education reflect upon itself. The notion of 'social capital' may help in that process.

Both web-based and local communities aspire to reach maximum effects. For many years researchers tried to increase productivity in many fictitious situations with increasing degrees of successes and failures. A typical failure negating productivity in virtual communities is the absence of a robust analytical framework.

This book provides you with a robust analytical framework for analysing social capital in the context of virtual communities. The approach presented in the book is extensible to the understanding of other social systems. This is a 'must' for any organisation that lets people engage in virtual communities. The possibilities of using virtual communities with the increasing support of technologies such as Web 2.0 are endless, justifying why research into these communities has increased. This is the first book that provides a comprehensive analysis of social capital in geographical communities and extrapolating its approach towards virtual communities. The book also provides researchers, students, managers and co-workers to imagine the societal changes to come.

Part I of the book makes a thorough theoretical analysis and synthesis of social capital. Part II discusses various types of virtual communities together with the needed new technologies.

Its two sections are invaluable to researchers, students and practitioners interested in exploring the potential of social software and virtual communities for enhancing social engagement and community.

Part III gently confronts the reader with computational modelling and procedures for building a Bayesian Belief Network. It is a research tool for understanding complex social systems. This part of the book would be of interests to those who are interested in building complex and dynamic models. The most typical value of the book is its careful- and elegant presentation of the model of social capital and the procedures to validate it. You will find it in Part IV of this book.

Wishing you as a reader as well as the book's authors a productive role in the future now that social benchmarks are needed to supplant the harm of financial distrust of our modern times.

Piet Kommers
Professor, Chair of the Web-based Communities Conferences
Executive Editor of the International Journal of Web-based Communities

Piet Kommers *is associate professor at the University of Twente in the Netherlands, as well as adjunct professor in the Faculty of Computer Science at Joensuu University (Finland). Professor Kommers served as advisor to the Ministry of Education in Singapore and several UNESCO International Projects* *on Educational Technology. Currently, he lectures in the fields of media, technology, communication and education. Dr. Kommers' early research focused on conceptual representations for learning and exploration of virtual reality environments to support learning. He developed several techniques including cognitive style effects that could be derived back to differences in students' short term memory capacity. For more than twenty years, Professor Kommers has worked on various large-scale European research projects. He has organized numerous conferences, initiated new scientific journals covering a variety of areas on virtual presence, explorative learning environments and web-based communities. His work appears in many European and International Scientific Conferences, book chapters, and journal articles. In addition, he has published six books and was awarded as Honorary Doctorate by Capital Normal University in Beijing in 2000.*

Preface

Working together collectively as communities to address shared problems is necessary if individuals in societies need to quickly reach certain goals and attain specific outcomes. Communities are social systems intended to serve specific purposes. They serve as environments for discussing and tackling important issues in societies such as reduction of crime rates, the reduction of pollution, the eradication of poverty and diseases and housing problems, economic crisis and only to mention a few. In tackling any of these issues, communities are used as platforms for developing social mechanisms, encouraging the spirit of cooperation and collaboration among their populace and instilling and fostering a sense of community, within a geographical neighbourhood, to improve the quality of life.

Throughout history, communities have demonstrated various ways to help their members achieve immediate and long term goals. The most successful communities often foster cordial and collegial relationships among their members, by building awareness, establishing shared understandings, cultivating trusting relationships and encouraging members to follow a certain shared set of social protocols.

Dating back to the Stone Age, the notion of a community was limited to a particular geographical location and it was predominately characterized by collocation, co-presences and shared social and cultural values. It was also characterized by shared beliefs, norms and traditions. The Hunters and Gatherers communities typically served as a good example of one of the oldest forms of human communities. Hunters and Gatherers primarily used communities as protective shields and silos for survival—for gathering and sharing limited resources in what had been very harsh environmental conditions. Furthermore, the Hunters and Gatherers also used communities as military barricades for defence and for protecting their environments in order to maintain territorial integrity. Throughout the Palaeolithic time, humans used communities to socially and politically distinguish one group from another, one tribe from another, one band from another, one clan from another and so on.

The academic discourse on communities has a long tradition in sociological theory, reflected in the work of Durkheim, Marx, Weber and Tonnies among others. These early scholars were primarily concerned with the loss of place-based community and the weakening of the face-to-face relations of "Gemeinschaft"—or an association. However, the discourse around the decline of face-to-face communities and the growing sociological concerns about their implications to contemporary societies did not gain much traction until the beginning of the 1990s. This is when the idea of communities based on geography or place shifted dramatically to communities based on common interests formed among distributed groups supported by various kinds of online technologies.

Similar to their predecessors, modern communities are social systems, manifesting certain shared characteristics; but the ultimate nature of their goals might not be the same. For example, some communities are goals specific (e.g. communities based on preservation of language, culture or traditions) while others might not have clearly stated goals to achieve. More specifically, communities defining membership along professional lines (such as research communities) might not have collectively defined goals and their members might not necessary live in the same location, work in the same building, or share the same culture or language. But members in these kinds of communities might be collectively interested in advancing knowledge and science in their respective disciplines or areas of research. Communities with members sharing certain ethnic characteristics such as language, culture and systems of beliefs might not have clearly immediate stated goals to achieve, but members might still be strongly united by their tribal or nation bond.

The permeation of new technologies into mainstream societies facilitated new forms of communities that are not restricted to physical dimensions, but they are rather situated in virtual space. Perhaps the most profound success of the new technologies in facilitating communities online is their ability in fostering synchronous and asynchronous communication and their power to deliver information in various formats (videos, audios, text and graphic images).

Furthermore, the emergence of these new forms of communities (virtual communities) has not only challenged our thinking about the meaning and purposes of communities, but they also present new grounds for exploring new forms of social relationships online. Many researchers, scientists, practitioners, community architects, software developers, and educators are becoming increasingly aware of the fact that the health of any community is intimately connected to the way people relate to each other.

For more than two decades, researchers have employed different approaches to examine and describe various types of relationships among people in communities by using social capital as a conceptual and theoretical tool. Social capital, the stock of productive social relationships among people, lies at the heart of any community, and it is the most important mechanism for creating and maintaining useful and productive social ties, binding people together in communities.

BOOK MOTIVATION

Social capital is arguably the most critical theory to emerge in the Social Sciences and the Humanities in the last two decades. Social capital emphasizes the importance of social networks, communication, trusts, shared understanding, collective social protocols and the symbolic and immaterial exchanges of information and relationships that strengthen communities. This book represents a landmark consideration of the origin, diverse meanings, types, dimensions, components, measurements methods, sources, and positive and negative consequences of social capital, with a particular emphasis on how to model social capital within virtual communities. Informed by past and ongoing research, social capital in virtual communities is an evolving concept, one that includes constructs such as social networks, trust, various forms of awareness, engagement, shared understanding, and social protocols. In many writings, the fundamental message social capital attempts to convey is that some value can be derived from productive social relationships and that the extent to which people are embedded within social networks and communities can help to enhance their lives.

Most of the ideas presented in this book are based on a decade of research into social capital and virtual communities. The guiding philosophy motivating this work is founded on the belief that social capital holds a great potential for understanding social and technological development in virtual communities. It is a glue that keeps people together in communities, creating a stronger zeal for building a healthier, more tolerant communities built on respect of individual differences, valuing and recognising individual achievements and celebrating diversity and community success. Among other benefits, social capital enables people to collaborate and learn from each other in a collegial community spirit.

Furthermore, in a society with much information overload, social capital serves as a pipeline for channelling useful information and as a filter for processing and transmitting information and knowledge to community members. Widely applied in many areas of research, social capital helps to ease transaction costs in business by encouraging a trusting environment, loosening communication surfeit and speeding the flow of information within a community. In education, social capital enables students to collaborate with each other, teachers to work together with communities and effective parental involvement in school affairs. Furthermore, a plethora of research has demonstrated that communities with a high stock of capital are healthier, have lower crime rates and the people within these communities tend to be more respectful of each other. Within the civic discourse, when people are actively involved in community activities, they are more likely to participate in voting, become involved in community peace corps and volunteer in most important community projects.

Furthermore, one of the globally growing issues that perhaps had some negative impact on the rate development on a global scale is the gap between those who possess technology skills and those who do not. This is known as the "digital divide" and the "digital dividend". For many years, international organisations such as the Organisation for Economic Co-operation and Development (OECD) and the World Bank have explored ways of bridging the divide. In communities with high social capital, when people work and learn together the "digital divide" and the "digital dividend" can be increasingly reduced; the more people exchange information among themselves and support each other as a community, the better they can build from each other's strengths.

These few instances of the benefits of social capital demonstrate the growing attraction to the theory in addressing critical problems in communities. This book aims at exploring the underlying mechanics of social capital in order to accurately understand the theory and to better extend it to virtual communities. While it is too soon to conclude that social capital is an accurate analytical "paradigm" for addressing social issues in virtual communities, it is fair to suggest that social capital provides a potential framework, that once properly defined can help us accurately analyse and improve the quality of life in virtual communities.

ABOUT THIS BOOK

James Kouzes, Chairman Emeritus of the Tom Peters Company, Business 2.0 in September 2000 stated that, "the new currency won't be intellectual capital. It will be social capital - the collective value of whom we know and what we'll do for each other". He pointed out that when social connections are strong and numerous, there is more trust, reciprocity, information flow, collective action, happiness and greater wealth.

The main purpose of this book is to bring to the table a discussion on "the new currency", to introduce social capital theory as a way to think about social issues that are critical to effective social engagement, social networking, knowledge sharing and community building in virtual communities. The book aims at engaging scientists and practitioners from diverse disciplines, to explore the potential of social capital in virtual communities. The insights presented in the book are essentially interdisciplinary, drawing from applied Artificial Intelligence, Human Computer Interaction, Educational Technology, and the disciplines of Economics and Sociology, thus, providing a broader perspective on the issues addressed. The book is founded on research and offers an original solution to the problem of refining the concept of social capital in order to utilize it in the examination of social issues in virtual communities by constructing a formal Bayesian Belief Network model.

WHY A BOOK ON SOCIAL CAPITAL IN VIRTUAL COMMUNITIES?

Why not open up a dialogue on social capital in virtual communities? There are essentially many reasons to write this book at this time. Some of these reasons are highlighted in the following paragraphs. First of all, this is the first complete and comprehensive book solely devoted to analysis of social capital in virtual communities. Beginning with the context of the analysis of the issues presented in the book, virtual communities are becoming increasingly accepted and useful social structures in modern societies.

They are especially popular in the areas of Business and Education. Business organisations deploy many virtual communities to offer support to their customers for them to be able to discuss product issues. In July 2008, researchers at Deloitte carried out a study of more than 100 businesses ("Tribalization of Communities") to investigate the state-of-the art and the business purpose of virtual communities in these organisations. They found that businesses tend to support virtual communities to enable members to connect with likeminded people and to help others in the community.

With the permeation of technological dimensions into social interactions, Web technologies are increasingly empowering customers with powerful platforms, providing them with a collective voice for evaluating products and making recommendations to others interested in the same products. For example, Amazon effectively utilizes Web 2.0 technologies to provide to its virtual communities of users a platform for product reviews and recommendations of products for other customers.

Furthermore, businesses are now adopting various Web technologies as part of a broader business practice to forge tighter relationships with customers and suppliers and engage employees more successfully. In addition, now not only are they using more technologies, they are leveraging them to change management practices and organizational structures.

Second, businesses have also begun to use virtual communities to engage with customers and employees for brand discussions, idea generation, and product development and innovation. They are not only being used to solicit product development ideas but they also serve as an early warning system for product issues. The added value of virtual communities to business then is beyond doubt.

Third, in academia, researchers are not only able to easily keep up to date in their respective fields but they are also able to share important data through virtual communities. For example, allowing for synchronous or asynchronous collaboration, virtual communities can increase the awareness of the value of research, share visions of excellence and build the culture of science among researchers in different disciplines.

Looking at the exponential growth of virtual communities and their immediate application to many areas, it became clear that a book on social capital in virtual communities was not only desirable, but also necessary. Extending social capital to the analysis of virtual communities helps us to understand the nature of social and knowledge networking and networks and how social capital informs our understanding of information flows among members.

Fourth, the literature to date on social capital and virtual communities is partial and can be found in collections of book chapters, journal articles and conference papers. It is time for a complete and hopefully a useful book on the topic to assist those interested in exploring social issues in these communities. Bringing together volumes of information regarding social issues in virtual communities in one comprehensive volume, this book is also one of the few that provides a complete and comprehensive introduction to two major types of virtual communities in education and business (distributed communities of practice and virtual learning communities) in which the context of discuss of social capital is situated in the book.

Finally, while social capital is a growing research area, with fascinating contradictions and ambiguities, there is no precise scientific definition of it. This poses many challenges for extending the concept to virtual communities. The challenges are: (1) the existence of many surrounding components, each of which operates variably in relation to other components. (2) Each of the various components which constitute social capital influences the level of social capital differently depending on the type of the community. (3) Identifying the key components constituting social capital and factoring in those more influential components is critical to our understanding of how to improve virtual communities. However, it might not be possible to accurately understand the various constituents of social capital in virtual communities using traditional Social Science scientific methods, some which are already under substantial criticism.

THE APPROACH TAKEN IN THIS BOOK

This book broadly examines what constitutes social capital in place-based (geographical) communities and extends this understanding to virtual communities, providing an in-depth description of the nature of social capital in virtual communities. This book begins with a description of social capital, followed by delineation of its fundamental components in place-based communities. Components unique to virtual communities are then identified. These discussions serve as a basis for the construction of a Bayesian Belief Network model of social capital. Described in detail is the procedure for modelling social capital as well as the processes involved in validating the procedure.

BOOK AUDIENCE

Primarily intended for advanced undergraduate and graduate courses on virtual communities and social capital, this book will be useful to applied computer science or educational technology programs. However, since virtual communities and social capital are research issues gaining traction across disciplinary borders, the Social Sciences and the Humanities might find some materials relevant. The materials in the book are primarily targeted at university/college professors, graduate students and Educational Technologists; researchers in the areas of Human Computer-Interaction, Social Media and Applied artificial Intelligence.

The Bayesian Belief computational modelling approach presented will primarily appeal to those interested in Bayesian and modelling computational techniques to analyse and model complex social systems. The chapters on social capital and virtual communities will appeal to those interested in social capital in place-based and virtual communities.

ORGANIZATION OF THE BOOK

Due to the diversity, breadth and depth of debate on the theory of social capital, the book is divided into four sections. Section I is concerned with theoretical analysis of social capital in place-based/conventional communities. There are five chapters in Section I. The chapters are intended to provide the reader with a broad outlook of the theory, debate, and classical work on social capital. The section does not pretend to cover all the research done on social capital, a goal which is impossible to achieve given the rising popularity of the theory and the vast amount of research conducted and situated in many applied sciences. Instead, this section covers the most important work on the theory leading to the motivation to extend the debate to virtual communities.

Section II provides a detailed description of virtual communities, focusing mainly on two types of virtual communities; virtual learning communities and distributed communities of practice. Work on these two types of virtual communities is drawn from prior research. The section also discusses more recent technologies currently used to support virtual communities. Overall, there are three chapters in this section, all of which are intended to provide the reader with context in which the discussion on social capital in virtual communities is situated. The section also aims at familiarising the reader with more cutting edge social software supporting virtual communities. The section also presents emerging areas in knowledge management where social capital has many underexplored opportunities.

Having understood the theory behind social capital and all debate on what it is, in addition to gaining more knowledge on the context in which social capital is discussed in the book, Section III delves into basic mechanics of Bayesian belief networks and establishes a foundation for building computational models. This section is particularly critical to those readers who are interested in understanding Bayesian belief networks and basic knowledge of modelling. Three chapters are covered in this section. It is assumed that chapters presented in this section prepare the reader to understanding materials presented in Section IV.

Section IV covers materials that constitute the main theme of the book; computational modelling of social capital in virtual communities. This final section of book presents the ideas, procedures and techniques used for building a model of social capital. The sections also include discussions on processes involved in conducting sensitivity analysis and model validation. This section also concludes the book and it includes discussion on some of the implications of the theory of social capital in virtual communities.

Acknowledgment

I am grateful to many people for making this project possible. I would like to thank Dr. Richard Schwier, Dr. Gordon McCalla, and Dr. Jim Greer who have positively influenced my scholarly interdisciplinary ideas. I am also indebted to Dr. Martin Mulder for inspiring my research career. Special recognition goes to my friend and colleague Dr. Diego Zapata-Rivera for tremendously stimulating discussions and collaboration on early work on Bayesian Belief Network. My involvement with the International Centre for Governance and International Development at the University of Saskatchewan under the mentorship of the Dr. Asit Sarkar helped in stretching my views on community technologies to new frontiers of Social Sciences and the Humanities especially within international development. Most of the ideas are presented in this book. I would also like to thank Dr. Piet Kommers for honestly undertaking the task of writing the foreword of the book.

Further, I would like to thank the two anonymous reviewers for taking their valuable time to review the book and provided me with honest and highly valuable feedback. Special thanks also go to IGI Global publishing team, whose contributions throughout the whole publication process. In particular, I am deeply indebted to Julia Mosemann who continuously provided support via e-mail and kept the project on schedule, but most importantly for her catalytic and facilitative role from the inception of the book to the finished product that you are now holding in your hands. Thanks to Jennifer Weston for helping with the enormous task of marketing the book, and to Jamie Snavely for editorial help. I also appreciate Nova Spivak of radarnetworks.com for giving me the permission to use the progress graph of versioning of the Web technologies in the book.

I was quite fortunate to be able to lecture on a few courses while writing this book. I am greatly indebted to Dr. Veronika Makarova, Dr. Richard Julian and Dr. Leonard Proctor for offering me the opportunities to lecture in their undergraduate programs. Special recognition goes to Dr. Beth Horsburgh, Dawn Sinclair, Donna

Mitchell and all of my colleagues in the Office of the Associate Vice President Research-Health (University of Saskatchewan)/Vice President Research and Innovation (Saskatoon Health Region).

I would like to thank my late father Daniel Motidyang Lo-Kuri Soma as well as Mama Helena Ropi and Mama Margret Kiden for being the cornerstone of my education. I am grateful to all my brothers and sisters for their love and support throughout the years. Special thanks to Alakai Joseph Sekwat, Roda Kade Daniel, Cecilia Muja Daniel, Dr. Stanley Mogga Josephson and James Wani-Kana for immeasurable support during my early years of college. Additionally, I would like to express my heartfelt gratitude to Mr. and Mrs Louis and Claudette Lavergne and their family; Anne Lavergne, Denis Lavergne and Thomas Lavergne for their constant support and encouragement. I am also grateful to my gorgeous girlfriend Michelle Lavergne not only for her unconditional love, patience and support, but also for editing the first draft of the book. And finally, thanks to those silent contributors, you know where you are to you know who you are.

Sincerely,

Ben K. Daniel

Section I
Theory and Application of Social Capital

As social capital has entered discourse in many disciplines, alternative definitions have been proposed. Social sciences and humanities research has sought to define and empirically investigate social capital in a number of different ways. At best, current definitions of the concept can be generally categorised into two analytical levels: macro and micro. On the macro level, social capital is treated as the institutions, relationships, and norms that shape the quality and quantity of social interactions. On the micro level, social capital is a set of connections among individuals—social networks and norms of reciprocity and trustworthiness that arise from such ties.

There is a great deal of work written on the theory of social capital. Much of this work has generated more controversy than consensus and ranges from conceptualisation, i.e., what is it, what are its variables and dimensions, its operationalisation and measurement issues. A considerable body of literature has also been devoted to differences and similarities of social capital to classic economic forms of capital.

Section I, divided into five chapters, provides a conceptual and theoretical background to the theory of social capital as well as the logic of extending this theory to virtual communities. The theory of social capital is introduced in Chapter I. Chapter I also explores the theoretical development of the notion of community. Chapter II synthesizes and presents various conceptualisations of social capital, identifying key shared variables underlying all definitions which then are compared to other forms of capital. Examples of applications of social capital can be found in Chapter III. These applications include in education, technology, business, international development, public health, the digital divide and e-commerce.

Chapter IV elucidates approaches used for measuring social capital as well as challenges associated with these approaches. The approaches include qualitative, social network analysis, content analysis and quantitative approaches. Also discussed are indicators and sources of social capital. A detailed discussion of trust, both its types and sources, as a key proxy for measuring social capital and the limitations involved is provided in Chapter V.

Chapter I
The Roots of Communities and Social Capital

INTRODUCTION

Communities are important social systems accountable for sustainability and continuity of humanity. They provide a variety of support to their members, ranging from physical to emotional. Communities also enable individual to gain collective and meaningful personal influence on decisions affecting their lives. Decisions may be made regarding education, health care and economy. Communities naturally blossom when members work together to advance collective goals. There is no shortage of scientific literature on various ways in which communities emerge or developed and the purposes and roles they play in modern societies.

Fundamentally, communities evolve when people identify with each other; grow a shared sense of identity, shared culture, language, folklore and professional practices. Communities also develop when members identify with each other, build collective conscience and identify common goals—the village council, for example can work to fight crimes and social injustice. In other instances, communities evolve when members are interested in the same activities such as gardening, sports or music. There are also occasions, where natural or human disasters occur, people might come together to support each other and collectively repair any damage made to their lives.

Though communities are to all intents and purposes immutable social system, they are not just empty social boxes waiting for people to populate. They are abstract social systems, where groups of people create shared identities, values, norms, and beliefs to systematically regulate their own behaviours. Equally, communities are not physical things that can be visibly grown, but rather entities that existed before their current members joined and likely will continue long after they are gone, as new members will have joined. Communities can pave ways for unprecedented synergies and strategic alliances as seen in many business and social organisations today. Communities created along this line serve a complex intertwined web of healthy and mutually supportive relationships among its members.

Since, communities are abstract social systems, the way they emerge, develop, change, and revitalises themselves, serving as focal interests to some individuals but remains mystery to many researchers. It is for this reason social capital is often used as an explanatory paradigm for the inner workings of communities. The theory of social capital attempts to provide us with appropriate lens to examine the complexities of communities, especially how people build relationships in them.

This chapter provides an overview of what constitutes a community. It provides some background context to the theory of social capital. More specifically, this chapter reviews social capital within place-based communities and the logic for extending it to virtual communities. The chapter also outlines the goals of this book, its intended audience, and the utility derive from a model of social capital.

EARLY WORK ON THE CONCEPT OF COMMUNITY

The concept of community has been a major concern of Sociological research since the beginning of the discipline (Wellman, 1982; Ferlander, 2003). The concept started mainly as one way of expressing anxiety about the social effects of industrialisation (Nisbet, 1962) and was distinguished from other social systems such as society. Early work on the distinction of community from society can be found in the social scientific work by Ferdinand Tonnies in the 1920s. Tonnies' distinction between Gemeinschaft (community) and Gesellschaft became the baseline for later discussions regarding the semantics and pragmatics of community.

Tönnies discussion on the distinction between community and society in a context of reflecting on different forms of grouping, particularly those capable of distinguishing between pre-industrial society and society developed after the 18th century and most particularly from 19th century onwards. For Tonnies, Gemeinschaft refers to the closeness of holistic social relationships. Gemeinschaft exists by the subjective will of the members which affirms conditions of mutual dependence among them (Tonnies, 1925). Communities organised around ethnicity, language and culture or those communities with membership based on ascribed status are examples of Gemeinschaft communities.

Gesellschaft on the other hand are more instrumental types of relationships typical of industrial society and are based on common traits and/or activities. Communities organised around work, musical endeavours or those communities with membership based on achieved status are examples of Gesellschaft. They are Gesellschaft because of some common external characteristic. Analysis of the notion of a community along these lines implies that a community signifies a form of grouping based on proximity, shared experiences and ways of living. Similarly, communities regarded as Gesellschaft draw its membership based on achieved status rather than ascribed.

Scholarly work of founding Sociologists such as Emile Durkheim and Max Weber covered significant theoretical discourse on the notion of a community. For Durkheim, a traditional community was a small, clan-based homogeneous agrarian settlement held together by mechanical solidarity. Mechanical solidarity referred to the simple social bonds that emerged from common traditions, beliefs, skills and activities that resulted from, in-group similarity of traditions, beliefs, skills, and activities; and between group dissimilarities.

Further, strong communities are more evident in small villages where everyone walks, talks, exchanges goods in a local economy freely. Durkheim described these types of communities as "collective conscience", implying that the interests of the individual and the group are aligned and merged through shared representations and a united moral vision. The collective conscience reflected in the work of Durkheim is pillars in the creation of relations among individuals. Durkheim's description of community membership through his concept of collective scruples is still relevant today, if we consider communities built around tribal, ethnic or racial communities in big cities in our modern states.

Max Weber, another influential Sociologist suggested that we examine the meaning of communities and their overarching purposes rather than studying their structural properties alone. This will involve analysing ideas, especially the understanding of what constitutes a community, and the role of change for the meaning of community. Weber used the concept of "Verstehen" to discuss the meaning of community symbols, artefacts and their underlying meaning for social relationships. Further, according to Weber, every community is uniquely determined by its cultural orientation, underlying social values and the importance members attach to collective social bonds. He contested that every community has symbols which represent certain objects that have unique meaning to its members. Understanding the unique meaning of these symbols is therefore critical to understanding a particular community.

The notion of community is also discussed in political theory. Andersen (1991) in his seminal work on nationalism used the concept of a community to describe democracy. He argued that nations are imagined communities because members (e.g. citizens of a country) will never know all of their fellow-members yet in the minds of each member lives the image of their communion. He further noted that a nation can be regarded as a 'community' because, regardless of actual inequities, whether it is sociological and/or technological, the nation is always conceived as a deep, horizontal comradeship' (1991, p.7).

Within the political conceptual parameters of the concept of a community, imagined community helps individuals to feel a strong sense of community with people whom they have not met (Kanno & Norton, 2003). Instances of an imagined community are noticeable in contemporary societies. For example, it is not unusual for people to identify themselves with their nationalities in the company of foreigners. For instance, a Canadian is more likely to present himself or herself as "I am Canadian" to non-Canadians and not to other Canadians because the feeling of "Canadianism" is inherently assumed in every Canadian—an imagined sense of a national community, one which is more than inculcated into the political culture but into the social configuration of system of cultural beliefs. That feeling of being Canadian inside the individual can be attributed to a sense of achievement, pride in national political culture and thus a sense of an imaginary community. Although such a feeling is embedded in the innermost feelings of most Canadians it might not be obvious to outsiders or people who are not Canadian and have no idea what it is to identify with Canada.

MODERN MEANING OF A COMMUNITY

In academia, discourse on the tone of community has taken many different connotations so much so that some scholars have argued variation in meaning has rendered the term almost meaningless (Hillery, 1955). In the early 70s Bell and Newby (1973) observed that: "the concept of community has been the concern of Sociologists for more than two hundred years, yet a satisfactory definition of it, at least in Sociological terms appears as remote as ever" (p. 21). Poplin (1972) further observed that the fact that the term community can be used in several and yet different ways diminishes its usefulness for purposes of scientific communication and theory building.

But what is a community? Originating from two Latin words, the term community means "with gifts," implying a general sense of altruism, reciprocity, and beneficence, directly resulting from people working together as a group. Etzioni (1993) defined the term community as a web of affect-laden relationships among a group of individuals. Relationships criss-cross and reinforce one another (as compared to one-on-one or chainlike individual relationships). This characterization of a community suggests two dimensions, the first one entails that any community is committed to a set of shared values, norms, and meanings, through a shared history, and the second dimension rests on the expectation that a community has an identity, operating within a particular cultural setting.

In a study of what constitutes community among people of different social and ethnic backgrounds, MacQueen, McLellan, Metzger, Kegeles, Straus, Scotti, Blanchard & Trotter (2001) found out that most people define a community as a group of people with diverse characteristics who are linked by social ties, shared common perspectives, and who are willing to engage in joint action. Thus a sense of a place, something that could be located and described was considered to be an important characteristic of a community.

For the sake of conceptual precision in this book, a community is broadly regarded as a social system that includes almost any gathering of people within certain physical or virtual parameters. Along this spectrum, a community may refer to a group of people who feel a close connection or belonging to a specific group. Community may also refer to a group who have common values and/or a common general geographic location or interests. However, this conceptualisation also includes individuals who share characteristics, regardless of their location or type of interaction.

Community is further distinguished from the concept "communitas". In communitas, members strictly adhere to group norms and are expected to forgo their own will in favour of a group, in which he/she belongs. Typical examples of communitas are closely tied groups that are willing to sacrifice their lives for a belief system (e.g. members of certain religious cult and social doctrines). Communitas are important Sociological and Theological social entities. Where members share a feeling of great social equality; solidarity and togetherness and building a strong fortified boundary from other social groups or systems that manifest opposing values or norms. Members of communitas often consider themselves internally more cohesive from members of a community. They find ways in which they act together and protect themselves from an external threat or simply "the common enemy". In strict doctrines of communitas, no one is intentionally marginalized; decisions are meant to equally benefit all. Anthropologically, speaking communitas suggests a transitional phase of the development of communities (mechanical solidarity) enabling themselves to find unique solutions for living together and preserve the shared common values and norms which are strongly conservative, unalterable and unchallenged.

Further, the notion of communitas underpins Emile Durkheim's work on suicide. For Durkheim, people have a certain level of attachment to their communities through social integration Durkheim regarded altruistic suicide[1] as the result of too much social integration of individuals into community structure. In his view people were willing to self sacrifice when they lose sight of their individuality in favour of group or their community interests. An example of altruistic suicide would be members of the military who are willing to sacrifice their lives in order to conform to military ethical codes of law (fear of court martially resulting humiliation from peers or simple act of bravery). Other examples would be people with religious beliefs that oppose medical procedures (e.g. blood donation or transfusion) and the act of caring for sick member of a family, even when it is a burden, or accepting care from family members even when it is hard on the family.

Despite differences in conceptualisation of communities, it is reasonable to state that all communities have shared characteristics including; well defined boundaries with easily identifiable members, implicitly or explicit social protocols, shared sense of identity, language and artefacts, and a life span be it determinant or indeterminate (Becker & Mark, 1999). Though communities may be similar in size and density, they can vary widely not only in terms of their social configurations but also in terms of member familiarity with other members. For example members of one community can live within a certain physical area, and know each other well enough, while in other communities, members may simply self identify themselves with the name of the community, not knowing other members of that community.

Depending on the terms of membership, communities can show different patterns and rates of growth. Communities also vary structurally with some having more hierarchical, rigid lines of power and interaction whilst others are more horizontal and fluid. For example, the more people come together the more they find other ways that they are linked. That is, when a person first comes to a community they are drawn by common interest of the community. As they interact with other in-dividuals, they find similarities with people in the community and create a deeper sense of belonging and thus the community grows.

SOCIAL CAPITAL AND COMMUNITY CONNECTIVITY

Communities generally exist to look after the wellbeing of their members through the pursuit of collective goals. Some communities, however, are more successful in helping their members in achieving collective goals more than others. Why are some communities more successful in achieving collective goals than others? This book seeks to address this major question by using social capital to understand relationships among community members and how that can ultimately influence the performance of communities.

To better understand the performance of any community, it is critical to realize that any community is based on the relationships that form among its members. The theory of social capital purports that productive resources necessary for community success do not only reside in physical or economic capital but also in social relations among people (Coleman 1988). In other words, social capital suggests that a community with people who developed strong social relationships among themselves can accomplish much more than a community with poor social relationships, even if they have abundant human, physical and financial resources available.

For many years, the theory of social capital has been central for investigating different communities' performances. Research has shown that social capital helps communities reduce crime rates, help children achieve high educational scores, help people to access and acquire important technological skills, help to increase information literacy and provide better public awareness on issues of community concern. Further, an important aspect of social capital for Social Scientists is that it enables people to build communities, commit themselves to each other, feel a greater sense of belonging, and knit a particular social fabric. Social capital operates on different levels but some its outcomes are evident in many aspects of day to day activities. For example, in a well-connected community with dense social networks, social capital can be seen in a group of neighbours when they informally keep an eye on each other's homes or when survivors of breast cancer come together to form awareness and support themselves. Social capital can also be seen in those groups such as soccer teams, football leagues, bowling leagues and a group of computer programmers willing to share source codes with each other.

THE ORIGIN OF THE NOTION OF SOCIAL CAPITAL

Though the notion of social capital gained popularity in the twenty century, the idea is neither new nor original. In fact, analysis of the literature revealed elements of the theory of social capital dated back to the work of Karl Marx (1818–1883), Max Weber (1864–1920) and Emile Durkheim (1858–1917). A great deal of work in Sociology suggests that Durkheim's work on anomie and social cohesion and Marx's writings on the concept of Class, were some of the precursors of the contemporary social capital (Portes 1998). More specifically, Durkheim's emphasis on group life as an antidote to anomie and self-destruction and Marx's distinction between an atomized "class-in-itself" and a mobilized and effective "class-for-itself" are some of the prime examples of classical intellectual discourse predating social capital.

However, in Sociological theory, a number of social theoreticians seem to legitimatized that the first formalisation of social capital goes back to the work of Hannifin (1916; 1920), who invoked the concept to explain the importance of community participation in enhancing school performance. Others maintained that after Hannifan's work, the idea of social capital disappeared from the Social Sciences debate, surfacing occasionally, but without arousing any particular interest. There are also reports suggesting that Scientists such as the French Sociologist

Pierre Bourdieu (1986) followed the Marxist conception of social capital and more recent American Scholars such as Etzioni (1993) and Putnam (1993) followed the communitarian tradition in explanation of social capital.

Conceivably, social capital was brought once again to spotlight by a team of Canadian Urban Sociologists (Seely, Sim & Loosely, 1956) who used it to describe culture in urban communities (Homans, 1961). Later Jacobs (1965) writings on social capital helped increased the exposure of the concept and rejuvenated its intellectual discourse among many Social Scientists, who subsequently used it in various contexts, primarily to describe trust, shared understanding, reciprocal relationships, social network structures, common norms and cooperation, and the roles these entities play in various aspects of many geographical communities.

In her work, Jacobs (1965) highlighted the central importance of networks of strong personal relationships that develop over a period of time, adding another interesting dimension to the application of social capital in examining social relationships. Relationship embedded within social capital, Jacobs indicated provided a basis for building trust, cooperation, and collective action in communities and groups. Jacobs (1971) later used "social capital" as a metaphor in describing communities' ability to organize themselves into self-governing social entities to overcome political problems. Six years later, this was followed (Loury, 1977), who used social capital to explore interactions in relation to income distribution. Perhaps what is more perplexing is that none of these scholars cited earlier work on the subject, but all used the same umbrella term to encapsulate the vitality and significance of community ties—social capital.

The historical development of social capital is mundane and inaccurate; however, this is less of a concern in the book, instead the focus is geared towards understanding the contributions of various earlier writers to the development of the theory of social capital on one hand and what actually constitutes our basic understanding of social capital. The most notable contribution to theory of social capital in the twenty century was made by Robert Putnam, who helped in philosophical and scientific exposition of the theory, provoking more intellectual discourse around the basic elements of the theory and extensive exploitation in many domains. Putnam used social capital theory to explain failure in civic engagement in Italy in the 1990s. He argued that in Italy the level of social capital determined the quality of civic life in the cultivation of democratic society. After his work in Italy, Putnam turned his attention to the analysis of social capital in the United States of America, which he believed was declining. He attributed the decline in social capita to lack of civic engagement and public trust in American political culture.

Throughout his analysis, Putnam maintains coherent views that social capital is more than a stock of capital but rather as a theoretical analytical tool capable to be used to explain why certain communities and groups are performing better than others. In other words, the presence of social capital in any community enables people to socially connect to each other, to work together, to achieve things they would not achieve alone, share important information and knowledge overtime and develop trusting relationship among themselves, which are all important in the determining of how well they work together to benefit individuals and the whole community.

Since Putnam's seminal work on social capital, numerous researchers, from different disciplines used the theory to explain community engagement in different contexts. Due to its conglomerate and perplexing nature, coupled with a general appeal and ability to describe operational activities in communities, researchers used the theory often broadly a tool to analyse vital issues pertinent to effective community functioning and sustainability. In spite of its growing popularity, social capital remains a tenuous theory and mostly limited to describing social issues in geographical communities. Furthermore, to date, most of the approaches taken for measuring social capital are problematic and to some extent unrealistic—creating validity and misinterpretation issues. Further secondary data often used in the analysis of social capital are often developed for different purposes and re-using them might have been significantly reduced in meaning and scope resulting to misleading interpretations of what constitutes social capital.

The introduction of the Internet as a socially engaging medium, especially during the second wave of the World Wide Web tools marked an interesting period in the transformation of the way people form communities and how they relate to each other. This period was marked by the proliferation of various social networks and online groups. It then became necessary to extend the analysis of social capital to virtual communities, to guide our thinking about how people interact, relate to each other and share information and knowledge in virtual communities (Daniel, McCalla & Schwier, 2002). Oldenburg (1991) attributed the decline of social capital to the lack of what he referred to as "a third place'. He pointed out that the "third place" is central to interpersonal integration; it is a place where people can gather, put aside the concerns of work and home, and hang out simply for the pleasures of good company and lively conversation. In his view "a third place" can be a coffee shop, bar, town hall, anywhere away from both work and home. Further, "a third place" is essential for identification and belonging, social support, participation, and inclusion. The third place is the heart of a community's social vitality and the grassroots of democracy. Common features of "a third place" the main activity is socialisation. It is a neutral place acting as a home away from home. It has a low profile with a playful mood (Schuler 1996, p.42). The "third place" serves as a platform for communication discussed by Rheingold (1998) in the 'World Earth 'Lectronic Link' (WELL) and it potentially contains abundant amount of social capital.

SOCIAL CAPITAL IN VIRTUAL COMMUNITIES

In a conventional society, communities are evoked by geographical closeness for instance; villages, neighbourhoods, and towns are natural occurrence of place-based communities. The foundation of a community might even be organisational as in the case of churches, schools, and clubs (Rheingold, 1993, Smith & Kollock, 1997). By contrast a virtual community is a social network, a group of people who are trying to achieve something through the use of technology. These communities are emergent and are mainly determined by their interconnectivity by computer technologies and associated media. It is any aggregation of individuals who are interested in making connections among themselves through new technologies to achieve certain implicit or explicit goals.

The emergency of a wide variety of Web technologies in the last three decades have ignited new forms of social interaction, increasingly resulted to formation of various types of virtual communities and knowledge networks, with members' activities primarily conducted online and under distributed circumstances. Looking at the traditional notion of community, Putnam (2000) noted that the traditional community and social relationships are losing importance or even vanishing altogether, especially in urban areas. He observed a shift in community and social relationships away from local anchors and towards the Internet and its related Web technologies, signalling a potential revival and renewal of social capital. For Putnam (2000), these technologies are ambient into our social fabrics to an extent that it is hard to imagine solving our contemporary civic dilemmas without them. Perhaps as early as 1999, Anderson's (1991) in his work on imagined communities described how different technologies, such as national newspapers, contributed to the development of national and regional consciousness among early nation-states.

Other Scholars also indicated that the Internet enhances and facilitate the flow of social capital and it has invariably a positive effect on people's lives, creating new forms of online interaction and with potentials for enhancing offline relationships (Quan-Hasse, Wellman, Witte & Hampton, 2002). They argued that with the Internet, social relationships can be virtually conducted anywhere, at anytime and on any platform (through the use of desktop computers, laptops and handheld devices, Blackberry, ipod etc). The portability of interaction and their sustainability make the concept of a community mutable. For instance, virtual communities are global in nature and their presence never requires shared physical and temporal space anymore. Instead, virtual communities are created to enable people regardless of where they are situated, to learn from each other and share knowledge.

In virtual communities, often people who have similar interests in learning or advancing their understanding of a certain domain team up and form groups virtually regardless of geographical locations and time constraint, essentially, these people form communities to share ideas and goals (Schwier, 2001). Another aspect, which characterizes virtual communities, is the nature of social interaction, which tends to revolve around shared knowledge, artefacts, problems and solutions (Nichani, 2000).

The increasing popularity of social capital in new disciplines such as Computer Science and Educational Technology in particular are linked to two reasons: the emergence of new socially oriented computing approaches aimed at better understanding the social dimensions of people in order to effectively build technologies that can promote collaboration, knowledge sharing and learning and the ability of virtual communities as hubs for knowledge sharing and learning.

Within virtual communities, social capital provides us with different ways of examining and better understanding of how people interact with each other, share information and knowledge. An important aspect of social capital in virtual communities is in describing how to invest and harness productive online social interactions. Unlike economic capital, the more people invest in social capital the more it grows. Further, the fact that membership in virtual communities is not restricted by traditional constraints such as culture, ethnicity, geography, time, etc., people have the possibility of becoming members of many virtual communities, providing opportunities to grow social connectivity and associated benefits.

Viewed from these perspectives social capital constitutes an important set of resources that accrue to individuals through their social network structure. It is a capital in its own right because it is not only a property of an individual but it is determined by how an individual relates to other individuals within a virtual community. Furthermore, within virtual communities, social capital can be regarded as an abstract hidden resource, which can be accumulated, tapped, and attained when people value relationships among each other, interact, collaborate, learn and share ideas.

This book introduces Bayesian modelling approach as a new way of examining and understanding the constituents of social capital and how they interact among each other to provide a clear and complete picture of social capital in virtual communities. The modelling approach presented in the book clearly identifies variables constituting social capital and isolating those variables that are more relevant to virtual communities.

BAYESIAN BELIEF NETWORK AND MODELLING OF SOCIAL CAPITAL

For many years, Scientists, Engineers, and Economists have built sophisticated probabilistic models of social and natural phenomena of various physical and abstract objects. While each individual might have different reasons for building models, a shared motivation for modelling is to be able to predict what was or is likely to happen when something else happened. For example, Economists would build an economic model that predicts changes in market prices as a result of human consumption habits, the amount of goods and services suppliers provide to retailers and government regulations (taxes) and their effects on an economy. Engineers would be interested in building models of new cars that provide more safety features during accidents. Natural scientists would be interesting in simulating a model of whether conditions in order to predict climatic conditions or environmental changes. Artificial Intelligence Scientists might be interested in building a computer model of cognitive dissonance. All these individuals would apply probability theory to observe how the models react to changes that are either intentional or incidental to the models.

Typically, probabilistic models consist of one or more tables of all the probabilities of all the possible combinations of states in the world the model is trying to emulate. However, in a situation where a model would have many variables tables can become difficult to manage, leading to computational complexity. For models of any reasonable complexity, the joint distribution of probability values can end up with millions, trillions, or unbelievably many entries. And so, the Bayesian Belief approach provides a better way to handle probabilistic complexity and to manage exponential growth of probability values within a network.

Bayesian belief networks are compact networks of probabilities that capture the probabilistic relationship between variables, as well as historical information about their relationships. The Bayesian Belief network approaches use causal dependency among variables to isolate irrelevant variables and reduce computational complexity. In using Bayesian Belief Network, the knowledge engineer (or the person who builds the model) does not need to be concerned about all possible configurations of states of variables within the model. Instead all that is needed to store and work with are all the possible combinations of states between sets of related parent and child nodes (families of nodes). Such a technique significantly reduces table space and number of probability values.

A Bayesian Belief Network approach is also concise and easily adaptable, such that a modeller can begin modelling with limited domain knowledge, and expand as new knowledge is acquired. Furthermore, in a situation where there are more variables, few variables can be modelled and more added as new evidence become available. In other words, a Bayesian belief network combines observed data with prior belief or knowledge to understand the inner working of a system, especially how it reacts to its outside environment.

The Bayesian Belief Network approach is suitable for modelling social capital and to effectively address three major problems associated with understanding social capital. First social capital is not scientifically defined, second analysis of social capital is limited to exploration of problems in place-based communities and third most of the approaches used for analysing social capital sometimes use secondary data collected primarily for other purposes, limiting their ability to address reliability and validity issues. A model of social capital serves as a decision-support tool for reasoning and to help researchers, policymakers and system designers to understand relationships in virtual communities in order to develop tools and processes to help people effectively engage in productive activities.

CONCLUSION

The discipline of Sociology has contributed enormous theories to the analysis and understanding of communities. Historically, the notion of a community was confined to geographical location and elements such as distance, time, culture and ethnicity had continued to be the determining factors defining communities and the conditions in which people acquire memberships in communities. Communities, regardless of space are necessary parts of human interaction where kinship and friendship ties are connected through common interests. These fundamental features also played a greater role in the horizontal growth of communities. Further, activities in communities that bring people together such as conducting meetings, socialising or resolving collective problems were limited to face-to-face settings.

For the last three decades, the introduction of information and communication technologies and their effects on group interaction, have transformed the notion of traditional communities. Communities have evolved into complex social systems, breaking the traditional barriers defining their boundaries and reducing face-to-face interaction and remodelling local spaces (e.g. time, distance, ethnicity, language and culture). In a networked society, people form communities when they identify the need to engage in a process of collective action, by sharing what they have and what they know with each other irrespective of their geographical location and ethnic background. Graham (1994) pointed out that communities in 'cyberspace' contain the same four critical elements that shape place-based communities, shared values, unity, intimacy and free expression. As networks transcend geography having a sense of community becomes ever more important. As networks transcend geography having a sense of community becomes ever more important for they promise a renewed sense of community and, in many instances, new types and formations of community.

Virtual community is used in this book as a metaphor for describing communities formed online of those coherent social groups whose activities are mediated by various kinds of information and communication technologies. The differences between virtual communities and geographical or place-based communities are becoming indistinguishable in intent. In the geographical world, communities are typically groups of people (a town, for instance) held together by some common identity or interest. Virtual communities are similar to geographical communities in that they too are comprised of people with shared identity or interests coming together for a shared purpose. This shared interest offers a strong forum for members of the community to build relationships and associations out of which they can learn from one another and make an impact on the society or culture they belong to. However, the mediating modalities of communication and definition of members are the two key elements distinguishing virtual communities from traditional geography based communities.

While a wide range of technologies are now capable of fostering various kinds of engagement, there is still a lack of robust mechanisms for analysing social engagement in virtual communities. Over the last decade, social capital has emerged as an important conceptual and theoretical framework for analysing social issues in communities. Social capital offers robust approaches that can be extended to the analysis of social phenomenon in virtual communities.

In order to extend the notion of social capital to virtual settings, the book offers a compressive review of the theory and suggests more precise, more complete and more tractable model of social capital. Variables constituting a model of social capital are grounded in the vast work on the theory. Chapter 2 presents a thorough review of the literature on social capital. The goal is to identify key variables constituting social capital.

REFERENCES

Anderson, B. (1991). *Imagined Communities: Reflections on the Origin and Spread of Nationalism.* London: Verso

Becker, B., & Mark, G. (1999). Constructing social systems through computer-mediated communication. *Virtual Reality, 4,* 60-73.

Bell, C., & Newby, H. (1972). *Community studies: An introduction to the sociology of the local community.* New York: Praeger Publishers.

Coleman, J. (1988). Social Capital in the Creation of Human Capital. *American Journal of Sociology, 94,* 95-120.

Daniel, B., McCalla, G., & Schwier, R. (2002). A process model for building social capital in virtual learning communities. *Proceedings of the International Conference on Computers in Education (ICCE)* (pp, 574-577). Auckland, New Zealand.

Etzioni, A. (1993). *The spirit of community: The reinvention of American society.* New York: Touchstone.

Ferlander, S. (2003). The Internet, social capital and local community. Unpublished Doctoral thesis, *Department of Psychology, the University of Stirling.*

Graham, G. (1994). Freenets and the Politics of Community in Electronic Networks. *Government in Canada, 1*(1). Retrieved December 12th 2008 from http://www.usask.ca/library/gic/v1n1/graham/graham.html

Hanifan, L. J. (1916). The rural school community centre. *Annuals of the American Academy of Political and Social Science, 67,* 130-138.

Hanifan, L. J. (1920). *The community center.* Boston: Silver Burdett.

Hillery, G.A. (1955). Definitions of Community: Areas of agreement. *Rural Sociology, 20,* 111 - 123.

Homans, G. (1961). *Social behavior: Its elementary forms.* New York: Harcourt, Brace and World.

Hunter, B. (2002). Learning in the virtual community depends upon changes in local communities. In K. A. Renninger & W. Shumar (Eds.). *Building virtual communities. learning and change in cyberspace* (pp. 96-126). New York: Cambridge University Press,

Jacobs, J. (1965). *The death and life of great American cities.* New Jersey: Penguin Books.

Jones, M.A., (1977). *Organisational and social planning in Australian local government:* Richmond: Heinemann Educational Australia. Pty Ltd..

Kanno, Y., & Norton, B. (2003). Imagined communities and educational possibilities: Introduction. *Journal of Language, Identity, and Education, 2*(4), 241-249.

Kollock, P., & Smith. M. (1996). Managing the virtual commons: Cooperation and conflict in Computer communities. In S. Herring (Ed.), *Computer-mediated communication: linguistic, social, and cross-cultural perspectives* (pp.109-128). Amsterdam: John Benjamins.

Loury, G. (1977). A Dynamic theory of racial income differences. In Wallace, P.A., Le Mund, E.. (Eds.). *Women, minorities, and employment discrimination* (pp.153-186). Lexington MA: Lexington Books.

MacQueen K.M, McLellan, E., Metzger, D.S, Kegeles, S., Straus, R.P., Scotti, R., Blanchard, L, Trotter II, R.T. (2001). What is community? An evidence-based definition for participatory public health. *AJPH, 91*(12), 1929-38. Retrieved November 14, 2008 from http://www.pubmedcentral.nih.gov/articlerender.fcgi?artid=1446907.

Mardsen, P.V. & Lin, N. (1982).

Nichani, M. (2000). Learning through social interactions (online communities). *Elearningpost.com*. Retrieved November, 25th from http://www.elearningpost.com/elthemes/comm.pdf

Nisbet, R. (1962). *Community and Power.* New York: Oxford University Press.

Oldenburg, R. (1991). *The great good place: Cafes, coffee shops, bookstores, bars, hair salons, and other hangouts at the heart of a community.* New York: Paragon House.

Poplin, D. (1972). *Communities: A survey of theories and methods of research.* New York: Macmillan.

Portes, A. (1998). Social capital: its origins and applications in modern sociology. *Annual Review of Sociology, 24*, 1-24.

Putnam, R. (2000). *Bowling alone: The collapse and revival of American community.* New York: Simon Schuster.

Quan Hasse, A., Wellman, B., Witte, J. & Hampton, K. (2002). Capitalizing on the Internet: Network capital, participatory capital, and sense of community. In Wellman, B. & Haythornthwaite, C. (Eds.), *The Internet in Everyday Life* (pp.291-324). Oxford: Blackwell.

Rheingold, H. (1993). *The virtual community: Homesteading on the virtual frontier.* New York: Addison-Wesley.

Schuler, D. (1996). *New community networks: Wired for change.* New York: ACM Press

Schwier, R. A. (2001). Catalysts, emphases, and elements of virtual learning communities. Implication for Research. *The Quarterly Review of Distance Education, 2*(1), 5-18.

Seeley, J.R., Sim, A.R., Loosley, E.W. (1956). *Crestwood heights: A study of the culture of suburban life.* New York: Basic Books.

Thompson, K. (1982). *Emile Durkheim.* London: Tavistock Publications.

Tonnies F (1925). The concept of Gemeinschaft. In Cahnman, W. J & Heberle, R. (Eds.), *Ferdinand Tonnies on Sociology: Pure, applied and empirical. Selected writings* (pp.62-72). University of Chicago Press, Chicago.

Wellman, B. (1982). Studying personal communities. In Marsden, P. & Lin, N. (Eds.) *Social Structure and Network Analysis*. Beverly Hills, CA: Sage.

ENDNOTE

[1]   Durkheim proposed this definition of suicide: "the term suicide is applied to all cases of death resulting directly or indirectly from a positive or negative act of the victim himself, which he knows will produce this result" (1982, p. 110).

Chapter II
Conceptual and Theoretical Foundations of Social Capital

INTRODUCTION

Social capital is a complex multifaceted and litigious theory, discussed in the Social Sciences and the Humanities. It is a theory which researchers have increasingly questioned its scientific legitimacy and yet paradoxically many other researchers continuously use it as a conceptual and theoretical framework to explain the structural and functional operations of communities. This chapter discusses work done on the theory. It covers some of the theoretical controversy with a goal of aligning its conceptualization and distinguishing it from other types of capitals.

This chapter presents the basic theoretical and conceptual foundations of social capital. The aim is to present the reader with a basic understanding of what constitutes social capital, by opening discussion about various forms of capital(s)—as discussed in the disciplines of Economics and Sociology. Second, the chapter discusses the origin of the theory as well as the work of key scholars who have contributed to the development of the theory. Furthermore, in order to identify the strengths and the weaknesses of the theory, the chapter provides the reader with analysis of benefits and shortcomings of social capital both as a theoretical and analytical tool for studying communities.

THE CLASSICAL ECONOMIC CAPITAL

Economics is a Social Science discipline concerned with how society allocates its scarce resources in the face of limited choices on the alternative use of the same resources to attain different outcomes. An underlying principle of opportunity cost—the ability to forgo certain decisions in order to attain specific outcomes is fundamental to Economic thought. This principle guides rational individuals to make wise choices in situations where there are shortages of resources.

The principle of opportunity cost is best illustrated by the example. In 2008, it seems the world's economy came to a state of recession. Nations in North America and elsewhere were faced by difficult choices regarding how much resource to deploy on national economy to avoid increasing failures in stock markets and curb an imminent economic depression. One possibility was to stimulate the economy through lending money to banks to maintain line of credits for individuals and businesses. Another possibility would be for a government to overspend or head for financial deficit. Each of these two possibilities has associated benefits and disadvantages. A rational government would make rational analysis and informed decisions in choosing either one of them. The expectation is that an informed and rational decision is considered cost-effective, yielding outcomes that would not subject the government at a great disadvantage or put its economy back to state of recession.

Making informed, efficient and effective choices are core to the basic principles of Economics. For hundreds and thousands of years, the discipline of Economics has enormously provided us with tools and knowledge to effectively and efficiently make effective choices that might have positive ramifications to a nation's well-being through paying close attention to how resources are produced and consumed. In Economics, resources are presented as goods and services. Many of the classic Economics theories are devoted to the explanation of resources (goods and services) understood as "capital". Economists treat capital as a human-made tool of production. It is a good or service produced for the use and more production of other goods and services. But Capital in Economics is only one of the three factors of production, the others being land and labor.

Together, all three factors of production are considered critical input to any economic production system. They are responsible for producing consumable goods and services. If a nation fails to carefully deploy goods and services, many social amenities will underperform. For example, health care systems will be enormously strained with long wait time, schools will be poorly equipped, physical and technological infrastructures such as roads and bridges, computer and telephone networks will not work efficiently. More than a resource, in Economics, a good or service is anything that satisfies a need (desire). Goods can be classified to tangible or intangible goods. Tangible goods are physical items such as cars, buildings and computers. Intangible goods include abstract objects such as medical care, labour and education; all of which are essentially referred to as services.

Goods and services are produced for one or two purposes. A good may be a consumer good used for immediate satisfaction of needs. Satisfaction of needs is the ultimate purpose of production in economic terms. A good can be a capital good produced not for immediate or direct consumption but for use in producing more goods. Capital goods such as computers or medical facilities are resources that have been produced and that when combined with other resources, such as land and labor, they produce more goods and services such as good national medical care system with reduced wait time and free access to physicians.

The concept of capital certainly has a long history in Modern Economics thought. The early founding fathers of Economics discussed several types of capital and how the notion of capital has contributed to the advancement of Economic theory. For example, Adam Smith, an early Economist and author of "the Wealth of Nations", distinguished between fixed capital from circulating capital, including raw materials and intermediate products. Fixed capital is physical assets such as a house; circulating capital is liquidation or cash flow. Additionally, Karl Marx another influential Economist, a Political Philosopher and a Sociologist, conceptualized capital in terms of variability. For Marx, the basic determining factor of human history is the economy and this is driven by the manipulation of capital.

According to Marxian Economic theory, humans right from their earliest beginnings are not motivated by grand ideas but instead by material concerns, predominantly the need to eat and survive. This is the basic premise of a materialist view of historical capitalism of the Marxist Economic school of thought. Marxian Economic theory also treats a variable capital as capitalist's investment in labour power seen as the only source of surplus value. Where as constant capital suggests investment in non-human factors of production, such as plant and machinery. Investment is also seen as the production of increased capital. In other words, to invest in goods and services, one must engage in production of resources, which are not to be immediately consumed, but instead used to produce other goods and services. Marx's ideology on capitalism and the politics of class system and how these determine social relationships, especially between those who are engaged in the production process (proletariats) and those who own factors of productions (Bourgeoisies), presents interesting evolution of capital goods and how these shape personalities and influence personal relationships in communities. Though his ultimate form of egalitarian society is a clear example of a powerful utopia, many social systems around the world are still struggling to achieve this (e.g. fair treatment for all, respect for diversity, equal pay for men and women and social and economic justices).

Economic capital is critical to the success of many social amenities especially businesses. It is unimaginable for any business corporation to stay in business for any period of time if it lacks some form of economic capital. Moreover, for any business to stay in business, it needs to determine how much products are being produced, how much it costs to produce them and the estimated market price for the products. This is often achieved through analysis of return on investment or added-value of productivity and gain and computed through cost-benefit analysis techniques.

CULTURAL CAPITAL

Bourdieu (1986), a prominent Sociologist known for his theoretical analysis of social capital, argued that capital exists in three fundamental forms: economic capital that can be directly convertible into money and institutionalized in the form of property rights; cultural capital that may be convertible into economic capital and institutionalized in the form of educational qualification; and social capital, made up of social obligations that can be convertible into economic capital and institutionalized in the form of a title of nobility (Bourdieu, 1986). Bourdieu defined cultural capital as knowledge that enables an individual to interpret various cultural codes. It is the knowledge, experience or connections one has developed through the course of one's life. He identified three distinguishable states of cultural capital, the embodied state which represents the knowledge and skills an individual possesses. It is the long lasting dispositions of the mind and body, the objectified state, which is expressed in a form of cultural goods, such as pictures, books, machines and the institutionalized state is represented by actual documents and other proof of cultural status. According to Bourdieu (1984) when people possess knowledge of certain cultural codes and participate in the arts, they can acquire cultural capital that serves to reproduce class hierarchies and societal structures of domination.

This analysis further suggested that people who possess cultural capital are likely to effectively use it to their benefits. For instances, use it to get a good job, make new friends from other cultures. It also follows that an individual who has widely travelled and interacted with many people from different cultures is likely to develop high cultural capital than those who simply learn about foreign cultures through watching television or reading books. This is more so, because cultural facts often displayed on media such as televisions might be slightly or grossly distorted, unrealistically and stereotypical presented. They might even lack empirical evidence to justify their validity. It is also possible that distortion is intentionally to attract wider audience for the sake of marketing. This is similar to those governments or nations that often display positive achievements to the outside world while muting those areas where they could be unfavourably judged (e.g. treatment of minority groups, housing conditions for the populace or the political culture associated with governance or the process for the development of fair governance model). Further, a cultural capital presents itself in some standard, though sometimes misleading ways of behaviour such as knowing how to "dress for success"; choosing hairstyle, physical appearance. Whether appearance is a valid yardstick for measuring cultural capital is an open issue of research and perhaps better left to be addressed in a book on cultural capital.

But in a way of summary, cultural knowledge, which is the basis of cultural capital, brings some benefits to individuals who can learn to master and use it properly to their advantage. It is obviously alienating to those who might not value it or unable to appropriately use it. For example, people who intentionally or incidentally deviate from a normal acceptable "dress" codes, might find themselves unfavourably judged. In fact, some people do not know how to dress for success. They do not even know the importance of doing so. For this reason, the acquisition of high cultural knowledge and fashion, including stylish dress, table manners are for most, stereotypically and judgementally valued capital. This is because appearance does not reveal itself to trust. In other words, get wearing clothes of certain calibre might not correlate to the innermost human behaviour—for example dressing up indifferently might falsely reveal individual behaviour.

HUMAN CAPITAL

Human capital is another form of capital, which includes skills and knowledge people gather from school experiences or while interacting with peers. T.W. Schultz, a famous Economist, in 1960 first introduced human capital in his article entitled: "Investment in Human Capital". Schultz's human capital theory suggested that both "knowledge and skill are forms of a capital, and that this particular form of a capital is a product of a deliberate investment." Schultz compared the acquisition of knowledge and skills to the acquisition of the means of production. His work was targeted at benefiting workers who no longer have to depend on others (the workers and the landowners); instead they can be in control of increasing their own productivity and earnings. Schultz made a direct link between an increase in investment in human capital, and the overall increase in workers earnings. He stated that an individual's income proportionately increase with more education. Becker (1993) later confirmed that human capital means investment in training, education, or even work experience. He mentioned that human capital describes how education and training in organisations act as most important investments that carry economic value in comparison to other forms factors of production (Becker, 1993). Human is capital is also found to be capable of increasing people's productivity and presents them with higher earnings (Light 2004). The notion of human capital also suggests that people with more human capital are generally more successful economically than those with less of it.

Since the introduction of the human capital theory in the 1960s, Economists have devoted a great deal of research into examining and developing various ways to measure and utilize it in a variety of settings. The notion of human capital" is similar to Karl Marx's concept of labour power: to Marx, capitalism workers had to sell their labour power in order to receive income (wages and salaries). And so the more human capital one possesses the more labour power is at one's disposal.

The notion of human capital is perhaps more widely used in the corporate sector. Human capital in the corporations is treated as intangible resources embedded within people. These include people's competencies and their commitment to organisations i.e. their skills, experience, potential and capacity to enhance productivity. The human capital asset captures all the people oriented capabilities needed for any business to succeed. This form of capital is considered as a source of competitive advantage. Human capital within the corporate sector is also based on the recognition that people in organisations and businesses are important and are essential capital assets that contributing to the development and growth and these resources should be equally valued similar to the way physical assets such as machines and money.

NATURAL CAPITAL

Natural capital constitutes another form of capital asset, which includes: natural resource– stocks of renewable and non-renewable resources such as minerals and energy, forests, water, fisheries; the ecosystems or environmental resources (e.g. systems that provide essential environmental goods and services such as atmosphere and waste absorption provided by wetlands; and the land) (the space in which human activities take place). In addition, nature and its beauty is another form of natural capital. For example, a view of a mountain range or sea shore, a park on a warm summer day and a sky full of stars on a clear winter night are all parts of the beauty of nature and they constitute natural capital of a country, which if used as tourists' attraction site, can bring in more cash flows (money).

The stock of natural capital can yield economic capital (goods and services over time). As discussed earlier in the chapter, goods and services are essential to the sustained health and survival of a national economy. Along with human capital and produced or manufactured capital (e.g., machinery, structures), natural capital is an input into the production of goods and services.

SOCIAL CAPITAL AND OTHER FORMS OF CAPITAL

Social capital is broadly thought of as the 'value' of social relationships. It is regarded as another form of capital generated through interaction and engagement and embedded within social relations and in a network structure. Like the others forms of capital goods and services, social capital is a particular type of functional and valuable set of resources available to individuals and groups. And since humans are sociable animals, an individual or a community with high stock of social capital are better off compared to those with less. People who are well connected to other individuals have easy access to other types of goods and services. They are likely to access employment opportunities, get vital information that can help them decide which college to send their children and how to better raise their children to be good citizens.

Many researchers have equated social capital to other forms of capital. For example, social capital is equated to economic capital by its ability to be invested upon, whether by an individual, a community or both (Adler & Kwon 2002). This means social capital is appropriable (Coleman 1988) and convertible (Bourdieu 1986). Further, the term "capital" in social capital is used as an analogy to economic capital (e.g. factors of production). It can be mobilized to facilitate individual and community activities (Adler and Kwon 2002) and similar to economic capital, social capital has to be managed and nurtured to be prosperous.

There are other features of social capital that differ from other forms of capital, one of these features is based on the realisation that social capital is totally depended on human relations. In other words, if relationship dies out among individuals, social capital is no longer nurtured and consequently fades away (Adler and Kwon 2002). Further, like economic capital, acquiring social capital can be a process of investment that takes some time to acquire. Acquiring social capital requires some form of social skills and effort to nurture and sustain it. Ultimately, people often connect with those they share similar ways of life, have certain things in common, are interested in the same things, view the world in the same way and so on.

Social capital is also contrasted with other forms of social capital in that it is less measurable. Further, unlike other forms of capital such as natural capital (natural resources), social capital is not depleted by use, but in fact depleted by non-use ("use it or lose it"). Further, compared to economic capital, the "social" aspects in social capital emphasizes that resources can not be treated solely as personal goods or services. In economic capital, people can own private economic resources without being connected to other people; however, nobody can own social capital without being connected to other people.

In other words, social capital resources reside in networks of relationships. If we think of human capital as what we know (the sum of what we own knowledge, skills, and experience), cultural capital as the lifelong accumulated experiences that we gather from the environment, coming into contact with people from other cultures, reading books and watching movies. Social capital could be enhanced by all of these but will not directly be equated to any of one of them. Since access to social capital depends on whom we know—the size, quality, and diversity of our personal and social networks. But beyond that, social capital also depends on people we don't know, especially those people we are indirectly connected to via our immediate or distant social networks.

A major distinguishing feature of social capital from other forms of physical or human capital is based on the communitarian approach to how it operates. Whereas physical capital refers to physical objects and human capital refers to properties of an individual, social capital refers to connections among individuals—social networks and the social protocols associated with expectations of reciprocal relationships and trust gluing people together. Social capital is also distinguished from other forms of economic capital because it cannot be traded on, or at least not in a context of open market systems. Another contrasting feature of social capital from economic capital, it is not a set of active social connections among people within a particular social network, which cannot directly be translated in monetary value or cash flow nor can it be transferred from one individual to another.

Further, in contrast to economic capital, where only those with sufficient resources can enjoy its benefits, anyone can build social capital—ranging from simple gatherings of street people, gang members, hate groups, or soccer hooligans to corporate executives and closed-ended snob groups. In addition, people can acquire social capital anywhere from meeting in the playground, in the church, in the mosque, at a friend's party, at the local grocery store, in the office, in the public square, local pub, in the library or online, the sky is the limit.

CONCEPTUALISING SOCIAL CAPITAL

For more than two decades, researchers have not consistently agreed on what constitutes social capital. In a nutshell, social capital in geographical communities is the connections in a community and because such connections can be both positive and negative, the former is often implied when people talk about social capital. Social capital also describes ways in which people interact and relate to each other. The simplest connections are connections to family, friends and neighbours. On a larger scale, we form connections through community and volunteer organizations; it is the ability of groups of people to form governments to deal with common problems, and the ability of people to form companies to create goods and services to satisfy the needs of the community. Within the academic community discussions on what constitutes social capital has gained more interest than what is scientifically known about the theory.

Writings on social capital, especially how researchers conceptualized it, vary considerably; depending on what questions the theory is intended to answer. In addition, social capital conceptually operates on two levels. It is either analysed on an individual property in connections to others or as a community possessions. Researchers often use one level during its analysis. In most of the writings on social capital, it is possible to distil three was to describe it as an input, process, output or all of the three. As an input, social capital is regarded as a means to an end. For example communities where most people know each other are likely to develop social capital. As a process, when people work together, they build and enhance social capital that can in turn be used to attain specific outcomes (building neigh- bourhood school, helping each other in times of need). As an output, communities with a rich social capital develop safe neighbourhood where its ingredients such as social protocols are embedded in the social structure of the community

Generally, speaking, the various definitions of social capital in the literature can be classified into three broad categories. The first category views social capital in terms of content of relationships people maintain with each other. The second cat- egory looks at social capital through the lens of the structure of the social relation- ships and the third category describes the types of associations or linkages people have with each (Adler & Kwon 2002). Taking into consideration the variations in theoretical conceptualisation, Table 2-1 presents a number of key contributors to the development of the theory, their views on what constitute social capital and the shared variables among their definitions.

DIMENSIONS OF SOCIAL CAPITAL

In order to gain a better understanding of the theoretical and conceptual founda- tions of social capital, in addition to the definitions provided above, it is worth providing three dimensions in which the definitions of social capital can be broadly be grouped. These include: structural, content and cognitive dimensions. This classification is similar to Nahapiet and Ghoshal (1998) views on social capital as knowledge framework.

The Structural Dimension of Social Capital

The structural dimension of social capital focuses on the configuration of social organisations of communities and factors such as roles, rules, precedents and proce- dures, which individually or collectively determine and regulate how communities

Table 2-1. Common definitions of social capital and key variables

Researcher (s)	Definition	Key variables
Hanifin (1916)	Tangible substances [that] count for most in the daily lives of people - namely good will, fellowship, sympathy and social intercourse among the individuals and families who make up a social unit.	resources, good will, fellowship, sympathy, social interactions
Putnam (2000)	The connections among individuals – social networks and the norms of reciprocity and trustworthiness that arise from them.	connections, networks, norms/social protocols, reciprocity, trust
Coleman (1988)	Supportive relationships among adults and children that promote the sharing of norms and values.	relationships, norms, shared values
World Bank (1999)	The institutions, relationships, and norms that shape the quality and quantity of a society's social interactions.	relationships, norms/social protocols, social interactions
Cohen and Prusak (2001)	The stock of active connections among people: the trust, mutual understanding, and shared values and behaviours that bind the members of human networks and communities and make cooperative action possible.	connections, trust, mutual understanding/shared understanding, shared value/goals, networks
Bourdieu (1996)	The aggregate of the actual or potential resources which are linked to possession of a durable network of more or less institutionalized relationships of mutual acquaintance and recognition.	relationships, resources, networks
Fukuyama (1999)	The existence of a certain set of informal values or norms shared among members of a group that permits cooperation among them.	informal values, norms/social protocols, cooperation
OECD (2001)	The network, together with shared norms, values and understandings that facilitates cooperation within and among groups.	network, norms, shared understanding, cooperation
Loury (1977)	Natural occurring social relationships among persons which promote or assist the acquisition of skills and traits valued in the market place.	social relationships, skills, traits
Woolcock (1998)	Information, trust and norms of reciprocity inhering in one's social networks.	information, trust, norms/social protocols, social networks
Resnick (2004)	Productive resources in social relations	resources, social relationships

operate. The structural dimension also examines a given social network and whether or not the interaction of individuals within a network leads to specific outcomes. Scholars who use the structural dimension of social capital as an analytical framework examine social relationships to determine whether such relationships serve as a resource and conduit for effective collaboration. In other words, in the structural dimension, researchers can relate whether or not social relationships organised in

Figure 2-1. Triangulating dimensions of social capital

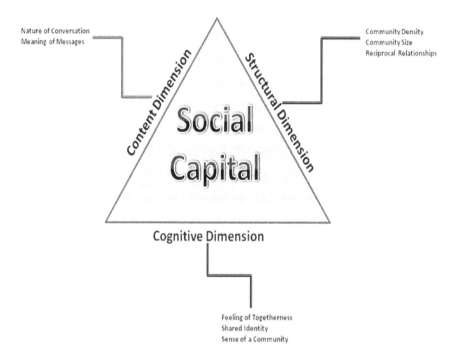

certain ways can lead to high social capital, they can investigate how people com-municate and connect with others.

The structural dimension of social capital manifests itself differently in different types of communities. It can reflect the disposition of power structures, relations and authority. For example, in some communities people's patterns of interactions are determined by the social position they occupy within the social structure of the community. Friedkin and Johnsen (1997) noted, the structural dimensions of social capital implies that people share information and interpretation by communicating and are influenced by each other as a consequence of their position in the social network. Moreover, the ability to interact with others in certain communities is determined along parameters such as age, social status and sometimes economic capital. The structural dimension of social capital is also culturally bounded to an extent that the ability to create or destroy social capital will depend on how power structures and traditional norms of association are engaged by field staff of external agencies (Hobbs, 2000).

The structural dimension of social capital helps us to understand how individu-als access information and their relational proximity to other individuals within a community (Pattison, 1994). Moreover the relational aspects of individuals in a community also suggest who they know and are likely to know. Further, through analysis of the structural dimension, it is possible to determine the nature, type and size of a community. Social network analysis topic discussed later in the book, is one of the common techniques scholars employ to investigate the structural dimension of social capital.

Similar to the notion of the Triple-Helix, a spiral model of innovation that captures multiple reciprocal relationships at different points in the process of knowledge capitalization and utilisation in Sociology (Etzkowitz & Loet, 1995), social network viewed from a structural dimension suggests organisations from different sectors can jointly work together to build a strong synergy and leverage their resources and each organisation maintains its unique identity. However, the structural configuration of the relationships has a strong bearing on their social cohesion which can ultimately affect their social capital. Besides, viewed from the Triple-Helix perspective, the structural dimension of social capital influences the way organisations interact with each other and it takes into account relationships at both an individual and the community levels.

Content Dimension of Social Capital

Whereas the structural dimension of social capital provide us with knowledge of the importance of location an individual occupies within a social network, the content dimension focuses on the content of the relationship an individual occupies within their social networks. In other words, the content dimensions reveals more knowledge of the quality of the connections, or the quality of social capital—i.e. what sticks social capital to tick. Using another analogy, the structural dimension of social can be regarded as a human biological system where as the content dimension is the blood that runs through the system and that gives the system life beyond its physical appearance or social manifestation.

The content dimension of social capital is strongly tied to the aspect and quality of communication and its role. The content dimension viewed from communication's perspectives advocates for understanding the content of communication among people. Communication is both a foundation for building useful and engaging relationship and a key mechanism in maintaining the continuity and sustainability of social capital within a community. Through communication many of the fundamental critical input factors for supporting social capital are created, nurtured or sustained. In addition, through communication, social protocols are made explicit, shared understanding or a common grounding for engagement is created among members of the community.

Cognitive Dimension

Cognition, a mental process of knowing including awareness, perception, reasoning and judgment are central to social relationships. Cognition deals with the internal structures and processes that are involved in the acquisition and use of knowledge, including sensation, perception, attention, learning and memory, language, thinking, and reasoning. In relations to social relationships, the cognitive dimension of social capital describes the relationships capturing the innate feeling people have towards each other and the things they need to do in order to get along well and work together toward achievement of common goals.

The cognitive dimension of social capital covers things such as norms, values, attitudes and beliefs. The structural and cognitive social capital can be treated as complimentary to each other in that any social system with some form and structure can help translate collective norms, social protocols and shared belief, resulting to well co-ordinated goal-oriented set of behaviours and expectations. Perhaps the most important aspect of cognitive dimension of social capital is in enhancing a common context and a shared language. In addition, the cognitive dimension to social capital involves analysing symbolic interaction within a group, through the use of stories to convey a sense of shared identity and sense of community.

TYPES OF SOCIAL CAPITAL

The variety in the definitions of social capital positioned along the three dimensions explicates different types, the most common being the distinction made between bridging, bonding and linking. Bridging social capital describes social capital that cuts across two or more communities, bonding social capital adhesively binds members of one community and linking social capital deals with connections that are bounded by power structures or class systems within a community.

Bridging Social Capital

In addition to connecting communities, or social groups, bridging social capital is forming relationships with distant friends, associates, and colleagues. Bridging social capital is characterized by weaker, less dense but more cross-cutting ties, and it can be found in business associations, knowledge networks, acquaintances, and friends from professional groups. According to Putnam (2000), bridging type of social capital though it manifests weak ties tend to be more diverse but are very important to "getting ahead" in groups,

Bridging social capital shapes heterogeneous groups of people with different backgrounds and it emphasizes the ability of communities to create 'bridges' connecting other sectors of society or communities that otherwise would have never come into contact. Concrete examples of social entities relevant to bridging social capital are mostly intercultural in nature. For instance, they consist of productive relationships between two or more relatively distinct organisations, two diverse human cultural groups, or two or more divergent academic disciplines. Since building a bridge implies making connections and often with entities that are culturally and physically different, the bridging type of social capital is more challenging to achieve. It requires distinctively understanding the cultures of two or more communities as they were and finding middle grounds where the two cultures meet. When effectively developed, however, bridging social capital helps two or more distinct communities to seamlessly work together as if it is one community. And in some cases the two communities mutate into a brand new form of community, one which might resemble a distributed community—both vertically and horizontally.

Another important example of bridging social capital can be seen in two academic domain groups (e.g. community of Nurses and Physicians) working together to develop effective health care systems. This interdisciplinary nature of diverse domains is becoming increasingly important within the academia and be regarded as communities spread along certain dimensions.

Despite challenges associated with building bridging type of social capital, many researchers see bridging social capital as one of the most inclusive and proficient levers of community living. The benefits of bridging social capital are similar to Granovetter's (1973) notion of the strength of weak ties, suggesting that weak ties are an important resource in making possible mobility of resources, persons, tools, and ideas, and can facilitate incoming information from outside sources and provide economic opportunities such as acquiring jobs or marketing products to a larger market sector.

Further, bridging social capital can be used as an extension cord connecting communities or other individuals that are more removed from the mainstream society. In addition, bridging social capital is closely related to thin trust, as opposed to the bonding (splitting) social capital of thick trust. For example, multicultural countries like Canada could use bridging social capital as a social mechanism for building linkages among its diverse communities, which are normally isolated from each other and to some extent lagging themselves from other different communities.

Bonding Social Capital

The bonding type of social capital is closely associated with both structural and content dimensions of social capital. Bonding social capital refers to horizontal, tightly knit ties between individuals or groups often with similar demographic characteristics. It describes a cohesive bond within members of the same community. And it is a cementing factor in homogenous groups such as close friends, family, ethnic, and religious groups. Social cohesion is one of the factors researchers use for measuring bonding social capital. It examines ties between people in groups and communities.

A number of researchers emphasize that a strong social cohesion within one group can be likened to a group's 'solidarity', and these 'bonding ties' can be detrimental if they are not balanced by suitable links to external information and knowledge through 'bridging ties'. So bonding ties causes the communication between people that builds a sense of cohesion or solidarity in a small group or community but they can be isolated, protecting themselves from to other communities. For communities with a strong bonded social capital, solidarity represents a social characteristic.

Portes and Sensenbrenner (1993) discussed another type of social capital linked to bonded social capital. They name it "bounded solidarity". Bounded solidarity describes groups that are closely cohesive either based on religious, ethnic or racial ties. Bounded solidarity is integral in garnering resources and increasing economic opportunities for their members and are potentially beneficial in facilitating the reciprocation of aid and enforcing norms that work towards the communal good. Bounded social capital can have latent consequences such as nepotism (giving job to family members, community or friends), corruptions (taking bribes or favours and in appropriate use of public funds) and outward discrimination. Bounded solidarity, similar to bonded social capital are used either maintain or challenge a status-quo.

Linking Social Capital

Linking social capital, the third type of social capital entails relationships formed between individuals and groups across different social strata of a hierarchy where power, social status and wealth are involved. It describes actual or potential links between people from different class or strata. For example, it describes people in positions of power and those who do not occupy power, people with political power and people with financial resources. Linking social capital is critical for leveraging resources, ideas and information beyond normal community linkages and it is essential for accessing support from formal institutions. It is different from bonding and bridging in that it is concerned with relations between people who are not on an equal foothold and within the same community.

Benefits of Social Capital

The widespread interests in application of social theory come with numerous theoretical justifications for its benefits. Many studies have provided sufficient evidence of the pervasiveness of social capital theory. They have offered useful impressions of its political, economic, social influence and recently technological utility. Community resilience demonstrated by the presence of social capital is prevalent when a natural disaster occurs within a community. The tragedies of Tsunami in South Asia that occurred in 2004 and the Hurricane Katrina in 2005 in the United States of America are two important examples demonstrating how social capital operates in times of tragedy.

In a relatively short time, in both tragedies, communities of victims living in other countries especially in North America and Europe, together with their friends and sympathizers quickly mobilised their social capital and raised enough money and other resources which were instantly channelled through humanitarian organisations to help victims of these two natural disasters. At the same time the social capital embedded in these communities was used to help people all over the world to quickly gain access to vital information about the situations where these incidents occurred and how more help could be mobilised.

There are also benefits associated with the environments in which social capital inhabits. Social networks in which social capital (structural dimension) resides, serves as a conduit for the dissemination of helpful information that contributes to the achievement of personal and community goals. For example, people who are well connected in a community are usually the first ones to receive valuable information. Maintaining a number of social networks means that one can have easy and faster access to information. A community with rich social networks therefore, breeds into its members an environment full of mutual confidence and the possibility to socialize and to develop benevolence towards each other.

In the corporate world, social capital is an indispensable part of achieving personal success, business success, and even a happy and satisfying life. Baker (2000) revealed that in most business organisations, pay, promotion, and accomplishments are largely determined by the structure and composition of one's personal and business networks. Baker's observations are in line with what is happening in many business organisations today. Many organisations place a great deal of emphasis on the way one interacts with co-workers and how well an individual associate with colleagues in the workplace. In today work environment, one's personal relationships with others, or simply ones social network can be used to determine the continuity of employment. It is observed that people with high social capital are likely to easily get good jobs. Such individuals also use their social networks to connect with others to access job information or get information from others about good jobs.

Research also shows that people with rich social capital are paid better, promoted faster at the early years of their careers (Baker, 2000; Burt, 2000).

Critical components of social capital reinforce human capital. In discussion of the benefits of social capital, Falk (2000) indicated that the networks, trust and shared values of social capital bring to life our human values, skills, expertise and knowledge. Social capital has a strong prevalence in the basic sociological unit of society—family. It provides the social infrastructure support for our lives in a web of elastic networks related to home, work, learning, leisure and public life and it is cement that can keep organisations together. Further, social capital helps maintain a healthy community.

Social capital allows individuals to draw on resources from other members of social networks to which they belong (Ellison, Steinfield, & Lampe, 2007). These resources can take the form of useful information, personal relationships, or the capacity to organize groups (Paxton, 1999). Access to individuals outside one's close circle provides access to non-redundant information, resulting in benefits such as employment connections (Granovetter, 1973). Moreover, social capital research-ers have found that various forms of social capital, including ties with friends and neighbours, are related to indices of psychological well-being, such as self esteem and satisfaction with life (Bargh & McKenna, 2004; Helliwell & Putnam, 2004).

Research done by the World Bank (1999) indicated that individuals who are well connected and have active trusting relationships with others in a neighbourhood are likely to behave in some acceptable social manners determined by the community. This research pointed out that professionals such as teachers, lawyers, physicians and police force are highly expected to confirm to certain ways of behaviour and are likely to be conscious of the fact that people in society are closely linked to them and that their behavioural patterns are constantly being monitored. The operation of social capital along these lines provides communities with a natural way of enforc-ing and preserving social order and the status quo and hence reducing delinquent or selfish behaviour within a community.

Social capital brings people together to engage in community affairs. It has the potential predisposition to create a warm and nurturing environment when it is used to encourage and strengthen involvement in society in a positive manner, and once accepted and used by majority members of a community. For example, when every individual is connected in a community, it can make people feel included and empowered. It can also encourage them to get more involved in community activities. The community benefits of social capital are extended to education. The mentoring, networking and mutual support often associated with high levels of so-cial capital in education is a key to success of many educational systems (Coleman, 1988). The World Bank (1999) confirmed that schools that closely involve parents, teachers and community tend to do better in comparison to those schools that do not. In addition, students tend to have higher tests scores in highly connected communities where teachers and parents work together.

The benefits of social capital are not limited to communities and educational systems. Social capital also presents business and industry many benefits. It facilitates cooperation and coordination, which minimizes transaction costs, such as negotiation and enforcement of social or business protocols, removing unnecessary bureaucracy. In some circumstance social capital promotes better knowledge sharing within business organisation, especially in the presence of trusting relationships among people and in the presences of shared frame of reference and shared goals (Prusak & Cohen, 2001). Further, social capital can connect together two or more communities separated by social or physical constraints. Further, diversity brought about by social capital, especially bridging or linking type of social capital is essential. When people from different communities connect with each other, they are likely to engage in some dialogue necessary for bridging cultural differences.

Shortcomings of Social Capital

Despite the benefits of social capital, there are also problems associated with the theory both theoretically and practically. In practice, social capital functions as "a double-edged sword". Close-knit communities with a high level of bonding social capital are often isolated from their larger society. And so the benefits that its members derive from the closely tight social network may begin to fall behind the costs. For example, exchange of knowledge or information can go smoothly but there is possibility of lack of sufficient diversity, resulting to circulation of the same knowledge, experiences and information possibly closing down doors for innovation and new knowledge. It is possible that people often get more innovative when they are removed from their environments and place into a different environment and association with the same individuals in a community can result to redundancy and circulation of the same information.

Further, highly cohesive communities exhibiting bonding types of social capital are not necessarily beneficial to a diverse society. Such communities might engender internal trust among their members while spreading hate to the larger society (examples include various kinds of gangs, racial hate groups, exclusive cults, and other criminal organizations) unless bridging mechanisms are instituted linking communities that are isolated within the same society.

Social capital, especially in "communitas", such as any form of strongly bounded community, can be used to coerce a culture of conformism, letting people to confirm to group norms even though some group norms might have vested interests and very destructive to advance of humanity, diversity and respect for individual differences and talents. This can be seen in communities with high social capital and where individuals' activities are condition upon strong values and norms.

The conceptualisation of social capital within the social network analysis does not differentiate between communities and social networks. While social networks are tight associations, they cannot automatically qualify as communities. For example, communities get initiated, develop and in some cases die (when members do not feel a need for a community or collectively do no longer feel a sense of a community) but they can still continue to associate with each other in one way or another. It is this association that forms a social network. Furthermore, social network approach to social capital assumes that communities solve group problems and provide individuals with plenty of social and economic benefits. However, the differences between a community and individuals members of a social network are not clearly addressed in the literature.

The effectiveness of a social structure in which social capital is located, depends for most part on the characteristics of individuals, the group they belong to, the structure of the group and the way members in a group interact with each other and the expectation of their community goals and shared norms of reciprocity. Many studies focusing on analysis of social capital tend to ignore effects of group characteristics on an individual's behaviour and the influence of an individual behaviour on the structure of the community. This is a major theoretical problem since in every community, the interplay between social capital and individual behaviour is enthralling but hardly explored. There are those individuals who can succeed socially and economically and their success might have nothing to do with whether they are relate to others in a community but rather success might be attributed to the results of hard work or wealth inheritance.

The treatment of social capital as "the sum of the actual and potential resources embedded within, available through, and derived from the network of relationships possessed by an individual or social unit", suggests that social capital exists at both the individual level and the group level. However, most of studies on social capital only focus on group level of analysis, measuring social capital through individual participation in community affairs (Putnam, 1999). Though in some cases, the social capital of a group depends on the social capital held by its individual members and without a group that provides the social context and social protocols to guide acceptable behaviour, an individual could not acquire any social capital.

Further, there are possible correlations between social capital and power structures. Social capital is both affected by and affects power structures. The ability to create or destroy social capital in any community is largely influenced by how power structures and norms of association operate. Synthesis of the literature revealed that social capital is equated to notions of strong or prosperous communities and most writers herald it as the glue that holds communities together. Yet, social capital remains an empirically elusive theory. In addition little is known about its fundamental variables and how they actually operate individually or together to provide collective benefits to communities.

The thinking that social capital is an end in itself is seriously flawed. Social capital is best understood as a potential means or instrument for achieving particular outcomes, rather than an objective outcome in itself. Indeed, social capital itself is value neutral, though this fact is loosely addressed in the literature. Briggs (1997) indicated that social capital has no right or wrong to it until some judgment is made about the ends to which it is expected to achieve.

From an economic point of view, social capital is only valuable for a rational individual (rational choice theory is an economic framework for understanding and often formally modelling social and economic behaviour) but not all people in societies are necessary rational or can effectively display a rational behaviour. In addition, some members of a community might not display rational behaviour all the time and some might not think in a rational order. In other words, social capital might not be used for attaining good intentions. As Putnam (2004) indicated that not all externalities accrued to social capital are positive. Similar to human and physical capital—knowledge of chemistry or aircraft can be used for deadly and destructive purposes, so can social capital. In fact, some social networks use social capital to raise money or resources to support criminal groups.

Popular economic analysis asserts that establishing corporate identities for good names is a way to establish markets for certain types of social capital (Tadelis, 1999). Companies that have earned a good reputation for the production of particular brands are likely to attract more investment. This line of economic thinking shows that social capital is a strong marketing tool, but the analyses lack the distinctions between trust, identity, reputation, and social capital itself.

Many research approaches treat social capital as a single entity. Moreover, social capital is a conglomerate of several variables and treating it as a single unit, do not contribute much to a clear understanding of what variables constitute social capital and how such variables should be measured and factored out. Furthermore, it is important to realize that social capital also requires investment in other forms of capital, for example, human capital (skills and knowledge) or economic capital (money). In other words, building social capital has its costs associated with it. For example, making new contacts and maintaining existing ones requires time and energy, and these obligations can become highly demanding when they are insufficient time and resources available.

Small communities might have high or bonded social capital but if they lack resources e.g. financial capital, necessary for building social amenities such as schools or if they lack the skills for attracting or building entrepreneurship that boasts up their economy, the amount of social capital they posses, might be equal to nothing less than poverty and isolation from the rest of the world. Research on ethnic entrepreneurs showed that social capital tends to be high in disadvantaged immigrant groups with distinct cultural characteristics but that unfortunately increases prejudice towards them (Portes & Sensenbrenner 1993; Woolcock 1998).

In modern economic thought, there are fundamentally three problems associated with negative effect of social capital. First, a strong embeddings in social networks can promote a closed social system and blind adherence to group norms even if some norms might exacerbate hate and distrust on an entire social system. In other words, people who are members of a closed system are likely to follow norms of operation since deviant behaviour might result to serious sanctions. Consequently, innovative and risky behaviour is not encouraged.

Second, safety nets provided by communities with increased bonded type of social capital, cannot encourage people to do their best on their own. Third, social capital can be viewed through rent-seeking behaviour and collusion. Rent-seeking behaviour is a phenomenon that happens when an individual uses resources to obtain an economic gain from others without reciprocating any benefits back to the community. Social capital understood though rent-seeking behaviour implies individuals can get involved in the extraction of uncompensated value from others without making any contribution to productivity, such as obtaining help from one's social network and refusal or inability to reciprocate or lack of contribution to the welfare of others in the community.

Benefits of social capital are limiting and do not extend beyond a social network's confines. The extent to which an individual can derive economic gains from social capital depends on the extent to which an individual is connected to others in the community (i.e., who an individual knows, how close his/her relationship is to others, and the resources available through these connections). For example, people who are well connected to people of power in a community can have access to information about job opportunities, which in turn provides them with personal economic gains.

Similar to other forms of capital, social capital is not always available to all members of the society. There is considerable evidence suggesting that there is an uneven distribution of social capital in societies, organised along such dimensions as social class, gender, age ethnicity and locality (Edwards & Foley, 1997). It is also argued that privileged groups in societies have higher levels of social capital when compared to marginalised groups (Putnam, 2002). Disadvantaged groups, such as immigrants, homeless, the less educated, those with disabilities and elderly people, may feel socially excluded from a main stream society and thus will not have high social capital.

Finally, one of the most critical limitations of social capital as a scientific theory is that there is no widely held agreement on how to measure it. The lack of standard measurement matrices has exacerbated failure to reach consensus on a standardized definition. Social capital is an abstract theoretical construct rather than a clearly tangible phenomenon. In addition, the components of social capital such as trust, shared understanding, social protocols can be directly observable and even measurable; however the interactions between these variables, constitutes another level of complexity rendering social capital itself imperceptible, and hence difficult to define and measure. It is not sufficient to only rely on trust as a single proxy for measuring social capital, since trust is a nebulous concept in its own and it tend to subsumes many other intermediary and often hidden variables.

CONCLUSION

In traditional economic theory, capital refers to factors of production and especially those we individually or collectively invest on to create durable assets. In most cases, capital is discussed with respect to those assets that can be used for productive purposes. Coleman (1988) described three forms of capital: physical capital, human capital, and social capital. Physical capital is the tangible and financial assets. This form of capital is relatively easy to measure in monetary terms; and it is this kind of capital that has been analysed in Economics and Accounting. The second kind of capital is human, which constitutes the characteristics of people and their skills and competence. Human capital can be perceived as the knowledge and educational background of the people. There are also those personal characteristics of people such as experiences and outlooks in life, constituting another form of capital—cultural capital. The third form of capital is social capital, implying how people relate to each other. Another type of capital that is rarely discussed in the economic or social theory is natural capital, which refers to collective value natures provides to humanity.

Physical capital is 'wholly tangible' and it is created by changes in materials in order to form tools that 'facilitate production', and human capital is 'less tangible' and created by changes in persons that 'bring about skills and capabilities that make them able to act in new ways' (Coleman, 1988, p. 100), social capital is less tangible yet for it exists in 'the relations among persons', 'unlike other forms of capital, social capital is inherent in the structure of relations between actors and among actors.

From overall analysis of current work presented in this chapter, it is safe to conclude that the meaning and utility, dimensions and types of social capital differ considerably, relative to the context in which it is investigated. In other words, the determinants of social capital are context specific and the consequences results from its structure and content might change over a period of time. And ultimately, no standard definition of social capital exists and this undermines it as a scientific theory. Despite its limitations, social capital has widely applied to solve many problems. Some of the applications areas where social capital has been used as an analytical framework are discussed in chapter III.

REFERENCES

Adler, P.S. & Kwon, S.W. (2002). Social capital: propsects for a new concept. *Academy of Management Review*, *27*(1), 17-40.

Bourdieu, P. (1986). Forms of Capital. In John G. Richardson (Ed.) *Handbook of theory and research for the Sociology of Education* (pp. 241-255). New York: Greenwood Press.

Edwards, B. & Foley, M.W. (1997). Social capital and the political economy of our discontent. *American Behavioral Scientist*, *40*(5), 669.

Etzkowitz, H. & Leydesdorff, L. (1995). The Triple Helix of University-Industry-Government relations: A Laboratory for Knowledge Based Economic Development. *EASST Review*, *1*(14), 11-19.

Falk, I. (2000). Human capital and Social capital: What's the difference? Adult learning commentary. Retrieved November, 15th 2008 from http://www.ala.asn.au/commentaries/Falk1810.pdf

Becker, G. (1993). Nobel Lecture: The Economic Way of Looking at Life. *Journal of Political Economy*, *101*(3), 383-409.

Bourdieu, P. (1986). The forms of capital. In Richardson, J.G. (Ed.) *Handbook of theory and research for the sociology of education* (pp. 241-58). New York: Greenwood Press.

Cohen, D., & Prusak, L. (2001). *In good company: How social capital makes organizations work*. Massachusetts: Harvard Business School Press.

Coleman, J. S. (1988). Social capital in the creation of human capital. *American Journal of Sociology*, *94*, 95-120.

Ellison, N. B., Steinfield, C., & Lampe, C. (2007). The benefits of Facebook „friends:" Social capital and college students' use of online social network sites. *Journal of Computer-Mediated Communication*, *12*(4). Retrieved December, 1st 2008 from http://jcmc.indiana.edu/vol12/issue4/ellison.html

Friedkin, N. E. & Johnsen, E. C. (1997). Social positions in influence networks. *Social Networks, 19,* 209-222.

Fukuyama, F. (1999, November). Social capital and civil society. Paper presented at the Conference on Second Generation Reforms IMF Headquarters, Washington, D.C.

Granovetter, M. S. (1973). The strength of weak ties. *American Journal of Sociology, 78*(6), 1360-1380.

Hanifan, L. J. (1916). The rural school community centre. *Annuals of the American Academy of Political and Social Science, 67,* 130-138.

Hobbs, G. (2000). What is social capital? A brief literature overview. *Economic and Social Research Foundation*: Retrieved November, 15th 2008 from http://www.caledonia.org.uk/papers/hobbs.pdf

Light, I. (2004). Social capital's unique accessibility. *Journal of the American Planning Association, 70,* 145-151.

Loury, G. (1977). A dynamic thgeory of racial income differences. In P.A. Wallace and A. Le Mund (Eds.) *Women, minorities, and employment discrimination* (pp. 153-186). Lexington, MA: Lexington Books.

Nahapiet, J. & Ghoshal, S. (1998). Social capital, intellectual capital, and the organizational advantage. *The Academy of Management Review, 23*(2), 242-267.

OECD (2001 Summer), The Well-being of Nations: The role of human and social capital, Paris. *OECD Observer,* No 226/227, 200.

Paxton, P. (1999). Is social capital declining in the United States? A multiple indicator assessment. *American Journal of Sociology, 105*(1), 88-127.

Portes, A. & Sensenbrenner, J. (1993). Embeddedness and immigration: Notes on the determinants of economic action. *American Journal of Sociology, 98,* 1320-1350.

Putnam R (2000). *Bowling alone: The collapse and revival of American community.* New York: Simon Schuster.

Resnick, P. (2004). Impersonal sociotechnical capital, ICTs, and collective action Among strangers. In. Dutton, W Kahin, B. O'Callaghan, R. & Wyckoff, A. (Eds.). *Transforming Enterprise.* Retrieved from November, 15th 2008 from http://www.si.umich.edu/~presnick/papers/xforment/chapter.pdf

Schultz, T. W. (1961). Investment in Human Capital. *The American Economic Review, 1*(2), 1-17.

Woolcock, M. (1998). Social capital and economic development: Toward a theoretical. synthesis and policy framework. *Theory and Society, 27*(2), 151-208.

World Bank (1999). Social capital research group. Retrieved November 15th 2008 from http://www.worldbank.org/poverty/scapital/

Chapter III
Social Capital Use–Case Application Areas

INTRODUCTION

Despite lack of meticulousness, social capital continues to occupy a central position in many discussions about community, trust and social networks. The multi-dimensionality and multivariate nature of social capital provides a foundation for explaining, although sometimes vaguely so, various social issues in communities and social networks. In most of the discussions in scientific work, social capital is continuously treated as either an output or an input. Researchers write about communities performing better due to higher levels of social capital, others attribute superior performance of social amenities such as national economy to the prevalence of higher social capital. Some writers mentioned the construct as a circumventing term to mean one or more of its core variables (trust, shared understanding, social protocols etc.) and their application to specific areas of interests, while others take a holistic view to describe all of its variables and their utility to addressing social problems anchored in communities.

This chapter discusses the application of social capital in a variety of contexts to solve community problems. This is by no means a complete comprehensive coverage of cases in which social capital is currently utilized, rather the cases presented here are considered sufficient to illustrate the growing relevance of social capital to many application areas. The goal of the chapter is to expose the reader to key application areas and to think about the practical and theoretical relevance of social capital to research and practice in other emergent cases.

MODERN APPLICATION OF SOCIAL CAPITAL

The increasing inspiration attracting the wide use of social capital is the nature of its elasticity in helping researchers to integrate ideas from various disciplines in order to tackle community problems. Concrete examples of researchers who have contributed to individual application areas mentioned in the Chapter are: policy and civic engagement (Putnam, 1993; economic investment (Sobel, 2002) and community development (Gittell & Vidal, 1998); Cohen and Prusak (2001) analysis of organizational development within business entities. The Organization for Economic Corporation and Development (OECD), the World Bank and The International Monetary Fund are three of the major organizations that have done a fair amount of work on social capital as measure of development and economic growth and as an indicator of educational achievement.

There is also a growing interest in employing social capital as a springboard for addressing the digital divide. Social capital has also been used as a way to illuminate the relationship between the micro level of educational experience and the macro level of social structures such as community contributions to educational achievement. Both Bourdieu (1986) and Coleman (1988) are instrumental in this regard. Daniel, McCalla and Schiwer (2002) presented work on the extension of social capital to examine social issues in technology enhanced learning environments. This chapter will elaborate on some of the major use-cases of social capital in modern life.

Community Development and Governance

In Economic discussions, the degree of development in most countries is determined by economic indicators such as gross domestic product (GDP) and total factor productivity. In the last decade, alternative indices covering various facets of social life and community associations are introduced into the equation of economic growth and productivity. Leading Economists and other researchers, principally, from the World Bank and elsewhere, pointed out social indicators such as community participation, are crucial to economic development and growth. They describe these indicators in terms of social capital which encompass multiple aspects of the social indicators that are decisive to community development.

Social capital promotes collective action which consists primarily of community-organized activities for building and maintaining infrastructure and for providing related public services. For example, instead of development experts engaging in building civil institutions in isolation from the communities in which these institutions are situated, social capital help them to include local mandates and take into account the contribution of voluntary participation in community activities. These are measured by the degree of community engagement and the resulting kinds of relationships individuals maintained (Putnam, 2000).

Furthermore, development experts view social cohesion as a vehicle of social capital necessary for helping people to work together to address common needs, overcome constraints, and consider diverse interests. Through social cohesion techniques, individuals and groups in communities can engage in civil resolution of differences in non-confrontational ways. Social cohesion also covers social inclusion approaches, which are more likely to promote equal access to opportunities, resources, and removes both formal and informal barriers to participation in community building.

Development approaches treat social capital as a community property capable of generating public benefit, facilitating achievement of higher levels of efficiency and productivity and economic growth. Researchers at the World Bank in particular have immensely contributed to the link between social capital and economic growth. They view social capital as a way to engage local communities to fully participate in the development of their society in their own terms.

Further, in order to amplify the chances of successful development initiatives, development practitioners designing interventions would benefit from information about the disposition and distribution of social capital. Moreover, with availability of better information infrastructure about how prevalent and effective local institutions are in terms of their capacity, leadership, and linkages, it became easier to assess implementation risks and opportunities.

The theoretical use of social capital to analyze development issues is largely informed by work on social network structures of individuals, groups and communities and forging productive linkages among people and organizations, both at the local and national levels. Further, from the economic development point of view, social capital is considered as a social investment critical to effective operation of communities and civil societies. Such an investment helps people to build capabilities and nurtures sense of belonging in communities and neighbourhoods.

In addition, there are other community development researchers who are focused on building social capital through the recognition of informal social networks such as family, friends and acquaintances. They consider informal social networks as critical to such problems as crisis management, getting work done quickly or living in good neighbourhoods. International, multinational and national institutions involved in development have also come to acknowledge that in order to effectively address community development and pave ways for smooth policy implementation, they needed to encourage grassroots community participation and focus on building community capacities and more importantly, urge community members to get involved at various levels of policy development and implementation.

Increasingly, the emphasis of social capital in relation to community development is concerned with the analysis of social issues critical to the enforcement of effective governance models. Research revealed a positive correlation between social capital, the quality of governance and economic growth (e.g. Putnam 1993, Knack & Keefer 1997; Knack 2000). Putnam (1993) work in particular, which was based on identification of a relatively small number of variables (e.g. density of civic engagement, newspaper readership and voting), was among the first to associate governance, civic engagement and social capital. Subsequently, his work led to increased interests in social capital theory and immense ramifications and acceptance of the theory in many domains.

In later work, Putnam (2000) analysed social capital and its role in fostering civic engagement and governance, suggesting that participation in community and civic activities are relatively linked and that social capital help individuals build connections beyond family and work. Participation in diverse organizations ranging from social clubs to sports teams provides enormous opportunities to develop better social relationships and ultimately increased civic engagement and good governance.

Policy analysts looking to reduce poverty and empower communities in the developing world tapped into the substantial promise of social capital to stimulate personal connections and building of social structures that enhance community involvement and high levels of trust. These initiatives are deliberate in terms of their long term impact on social change and development. Some concrete outcomes that are correlated to the influence of social capital in communities within the community development sphere include: better public health, lower crime rates, and more efficient financial markets (Adler & Kwon, 2002). In addition, those concerned with the role of social capital and civil society, collectively suggest that high social capital in any community is likely to encourage civic engagement and improve the quality of "good governance"[1].

Education

One of the earliest Sociological analyses of social capital is in connection to education and school achievements. Coleman (1986) and Bourdieu (1990) used social capital as a way to illuminate the relationship between the micro level of educational experience and the macro level of social relationships (policy intervention) and structures. Coleman (1980), in particular, developed the concept of social capital to conceptualize social patterns and processes that contribute to cultural disparities of student achievement. He argued that the educational expectation, norms, and obligations that exist within a family or a community are important sources of social capital that can influence the level of parental involvement and investment, which in turn affect academic success.

Coleman (1998) later demonstrated that schoolchildren's performance was influenced positively by the existence of close ties between teachers, parents, neighbours and church ministers. This insight has subsequently been explored in some depth through both a series of replication studies using other approaches (Field, 2005). Further, drawing from the work of Coleman and Bourdieu, social capital provides educators with the tools to scrutinize the role of communities in fostering education in novel ways. The World Bank has also done a fair amount of work on social capital and education. Researchers in the World Bank focused on social capital and community participation and how these impact school achievements.

Schuller (2001) examined the role of social capital and the development of partnerships between schools, Universities and other institutions. He argued that the kinds of relationships that can be derived from the partnerships between schools and Universities can affect the collective potential of human capital and subsequently social capital within those organizations. It must be noted that the levels of social capital in a broad spectrum and more distinctively, a bridging type of social capital is crucial in creation and maintenance of partnerships between schools and Universities. However, the levels of social capital between schools and Universities cannot be built to any extent without establishing trust and identifying shared understanding.

Further, within the educational milieu, the connection between social capital and lifelong learning has been a major focus of interest at least within the context of research endeavours in some European educational systems (Field, 2005). In North America, Putnam (1999) envisioned social capital not only in terms of enhancing civic engagement but as a lever for renewing school systems through educating children to engage in civic issues and to contribute to social development and learning of their communities. Furthermore, Putnam mentioned that the mounting interest in employing social capital within the educational sector through the development of civic programs, community service requirements and even extracurricular activities like sports and music, have long-term effects on the civic engagement of those students. He particularly stated that the decline in social capital in the United States of America might have been even sharper had it not been for the quality and strength of the higher education.

Putnam (2000) further noted that in the school system, social capital formation requires careful thinking about space for interactions. School buildings need to be built to enable easy and casual connections among people who might otherwise find themselves in isolated niches or working environments that are highly isolated from each other. Though Putnam made these observations within the context of school in the United States of America, his analysis has far wider ramifications to many other educational systems across the globe. For example, the link between social capital and education entails that countries with high stocks of social capital are more likely to produce students with better academic performance than nations with low stocks of social capital.

Researchers from the Organisation for Economic Co-Operation and Development (OECD) have done substantial work on the relationship between human and social capital. They suggested that the role of social capital in enhancing human capital is arguable. They indicated that well connected parents have the opportunities to provide their children with better educational opportunities. In addition to its role in international development and governance, the World Bank (1999) indicated that social capital illuminates the relationship between many levels of educational experiences.

Though social capital has been applied to the analysis of performances of formal educational systems, especially in developing countries and school achievement, the theory is extended to address community-based informal educational systems. This seemingly new area of research and application of social capital is perhaps more relevant to the analysis of how social capital interacts with learning and the infrastructure associated with supporting informal educational systems, since, an informal educational system is mainly concerned with the association and the quality of life from a local community perspective. It can be argued that success of any informal education depends mostly on how informal educators initiate and promote dialogue among individuals and groups, to cultivate environments in which people can build trust, develop shared understanding and work together as a community.

The Corporate Sector

For many years, it has been reverberated in both organisational and corporate learning literature that a commonly misinformed approach to knowledge management in many business environments is the ability to capture, mine, map, extract, record and store knowledge in computerised or databases systems for later access, sharing and reusability. More recently, a number of business organisations have realised that certain kinds of knowledge, especially the kind embedded within social relationship are critical to knowledge management and are part of implicit or tacit knowledge. Such knowledge includes intuition; heuristics and personal experiences gained through a long period of time cannot be easily captured, discerned or expressed in written form.

Numerous researchers in business organisations turned their attention to develop new approaches to address issues around knowledge management that are social in nature and more so, community-oriented. Community oriented approaches to knowledge management, championed by social capital are found to be more efficient and cost-effective. Today, many global leading organizations such as the International Business Machines (IBM), Microsoft, Shell, and others are either in the process or have already embraced community-oriented approaches grounded in the theory of social capital, to tackle knowledge management issues within their corporate environments. Researchers in these areas of knowledge management and corporate training develop new techniques for capturing knowledge, fostering learning or initiating and supporting social and knowledge networks. Their efforts resulted to the emergence of new theories of learning which are more towards group and community learning than individualistic centred (Lave & Wenger, 1991). For example, Cohen and Prusak (2001) pointed out that traditional knowledge management structures have masked the deeply social nature within organisations. They treated social capital as an alternative approach to unveil the rich nature of social relationships in social groups.

The development of social capital within organizations is necessary for the creation of intellectual capital and hence innovation. One of the main arguments in favour of social capital as an enabler of business operation are centred on the grounds that people with rich social capital are better informed, more creative, more efficient, and better problem solvers. With the right networks, people save time because they know where to get the information they need and they do not need to duplicate effort and reduce the over-use of overhead. Social networks also enable networks; organisations can foster cooperation and collaboration among its employees. In other words, an organisation with the tight social network of employees tends to do better than those with inadequate social networks.

Further, the best performers and the most profitable companies today tend to invest in social networks to generate more social capital. Increasingly it is argued that companies with rich social capital produce outstanding business results, e.g. higher sales, better quality products, more satisfied employees, greater profits, and superior market value. Social capital can encourage better knowledge sharing, high levels of trusting relationships in an organization and efficient business dealings and subsequent reduction in operational and transaction costs, due to this high level of trust and cooperative spirit. This can extend beyond individuals within organisations to organizations and their customers and partners.

The more tangible operation of social capital in many business organisations can also be seen in the way people continuously engage in conversation with each other around water coolers, open-plan offices or cubicles or escalators. There are many organisations that design open spaces to encourage informal interaction, where employees can freely socialise and to talk to each other about work and other issues of interest. Research pointed out that social capital can be a strong lever for knowledge sharing and that knowledge cannot be separated from the communities that create it, use it, and transform it (Verna, 2000). Production, sharing and dissemination of any type of knowledge within an organisation require conversation, experimentation, and sharing experiences with other people. Verna (2000) noted that in many business organisations, knowledge sharing and information exchange becomes more relevant especially as people move beyond routine processes into more complex and challenging issues in which they can rely on their peers and communities to which they relate to.

Digital Divide

In modern societies, information and communication technology forms the hub of social interaction, enabling people to engage in dialogue that fosters a sense of community. While benefits of technologies are enormous and evident in many realms of day to day activities, information and communications technology is rapidly becoming a barrier in many societies of the world, especially in poor communities and remote areas. Researchers, policymakers and pundits observed a growing gap between people who possess the skills and access to various forms of information and communication technologies and those do not. They emphasized that those with access and literacy skills are significantly advantaged over those who are less skilled in technology and do not have access.

Visionary social technologists such as Castells (2001) viewed the Internet as creating new forms of social organization, identity, inequality and power structures. He argued that claims in support of Internet are causing estrangement in societies. For example, without access to information and communication technology, those living in rural areas as well as people who are less literate and possess economic capital, are pushed to the margins of the disadvantaged sector of the society and therefore are pervasively falling victims of the digital divide. People who are more likely to experience the paroxysm of digital divide include digital immigrants[2]; the baby boomers, as well as late technology adopters. Development researchers view social capital and information technology investments as integrally related and interdependent. Many multinational organisations such as the World Bank and OECD are increasingly concerned that there is a great risk that information technology will exclude poor people and entire societies, making the gap between the rich and poor wider.

In the scientific discourse, researchers use the term digital divide as a theoretical phenomenon to describe the gap in technology usage and access. OECD (2002) referred to digital divide as a theoretical underpinning for defining a division between individuals and households at different socio-economic levels, regarding their chances and opportunities to access or use information and communication technologies. Digital divide does not only manifest itself in gaps in computer usage but also Internet access and affordability between different population groups, normally segmented along income, age, educational level and other parameters. In many countries, several efforts have been made to address the digital divide, focusing primarily on providing people with free access to computers or training on acquisition of information literacy skills. Though lower socio-economic groups are increasingly gaining Internet access, it is still possible that the digital divide will persist as new technologies become available.

Compared to content and cognitive dimensions of social capital, the structure dimension is the most relevant dimension of social capital driving the development initiatives in effectively addressing the predicament of the digital divide. The effectiveness with which structural social capital dimension, in the form of the associations and networks that fulfill this role depends upon many aspects of the groups, reflecting their structure, their membership, and the way they function (Grootaert, Narayan, Nyhan, Jones & Woolcock, 2004). The World Bank (2002) has recognised that information and communication is critical to community life and that access to information is being increasingly recognized as central to helping poor communities who have a stronger voice in matters affecting their well being. The utilization of social capital within the auspices of the digital divide is inclined to understanding the ways and means by which poor households receive information regarding market conditions and public services, and the extent of their access to communications infrastructure such as the Internet.

In many countries, a range of government policies are put in place to address the inequalities in computer technologies access and use since the late 1990s. The use of social capital and digital divide is a pedestal for examining new patterns of Internet use and adaptation of a holistic perspective on understanding of new forms and expressions of community and social formations. A successful digital divide policy approach requires a social capital framework, which recognizes that community assets include not only the formal skills of individuals and the tangible associations and institutions in a given locality. It also takes into account the informal proximity-based social clusters and intangible networks of 'weak-ties' relationships that people build and maintain through new media and network information and communication technologies.

Notley and Foth (2008) employed social capital as a framework to the analysis of issues of access and a broader understanding of the way the Internet and other information and communication technologies can be used to increase and strengthen digital dividend. Many countries have embarked in the development public programmes intended to provide access centres and technology expertise to people. In urban centres organisations such as the Young Men Christian Association (YMCA) and Young Women Christian Association (YWCA) (an umbrella organization of the global network of the YWCA, which act as an advocate for young women's leadership, peace, justice, human rights and the sustainable development both working on a grassroots and global scale), provides free technology access and technology training for those in need. Social capital plays a major role in these organisations, helping bridge the digital divide, through mobilisation of local capacity through voluntary participation. In other words, people who are technology literate and have the time, share knowledge with those that have fewer skills. However, the ability of social capital to bridge the digital divide through these organisations depends fundamentally on how people interact with each other, whether they are willing to get involved in neighbourhood associations activities and use their social network to enhance social communication to others in the community.

Public Health

Public health is concerned with the understanding and management of diseases and health related threats to the health of a community, in doing so; it pays particular attention to the social context of diseases and health. Public health focuses on improving health through society wide interventions using both clinical and social approaches. Public health mandates across the globe are increasingly recognising that health experience is shaped by genetic factors, individual lifestyles and a wide range of social, cultural, economic, political and environmental factors (WHO, 1999). In addition, research contribution from various individuals show that those who live in disadvantaged social circumstances have more illness, greater distress, more disability and shorter lives than those who are more affluent (Mackenbach & Bakker, 2002).

Most of the research in this area often begins with the assumption that people's wellbeing depends not only on clinical interventions but also social and particularly relational needs. Such needs include the need to belong, the role of social interactions in improving people's quality of life and in affecting individual's behaviour in relation to societal social protocols. A growing number of researchers agree that social networks and community involvement have positive health consequences. People who are socially engaged with others and actively involved in their communities tend to live longer and they are physically and mentally healthier than those who are isolated and maintain less contact with peers, neighbours, relatives and friends (Kawachi et al., 1997; Kawachi and Berkman, 2001). Putnam (2000) noted, the more integrated people to their community, the less likely they are to experience diseases such as heart attacks, strokes, cancer, depression and premature death.

As an information channel, social capital can promote more rapid diffusion of health information, increasing the likelihood that healthy norms of behaviour are adopted. The prevalence of social capital in a community can exert influence over deviant health-related behaviour, increase access to local services and amenities, and provide affective support and act as the source of self-esteem and mutual respect (Kawachi et al. 1999). Furthermore, Kawachi et al. (1999) found a strong correlation between indicators of high social capital and lower mortality rates. They found that communities with low social capital are characterized by a higher proportion of residents who report their health as being poor. Perhaps the strongest statement linking social capital and health is offered by Lomas (1998). He pointed out that the way people organize their society, the extent to which they encourage interaction among their citizens, and the degree to which they trust and associate with each other in caring communities is probably the most important determinant of public health.

In health research, there is growing recognition of the need to separate structural from cognitive social capital because the two components have different relationships with health outcomes. For example, generally speaking, high levels of cognitive social capital are associated with good mental health but high structural social capital is sometimes associated with poor mental health (for examples of studies and exploration of the hypotheses as to the reasons for these associations (De Silva et al., 2006).

CONCLUSION

Ferlander (2003) scrutinized the extent to which the use of information and communication technology can create or recreate create social capital and local community in an urban environment. She examined whether or not new technologies lead to new forms of social inclusion or to the creation of disparity in terms of access to information. Noticeably, as one can imagine, the areas in which social capital is currently applied are varied. Social capital has been used as an analytical tool for examining lack of civic engagement and economic development. It has also been used to determine the effectiveness of educational systems and knowledge networks. Further, the application of social capital has also entered business and industry, where social capital now plays a greater role in the analysis of organizational learning and knowledge sharing.

The digitization of social interaction in modern societies has created a disparity between those who have the skills to explore and garner the benefits from information and communications technologies and those who lack the skills and access points. Social capital is increasingly becoming an interesting analytical tool for explaining and indeed leveraging the disparity between those with access and those without access, as well as those who possess sophisticated information and communications skills and those without. Within contemporary social approaches to public health, community engagement remains central to improving health and healthy living. Further, educational policymakers and both classroom and online teachers have realized that the notion of social capital provides prolific grounds for reengineering teaching and tutoring methods.

The social capital approach to community development and civic engagement aims to build capacity in neighbourhood institutions, strengthen ties among communities, and assist citizens to work individually and collectively toward collective change. It encourages mass participation at various levels of a society in the design of development and civic policies that are more inclusive, more collaborative, and operationally more effective. Development advocates maintain that organizational support and social network activities are crucial for bridging and linking social capital. Social capital helps community development by engaging people to organize themselves and mobilize local resources to solve shared problems. The effectiveness of groups and networks and the extent to which they can help disseminate information, reduce opportunistic behaviour and facilitate collective decision-making depends upon many aspects of these groups, reflecting their structure, their membership and the way they function.

Education is perhaps under investigated area in relations to the prevalence of social capital. Educators who have explored social capital have explored it in a cyclical way, first as a social determinant of schooling and of human capital's accumulation. And second, the role of education in the creation of social capital. The application of social capital within analysis of educational institutions has sparked novel ways in which educational institutions are designed around communities and neighbourhoods. In increasingly diverse societies, using social capital as an approach to the analysis of schools and schooling has helped communities to tackle drop children's dropout rates in schools and to some extent sustain schooling.

This chapter provided examples of various use-cases of social capital. The increasing interest in using social capital in numerous application areas revolves around two key shared issues. First, individuals and communities can obtain needed resources and support from their network of social ties. Second, in combination with other human and financial resources, social capital can play a significant role in influencing social, economic, educational, technological and civic participation of people in communities. The varied examples of the application of social capital provided in this chapter also suggests that researchers view social capital differently and as a result, they have developed different approaches for studying and measuring the theory. The application of many approaches for measuring social capital paints a general picture on the difficulty relating to understanding the basic definitions, types and dimensions of social capital. Chapter IV provides some of the major approaches used to measure social capital.

REFERENCES

Bourdieu, P. (1986). The forms of capital. In J. G. Richardson (Ed.), *The Handbook of Theory: Research for the Sociology of Education* (pp. 241-258). New York: Greenwood Press.

Castells, M. (2001). *The Internet galaxy: Reflections on the Internet, business, and society.* New York: Oxford University Press.

Cohen, D., & Prusak, L. (2001). *In good company: How social capital makes organizations work.* Massachusetts: Harvard Business School Press.

Coleman, J. S. (1988). Social capital in the creation of human capital. *American Journal of Sociology, 94,* 95-120.

Daniel, B., McCalla, G., & Schwier, R. (2002). A process model for building social capital in virtual learning communities. *Proceedings of the International Conference on Computers in Education (ICCE)* (pp, 574-577). Auckland, New Zealand.

De Silva, M., Harpham, T., Tuan, T., Bartolini, R., Penny, M., & Huttly, S. (2006). Psychometric and cognitive validation of a social capital measurement tool in Peru and Vietnam. *Social Science and Medicine, 62*(4), 941–953.

Ferlander, S. (2003). *The Internet, social capital and local community. Unpublished thesis*: Retrieved November 22nd 2008 from http://www.crdlt.stir.ac.uk/Docs/SaraFerlanderPhD.pdf

Field, J. (2005). *Social capital and lifelong learning, the encyclopedia of informal education,* Retrieved November 22nd 2008 from www.infed.org/lifelonglearning/social_capital_and_lifelong_learning.htm

Gittell, R., & Vidal, A. (1998). *Community organizing. Building social capital as a development strategy.* London: Sage Publications.

Grootaert, C., Narayan, D., Jone, V., & Woolcock, M. (2004). *Measuring social capital. An Integrated Questionnaire.* Retrieved November 22nd, 2008 from: http://poverty2.forumone.com/files/11998_WP18-Web.pdf

Kawachi, I. and Berkman, L. (2001). Social ties and mental health. *Journal of Urban Health, 78,* 458–467.

Kawachi, I., Kennedy, B. P., Lochner, K., & Prothrow-Stith, D. (1997) Social capital, income inequality, and mortality. *American Journal of Public Health, 87,* 1491–1498.

Knack, S. (2000). Social capital and the quality of government: Evidence from the United States. *World Bank Policy Research Working Paper, 2504.*

Knack, S. & Keefer, P. (1997). Does social capital have an economic payoff? A cross-country investigation. *Quarterly Journal of Economics, 112*(4), 1251-1288.

Lave, J., & Wenger, E. (1991). Situated Learning: Legitimate Peripheral Participation. New York: Cambridge University Press.

Lomas, J. (1998), Social capital and health: implications for public health and epidemiology, *Social Science and Medicine, 47*(9), 1181-1188.

Mackenbach, J., & Bakker, M. (Eds) (2002). *Reducing inequalities in health: a European perspective.* London: Rutledge.

Notley, T. M., & Foth, M. (2008). Extending Australia's digital divide policy: an examination of the value of social inclusion and social capital policy frameworks. *Australian Social Policy, 7.* Retrieved November 22nd 2008 from http://eprints.qut.edu.au/archive/00012021/01/12021b.pdf

OECD (2002). Information Technology Outlook. Paris: *OECD Report.*

Putnam, R. (2000). *Bowling alone: The collapse and revival of American community.* New York: Simon Schuster.

Putnam, R. D. (1993). *Making democracy work: Civic traditions in modern Italy.* Princeton, NJ: Princeton University Press.

Schuller, T. (2001). The complementary roles of human and social capital. *ISUMA, 2*(10), 18-24.

Sobel, J. (2002). Can we trust social capital? *Journal of Economic Literature,* 40, 139-154.

Verna, A. (2000). *Knowledge networks and communities of practice. Organizational development, 32*(4). Retrieved November, 22nd 2008, from http://www.odnetwork.org/odponline/vol32n4/knowledgenets.html

Woolcock, M. (1998). Social capital and economic development: Toward a theoretical. synthesis and policy framework. *Theory and Society, 27*(2), 151-208.

World Bank (1999). *Social capital research group.* Retrieved November 22nd, 2008 from http://www.worldbank.org/poverty/scapital/

World Health Organization (1999). *Health 21: the health for all policy framework for the WHO European Region.* Copenhagen: WHO

Web Links

http://www.developmentgateway.com.au/

http://www.worldbank.org

http://www.imf.org

http://www.oecd.org

ENDNOTES

[1] The Australian Development Gateway asserted that "good governance" depends on transparency, accountability and equality in ways that are responsive to the needs of people. It is composed of the mechanisms, processes and institutions through which citizens and groups can articulate their interests, exercise their legal rights, meet their obligations and mediate their differences.

[2] A digital immigrant is an individual who grew up without digital technology and adopted it later. This is normally contrasted to a digital native, a person who has grown up with digital technology such as computers, the Internet, mobile phones and MP3.

Chapter IV
Approaches for Measuring Social Capital

INTRODUCTION

It is possible to measure how much an economic capital is worth, at least in terms of monetary value, through the use of sophisticated econometric tools, while conditioning other factors (Cēterīs paribus)[1], in comparison, measuring social capital is significantly more challenging and complex business. The complexity in measuring social capital relates to the fact it is an intangible concept, multidimensional and multivariate in nature.

Further as discussed earlier, social capital lacks a unified definition and dimension. To make matters more problematic, social capital is not a static construct that can be easily captured and conditioned during measurement, but rather it is a moving target, difficult to capture, without resorting to some assumptions and conditioning during measurement. It is unimaginable to condition and study individuals based on the number of their associations over a period of time, while keeping them away from making new friendship, leaving old relationships and withholding their associations until a study is completed.

Those researchers, who have attempted to measure social capital, resorted to the analysis of its indicators rather than the concepts underlying it. In addition while isolating social capital from its main indicators is attainable, and often with less degree of sophistication, separating its main components from each other posses another degree of complexity. Nonetheless, an exploration of the various ways in which researchers have measured social capital is critical to our understanding of the range of approaches and techniques available, to guide us when thinking about measuring social capital. This will also enable us to make informed decisions on the most relevant and appropriate approaches and level of measurement as per a variable or component of social capital.

This chapter presents some of the major approaches currently employed to measure social capital and the approaches used to achieve this endeavour. The chapter describes with illustration, the dimensions taken by each approach.

MEASUREMENT SOCIAL CAPITAL CONCEPTUAL

The analysis of current work on social capital revealed that there is still no one clear way to measure social capital. Many researchers have acknowledge that there is wide and growing gap between theoretical understandings of what constitutes social capital and the ways social capital is measured. In much of the empirical work to date, there is a growing criticism of whether it is even worth measuring the theory. It is this lack of consistent and unified approach for measuring social capital which leads to empirical confusion about the meaning, outcomes, validity and relevance of social capital as an analytical tool in many application areas.

Though the apparent lack of clarity in measurement is a source of confusion, it is also a source of unnecessary and sometimes unjustified critique of the theory. Another problem leading to inability to develop benchmark measurements is appearance of wide range of definitions; evident in the different ways the concept is operationalised. For example, Putnam (2000) examined social capital in terms of participation in groups (e.g., membership in voluntary organizations, local community clubs and political parties). Cote and Healy (2001) concentrated on structural aspects e.g. social networks, values, norms.

The World Bank (1999) used various measures, some of them relay on prevalence of various information and communication technologies. Researchers at the World Bank argue that maintaining and enhancing social capital depends critically on the ability of the members of a community to communicate among each other, with other communities and with members of their networks that live outside the community. Further, Robinson (1997) thinks that measures of social should focus on measuring contextual cultural issues. Given its multidimensionality and multivariate nature measuring a single variable within social capital such as trust does not provide us with adequate analysis of social capital.

CURRENT APPROACHES FOR MEASURING SOCIAL CAPITAL

Harpham, Grant and Thomas (2002) provided an elaboration of key issues involved in the measurement of social capital. They recommended that researchers need to ensure that measurement of social capital keeps speed with theoretical development. In this regard, the measurement of social capital can be focused along its dimensions: along structural, content and cognitive dimensions. The ability to come up with comprehensive approaches to measure social capital (for example, capturing the different dimensions noted above) is an unresolved issue. In addition, there is a growing concern suggesting that data used for analysis of social capital is not often primarily collected for that purposes. For instance, there are many studies that have examined social capital (e.g. Cooper et al 1999; Putnam, 1999) using secondary data collected in surveys, which were primarily intended to meet other objectives.

Further, a large household survey often conducted to examine the level of social capital in a community might include one question on "can people around here be trusted?" In which case, the objective was to examine trusting relationships people develop within a particular community rather than social capital per se. It is only recently that surveys explicitly designed to measure social capital have been implemented (see for example, Onyx & Bullen, 2001; Krishna and Shrader, 2000). Another key challenge associated with measurement of social capital is to ensure that determinants, consequences and outcomes of social capital (such as length of residence, satisfaction about services, being a victim of crime) are not mixed up with the measurement of social capital itself. These determinants are not uniform throughout communities and findings based upon these determinants are not likely to be generalised.

Without any doubt attempts to reach appropriate measures of social capital have resulted into the use of many approaches. These approaches can be conveniently group into quantitative, qualitative, social network analysis, content analysis and combination of two or more of these approaches. The four groups of approaches however, are summarised and presented in Figure 4.1.

Figure 4-1. Main approaches for measuring social capital

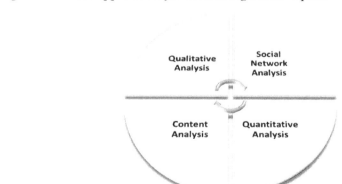

Quantitative Approaches

In general terms quantitative approaches employed in social research aim at measuring the objective and quantifiable aspects of a social phenomenon in a rigorous systematic and scientific manner. Quantitative approaches employ statistical procedures and models when analysing a phenomena. In quantitative approaches, the process and procedures of measurement and the conclusions made from observations provide the fundamental connection between empirical world and mathematical expression of quantitative statements describing relationships between variables

The emphasis of quantitative approaches in measuring social capital is on collecting and analysing secondary numerical data and concentrating on measuring the scale, range, frequency associated with occurrence of one or more of the key indicators of social capital. Indicators used in this approach include variables such as trust and civic norms of engagement. Examples of work that have employed quantitative approaches include the work of Knack and Keefer (1997); Narayan and Pritchett (1997); Putnam (1993) and Fukuyama (1999). These studies were commonly based on two measures. The first based on consensus of groups and group memberships and the second based on survey data on the level of trust and civic engagement. Employing quantitative measures, Putnam (2000) attempted to measure social capital by counting groups in civil society, using a number to track the size of memberships in clubs, bowling leagues and political hubs as they vary over time and in different geographical locations. He regarded social capital as the total sum of the membership in various kinds of groups and organisations. Fukuyama (1999) used similar approach but argued that the size of membership in communities might limit the kinds of outcomes a community can accomplish. He showed that families for example are good at socializing children but they might not necessarily be good at exerting political influence.

Fukuyama (1999) further observed that limitations in the accuracy and originality of data for examining social capital prohibit concrete enumeration of elements constituting social capital. He further, stated that it is nearly impossible to provide a complete and accurate census that registers the whole range of informal networks in which social capital can be found. In other words, Fukuyama noted that it is difficult to account for membership in many forms of social structures, especially those that are now connected to the proliferation of computer mediated communication technologies, a topic which will be discussed later in chapter VI of the book.

It is also possible that some individuals can hold overlapping memberships in multiple communities, so there is possibility of counting membership twice or many times. Fukuyama (1999) proposed internal cohesion and group or community context as qualitative measures to try resolve limitations of quantitative measures. It is also true that certain groups, particularly larger ones, can be characterized by internal hierarchy, a division of labour, status and functional distinctions. While the group may be united around some common interest or passion, the degree to which individual members are capable of collective action on the basis of mutual trust depends on their relative position within the organization.

Another important factor affecting sum of society's social capital is the way in which people relate to outsiders. Strong moral bonds within criminal groups in some cases may actually decrease the degree to which members of that group are able to trust outsiders and work effectively with them as discussed in the disadvantages of social capital.

In general, quantitative approaches used for measuring social capital are therefore, not without limitations. Those that relay on survey data are often affected by factors, such as the nature of questions asked, the number of individuals asked, and the expertise and experience of the researchers themselves. Fukuyama (1999) noted that coming up with a believable census of a society's stock of social capital is a nearly impossible task, since it involves multiplying numbers that are either subjectively estimated or simply nonexistent. Context is another key problem relating to measuring social capital. For example Fukuyama (1995) used quantitative measures to determine economic perspective for firms and society. Putnam (1993) concentrated on measuring political and policy performance. All these approaches were independently applied and they were intended to address problems in different contexts, the collective results of these studies can undermine the validity and credibility of final stock of relationship that can be deemed as social capital. It is in the light of these limitations that researchers have turned their attention to explore other approaches.

Qualitative Approaches

In broad terms, qualitative approaches seek to investigate a social or natural phenomenon using systematic and sometimes predefined set of procedures. They are intended to produce findings not determined in advance but are often applicable beyond the immediate boundaries of the study. Unlike quantitative approaches, the main strength of qualitative approaches is their ability to provide complex descriptions of how people experience a given phenomenon within some limited context. In addition, qualitative approaches are more subjective in nature and they include more subjective information about the subjects under study.

For many years, researchers have employed qualitative approaches to identify and describe intangible factors, such as sense of a community, nature of a community, the role of a community, social protocols, and participation in community activities, feeling of trust and shared understanding. More specifically, Social Psychology researchers often use qualitative approaches to examine and reflect on the less tangible aspects of a research subject, e.g. values, attitudes, perceptions. Although qualitative approaches are often mistakenly understood to be easy to employ and unscientific, such approaches are in fact difficult to apply and their interpretation of their findings is complex.

The use of qualitative approaches for studying social capital includes work done by Portes and Sensenbrenner (1993) who examined social connections among immigrant communities. Further, World Bank researchers employ qualitative approaches and tools for analysing social capital. For example work carried out by Dudwick, Kuehnast, Jones and Woolcock (2006) describes a qualitative approach investigating social capital based on six indicators: groups and networks; trust and solidarity; collective action and cooperation; information and communication; social cohesion and inclusion, and empowerment and political action. They suggested that these indicators reflect how social relationships act as a means through which individuals or small groups secure (or are denied) access to resources. They further noted that individuals, households, or small groups who have access to important resources, or who occupy key strategic positions in a community have more social capital than others and have better access to and control over valued resources. Implicit in the qualitative approach is the recognition that the distribution of social capital within any given community is unequal and often stratified, meaning that social capital can function as a mechanism for exclusion as well as inclusion.

Understanding groups and networks that enable people to access resources and collaborate to achieve shared goals is another important part of measuring social capital. Researchers have acknowledged that informal networks are rich sources of social capital and they manifest themselves in spontaneous, informal, and unregulated exchanges of information and resources within communities, as well as efforts at cooperation, coordination, and mutual assistance that help maximize the utilization of available resources. Informal networks can be connected through horizontal and vertical relationships and are shaped by a variety of environmental factors, including the market, kinship, and friendship. Social network analysis is one of the methods employed to measure social capital embedded in informal groups.

SOCIAL NETWORK ANALYSIS

Social network refers to a personal or professional set of relationships between individuals or organisations. It represents both a collection of ties between people and the strength of those ties. Often used as a measure of social "connectedness", recognising social networks assists in determining how information moves throughout groups, and how trust can be established and fostered. At the basic technical level, a social network can be presented as a graph based on a relational data model. A relational data model implies that data is arranged in some form of relation or in this case a matrix which is visually represented in a two dimensional table.

The data is then inserted into the table in the form of tuples or rows. A tuple is formed by one or more than one attributes, which are used as basic building blocks in the formation of various expressions that are used to derive meaningful information. There can be any number of tuples in the table, but all the tuple contain fixed and same attributes however with varying values. In social network analysis, the relational dimension between nodes *A* and *B* is recorded as 1 in the cells (*A, B*) and (*B, A*) if a tie is present between them; and as *0* if there is no tie. In other words, if the relation is directional, an arc (flow) from source **A** to link **B** and vice versa is recorded as *1* in cell (*A, B*), and a *0* in cell (*B, A*), this is also referred to as adjacency. *Adjacency* is the graph theoretic expression of the fact that two people, represented by nodes, are directly related, tied, or connected with one another (Robinson & Foulds, 1980). Formally it is presented as:

*Let n_i, $n_j \in N$ denote agents i and j in a set of N agents. Let a_{ij} denote the existence of a relation (arc) from agent i to agent j. Agents i and j are adjacent if there exist either of the two arcs, a_{ij} or a_{ji}. Given a graph **D** = (N, A), its adjacency matrix A(**D**) is defined by $A(D) = (a_{ij})$, where $a_{ij} = 1$ if either a_{ij} or a_{ji}, and 0 otherwise.*

The number of arcs (links) beginning at a node is called the *outdegree* of the node. And they suggest connections, and in our case initiation of engagement or discourse. Outdegree is measured as the row sum for the node in a dichotomous matrix:

$$\text{outdegree of actor i} = \sum_j a_{ij} \tag{1}$$

The number of arcs ending at a node is called the *indegree* of the node, indicating the reception of engagement. The column sum (for a node) in a dichotomous matrix measures the indegree of the node:

$$\text{indegree of actor j} = \sum_i a_{ij} \tag{2}$$

Wasserman and Faust (1994) suggested that a node is a transmitter if its indegree is zero and its outdegree is non-zero. A node is a receiver if its indegree is non-zero and its outdegree is zero, and it is isolated if both indegree and outdegree are zero. A graph can take on many forms: directed or undirected. A directed graph is one in which the direction of any given edge is defined. Conversely, in an undirected graph you can move in both directions between vertices.

Figure 4.2. An example of a social network

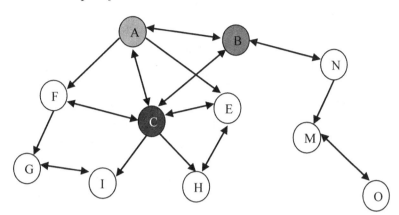

The criterion used for constructing a social network graph can be based on graph theoretic expression. The graph represents a directed graph with arrows indicating interaction and engagement between nodes (individuals) in the community. For example, if **A** sends messages to **C** and **C** does not send back any messages, then there is no reciprocal relationship between **A** and **C** But if reciprocal relationship exist two-way communication is suggested.

Social Network Measures and Matrices

Social networks are precursors to virtual communities. A social network is a social structure made of "nodes", which are generally individuals or organizations. A network maps the ways in which people and groups are connected to each other, through various relationships ranging from casual acquaintance to close familiar bonds. Social networks operate at many levels, from families up to the level of nations, and they affect the way problems are solved, and organizations are run. According to social network theory, the attributes of members are less important than their relationships to other actors within the network. Social networking also refers to a category of Internet applications to help connect friends, business partners, or other individuals together using a variety of tools. These applications, known as online social networks are becoming increasingly popular and are often used to strengthen existing relationships.

A fundamental strategy for understanding individuals within a social network is to evaluate the location of actors in the network. Measuring the network location implies finding the centrality of a node. Common metrics used include analysis of the degree, betweenness, closeness, boundary spanners, peripheral players and network centralization. Degree refers to the number of direct connections a node has (i.e., the number of nodes a node directly connects to the network and the number of nodes connecting directly to a node). For instance, if **X** has the most direct connections in a network, **X** is referred to as an active node in the network or hub or connector. It is also important to know what these connections lead to and how they relate to unconnected nodes. Betweenness determines the strategic location of a node. For instance, if a node falls in-between two constituencies, regardless of the number of direct nodes, the node plays a role of a 'broker' in the entire network. The metric of closeness refers to the distance of a particular node to others. Social ties provide many benefits, including companionship, access to information, and emotional and material support (Wellman & Gulia, 1999). Increasing the number of ties increases access to these benefits, although time and cognitive constraints preclude indefinite expansions of one's personal network.

The practical implication of location of a node in a network suggest that a node that is close to other nodes has excellent position to monitor information flow in a network and view what is happening in the network. Boundary spanners refer to nodes that connect their group to others. These are also nodes that usually end up with high network metrics. Boundary spanning actors are well positioned to be innovators, since they have access to ideas and information flowing in other clusters. They are in a position to combine different ideas and knowledge into new products and services. In Figure 4-2, **B** can be considered as a boundary spinner since it connects the main network and the subnetwork, **B** has direct link to the central node in the main network **C**.

Peripheral players refer to nodes that are on the periphery and those that have low centrality scores. Such nodes normally play the roles of vendors and contractors and they are good sources of fresh information. Network centralization, on the other hand, refers to individual central position in the network. Overall, centrality reveals the structure of a network. The relationship between the centralities of all nodes can reveal much about the overall network structure. One or a few very central nodes can dominate a centralized network and if these nodes are removed or damaged, the network quickly fragments into unconnected sub-networks.

Other social network analysis metrics include structural equivalence, which determines which nodes play similar roles in the network; cluster analysis which identifies cliques and other densely connected clusters, and structural holes which examine areas where there is no connection between nodes that can be used for advantage or opportunity. Other measures include determining a prestige of a network. A node's prestige in a network is essentially its reputation or influence arising from success, achievement, rank, or other favourable attributes of that individual node. Nodes with high prestige are important and they are those that are linked or involved with other nodes extensively. In practical sense a node with extensive connections (links) or communications with many other nodes in the network are considered more important than a node with relatively fewer connections.

Prestige can be considered as more refined measures of prominence of an actor that centrality measure. The differences between prestige and centrality are that prestige focuses on indegree connections while centrality deals with outdegree. The simplest measure of prestige of an actor i in a network (denoted by $P_D(i)$) is in fact its indegree of connectivity and it is given by:

$$P_D(i) = d_1(i)/n\text{-}1 \tag{3}$$

where $d_1(i)$ is the indegree of i (the number of indegree connectivity of actor i_1) and **n** is the total number of nodes in the network. Similar to centrality, dividing **n-1** standardizes the prestige value to the range from 0 and 1. The maximum prestige value is one when every other node links to i.

The measure of prestige of a node can be extended to examine the source of the connecting nodes as well as the content of the information embedded in the nodes. Examining the direction of connectivity and the nature of the connectivity can reveal the significant importance of the message as well as the status of the node(s) sending information and the node receiving the information. For instance, if **A** is a competent and knowledgeable individual in the network, and **A** interacts with **B** then it is more likely that **B** can acquire useful information from **A** and hence, both **A** and **B** can share important status in the network.

Distant can also be used as a measure of prestige entailing the degree to which one node is connected to other nodes of significant importance. For instances, nodes that are very close to nodes of high prestige are likely to have access to status in a community compared to those in a distant. Important or prominent actors are those that are linked or involved with other actors extensively. Though there exists a considerable variation in network-based approaches to social capital (see Adler & Kwan 2002), most approaches share the view that the structure of the network and the resources contained within it are critical to understanding of social capital of a community.

CONTENT ANALYSIS

For many years, content analysis is employed to understand a wide range of social issues in many domains. This approach is often used to determine the presence of words, concepts, and patterns within a large body of texts or sets of texts. In the methodological spectrum, content analysis approaches are more similar to qualitative approaches than they are to quantitative approaches, though they can also reveal certain instances of quantitative properties such as determination of reliability and validity. Through content analysis researchers can quantify and analyze the presence, meanings and relationships of words and concepts, then make inferences about the messages within the texts, the writer(s), the audience, and even the culture and time of which these occur.

Content analysis approaches also enables researchers to include large amounts of textual information and systematically identify their properties (e.g., the frequencies of certain groups of sentences and their meanings through inferences and the detection of the more important structures of communication or the content embedded in the messages). Moreover, the textual information being analyzed is often categorized according to certain theoretical frameworks, which inform the data analysis, and yielding meaningful reading of the content under scrutiny.

In general a content analysis serves as a critical to the exploration of social issues in virtual communities. Daniel and Poon (2006) employed content analysis to examine transcripts of online interactions with the intention of identifying components of social capital in virtual communities. The approach used for the analysis involved compiling a number of interaction transcripts and developing a coding scheme that takes into account the fundamental variables constituting social capital (such as engagement, interaction, shared understanding and trust). Though the variables were predetermined, grounded theory was applied to enable new themes to emerge from the data. Moreover the creation of the coding scheme was intrinsically related to a creative approach to variables that exert an influence over textual content.

SOURCES OF SOCIAL CAPITAL

There are several sources of social capital. For examples, political participation, civic leadership and associational involvement, volunteering, faith-based engagement, informal social ties, diversity of friendships, social networks, knowledge networks and indeed all kinds of community engagement signify the sources of social capital. In addition, some researchers treated shared belief as a source of social capital. Portes (1998) refers to shared belief as "bounded solidarity", a sense of community solidarity which results from collective shared experiences of community members. There are other sources of social capital such as "identification with one's own group, sect, or community can be a powerful motivational force (p. 8)". These particular sources constitute a cognitive dimension of social capital. Nahapiet and Ghoshal (1998) suggested that cognitive dimension of social capital serves as a resource and provide shared representations, interpretation, and systems of meaning among parties. It includes the shared ways of thinking and interpreting events. The cognitive aspect helps generating social capital that helps people exchange ideas, understand each other better, and get along better.

The World Bank identified several sources of social capital for its own work on development (for social and economic development purposes). These sources are drawn mainly from research and practice and they include:

- **Families:** This is considered to be the main source of social capital and an enabler of economic and social welfare for its members, the family is the first building block in the generation of social capital for the larger society.
- **Communities:** Built around effective social interactions, requiring deep engagement among neighbours, friends and groups generate social capital and the ability to work together for a common good. According to the World Bank, communities are critical in alleviating poverty and increasing social capital among the poor as social capital, substituting it for human and physical capital.
- **Firms or simply business:** Building and sustaining efficient organizations like firm's demands trust and a common sense of purpose, i.e., social capital. Social capital benefits firms by reducing transactions costs, but can also have negative effects for a firm and society.
- **Civil society:** Social capital is crucial to the success of any non-governmental organization because it provides opportunities for participation and gives voice to those who may be locked out of more formal avenues to affect change.
- **Public sector:** The public sector, i.e., the state and its institutions, is central to the functioning and welfare of any society and can be enhanced by social capital.
- **Ethnicity:** Ethnic relations are discussed as sources of social capital in many studies. For example, within immigration, micro enterprise development, tribal nepotism or racial conflict, ethnic ties are a clear example of how actors who share common values and culture can band together for mutual benefit.

Clearly there are many sources of social capital in addition to the ones listed by the World Bank and others; it is beyond the scope of this book to provide more comprehensive coverage of the sources of social capital.

INDICATORS OF SOCIAL CAPITAL

Though social capital has given rise to an unprecedented excitement among researchers concerned with social issues in many application areas, lack of solid indicators continues to generate much controversy and debate on the validity of social capital as a scientific theory. Lack of clarity in conceptualising and in determination whether social capital is an input, process, output is a critical difficulty in relation to determining solid indicators and comprehensive sources of social capital.

Stone (2001) provided some interesting indicators of social capital. She grouped social capital indicators into 'proximal' and 'distal' groupings. She suggested that 'proximal' indicators of social capital are in fact outcomes of social capital related to its core components of social networks, trust and reciprocity. Examples of these include the use of civic engagement as an indicator of social networks. This approach was made famous in Putnam's (1995) analysis of civic decline in America, which was based upon membership of formal associations and groups. Actions associated with a display of confidence in others, an outcome of a norm of trust (see for example Onyx and Bullen 2000), as well as reciprocal acts or exchanges, an outcome of a norm of reciprocity, are also used as proximal indicators of social capital. '

Distal indicators are outcomes of social capital, which are not directly related to its key components. Examples of distil indicators include: life expectancy; health status; suicide rates; crime rates; participation rates in tertiary education; employment and unemployment rates; family income; marital relationship formations and dissolutions; business confidence; job growth and balance of trade (Spellerberg 1997).

Proximal and distal indicators are relied upon frequently in social capital research, particularly in studies reliant upon secondary analyses, where existing data is limited. While useful in some ways, the mixture, use and misuse of indicators in social capital research to date, and lack of theoretical precision used in the selection of indicators, has led to considerable confusion and problems in identifying what social capital is, as distinct from its outcomes, and what the relationship between social capital and its outcomes may be.

Despite problems in identifying common indicators for measuring social capital, there are at least three common trends, which are beginning to emerge. One trend relates to looking at participation in community as an indicator of presence or absence of social capital. Participation of this kind can be treated in terms of activities, especially through neighbourhood or parent school associations, volunteerism in community affairs, sports leagues, advocacy groups or other forms of social activism. The other involves participation in political life, including participating in elections and signing petitions.

CONCLUSION

Despite the growing amount of research coupled with increasing interest, the definition of social capital has remained elusive and so are its indicators for building solid measurement approaches. It seems the diversity in approaches enable researchers from various disciplines to use the theory to mean different things to facilitate thinking in interdisciplinary and multidisciplinary research areas. The conceptual vagueness of social capital has impacted the development of a standard measurement and thus caused impediment to both theoretical and empirical research. Examining the literature it seems there are various reasons why a standard measure for measuring social capital hasn't been developed:

- First, social capital consists of many components and each component seems to have many dimensions.
- Second, social capital is considered as the property of groups or communities or individuals and doing analysis on one level undermines the importance of the other.
- Third, social capital can be sources of productive relationships and productive relationships can be measured by the level of social capital in a community, making it both an input and an output of social relationships.
- Fourth, most of the previous attempts to measure social capital were based on secondary analyses. Much social capital research to date falls within this category, yet – not surprisingly – is inherently limited as data gathered originally for purposes other than the study of social capital are unlikely to provide conceptually thorough measures of it.
- Fifth, the ad hoc mixture of measures, indicators and outcomes drawn upon in secondary analyses have no doubt contributed to the confusion which exists between social capital theory and measurement, despite providing some early indications of the usefulness of social capital as a concept.
- Sixth, there are the earliest attempts at primary data collection for the study of social capital. These are fewer in number yet extend what may be learned via secondary analysis as they add sophistication and precision to data collection (Stone, 2001).
- Seventh, when thinking about measuring social capital, a clear understanding of the context and purpose of the measurement should be clearly determined.
- Eighth, before, embarking on measurement issues, it is necessary to clearly identify the fundamental variables constituting social capital. Unfortunately, this requires that social capital has to be clearly defined and a standard definition is still missing.
- Ninth, understanding the limitations of measurement and level of analysis and ensuring that the results are interpreted within the limitation and the context in which measurement is carried out.
- Tenth, there is a need to triangulate results using alternative methods or corroborating data through collection of other kinds of data.

- Finally, viewing social capital as input-output is theoretically important but it makes it scientifically incoherent and methodological difficult to use.

Despite its obvious importance, current understanding of social capital is much less advanced than for the other types of capital such as physical capital, financial capital and human capital. Without a clear conceptual understanding of what is meant by social capital, it is not possible to measure or report on it and scientific discussion of the term is meaningless. In addition, social capital theory has always also given rise to much controversy.

This chapter has presented some of the major approaches researchers currently use to examine social capital. It has identified several sources and indicators of social capital as well as the problems associated with measurement of the theory and over reliance on single measurement unit such as trust. In chapter V, the concept of trust is analyzed in relation to measuring social capital.

REFERENCES

Adler, P. S., & Kwon, S. W. (2002). Social capital: propsects for a new concept. *Academy of Management Review, 27*(1), 17-40.

Cooper, H., Arber, S., Fee, L., & Ginn, J. (1999). *The influence of social support and social capital on health: a review and analysis of British data.* London: Health Education Authority.

Daniel, B. K., & Poon, N. (2006, July). Social Network Techniques and Content Analysis of Interactions in a Video-Mediated Virtual Community. *Proceedings of the 6th IEEE International Conference on Advanced Learning Technologies, Kerkrade, Netherlands.*

Dudwick, N., Kuehnast, K., Jones, V. N., & Woolcock, M. (2006). *Analysing social capital in context. A guide to using qualitative methods and data.* Retrieved November 15th 2008 from http://siteresources.worldbank.org/WBI/Resources/Analyzing_Social_Capital_in_Context-FINAL.pdf

Earls, F., & Carlson, M. (2001). The social ecology of child health and well-being. *Annual Review of Public Health, 22*, 143-66.

Fukuyama, F. (1995). *Trust: The social virtues and the creation of prosperity.* New York: Free Press.

Fukuyama, F. (1999, November). *Social capital and civil society.* Paper presented at the Conference on Second Generation Reforms IMF Headquarters, Washington, D.C.

Harpham, T., Grant, E., & Thomas, E. (2002). Measuring social capital in health surveys. *Health Planning and Policy, 17*(1), 106-111.

Krishna, A., & Shrader, E. (2000). Cross-cultural measures of social capital: a tool and results from India and Panama. *Social Capital Initiative Working Paper no. 21. Washington DC: World Bank.*

Onyx, J., & Bullen, P. (2001). The different faces of social capital in NSW Australia. In Dekker, P. & Uslaner, E.M (Eds). *Social capital and participation in everyday life* (pp. 88-111). London: Routledge.

Nahapiet, J., & Ghoshal, S. (1998). Social capital, intellectual capital, and the organizational advantage. *The Academy of Management Review, 23*(2), 242-267.

Portes, A. (1998). Social capital: its origins and applications in modern sociology. *Annual Review of Sociology, 24*, 1-24.

Putnam R. (2000) *Bowling alone: the collapse and revival of American community.* New York: Simon and Schuster.

Putnam, R. (1993). *Making democracy work: civic tradition in modern Italy.* Princeton, New Jersey: Princeton University Press.

Robinson, D. F., & Foulds, L. R. (1980). *Digraphs: Theory and Techniques.* New York: Gordon and Breach.

Spellerberg, A. (1997). Towards a framework for the measurement of social capital. In Robinson, D. (Ed.). *Social Capital & Policy Development Institute of Policy Studies*, Wellington, New Zealand.

Stone, W. (2001). Measuring social capital towards a theoretically informed measurement framework for researching social capital in family and community life *Research Paper No. 24, February 2001 Analyzing Social Capital in Context: A Guide to Using Qualitative Methods and Data.*

Wasserman, S., & Faust, K. (1994) *Social Network Analysis: Methods and Applications.* Cambridge: Cambridge University Press.

Wellman, B., & Gulia, M. (1999). Net Surfers don't ride alone: Virtual communities as communities. In M. Smith & P. Kollock (Eds.), *Communities in Cyberspace* (pp. 167-194). New York: Routledge.

ENDNOTE

[1]   Is a Latin phrase, translated as "with other things the same." It is commonly rendered in English as "all other things being equal." A prediction, or a statement about causal or logical connections between two states of affairs, is qualified by ceteris paribus in order to acknowledge, and to rule out, the possibility of other factors which could override the relationship between the antecedent and the consequent

Chapter V
Trust and Social Capital

INTRODUCTION

Regardless of any approach taken for examining social capital, researchers continuously converge on some key issues such as trust and yet diverge on several
others about concrete and consistent indicators for measuring social capital. Many
researchers believe that presence or absences of social capital can be solely linked
to trusting relationships people build with each other as well as social institutions of
civil engagement. It is not clearly known however, whether trust itself is a precondition for generating social capital or whether there are other intermediary variables
that can influence the role of trust in creating social capital. In addition, similar
to social capital, the definition of trust is problematic and it remains a nebulous
concept and equally, with many dimensions.

Interests in the analysis of trust are wide spread among many disciplines, notably
policy analysis, economic development, reliability and security of distributed computational systems and many others. The variety of approaches currently employed
to investigate trust and different interpretations of its role in fostering social capital
has resulted into a diverse array of knowledge about the concept and its relationship
to social capital. This chapter provides a broader overview of work on trust. It discusses how researchers have used trust as a proxy for measuring social capital.

THE NATURE OF TRUST

Any concept that is multidisciplinary in nature, enabling people to approach it from
many angles is open to a wide range of interpretation. Such a concept can often be

technically challenging to precisely define against any scientific standards. In all accounts, trust is a concept in search of consistent definition and common identity. There are many disciplines contributing to our understanding of the concept. The disciplines range from the Social Sciences and the Humanities to the Natural Sciences. Figure 5.1 shows some of the key prevalent disciplines contributing to research on trust.

The miscellany in analysis of trust has added more complexity in its interpretation, which has resulted into development of various conceptual approaches describing it. Deutsch (1958) approached trust from the discipline of Psychology and viewed it in terms of individual trusting or distrusting behaviour. His approach was primarily based on cost benefit analysis, treating trust as an outcome of carefully weighing alternative costs of decisions individuals make. According to this approach, an individual develops trusting behaviour when he/she perceives that the occurrence of a particular event is contingent on the behaviour of another person and that the occurrence of the event itself is associated with certain benefits and risks.

Luhmann (2000) a Sociologist, took a different perspective and considered trust as an important variable necessary for effectively mediating interaction and as a means of reducing complexity in society. He believed that every time people face a simple or complex decision-making situation, they make assumptions taking into account the particular situation and the environment in which the situation occurs. Such a complex decision-making requires a great deal of trusting behaviour.

Further, Barber (1983) believed that trust is deeply rooted in a society and the culture associated with it. He argued that trust is not only limited to an individual's perception, neither can it be reduced to cost—benefits analysis associated with

Figure 5.1. Core disciplines investigating trust from unique perspectives

determining rational behaviour and choices. Instead, trusting a person is a future investment a person makes and it is also related to reciprocal relationships associated with the investment. According to Barber (1983), three fundamental expectations are tied to conditions necessary for building trust:

- Expectation of persistence and fulfilment of natural and moral social orders
- Expectation of "technically competent role performance" from those which we interact with in social relationships and systems
- Expectation that partners in interaction will carry their fiduciary obligations and responsibilities, that is, their duties in situations to place others' interests before their own (Barber, 1983)

Gambetta (1990), another well recognized contributor to research on trust, established mathematical abstractions and representations of trust. This was achieved by building a mathematically computable and tractable model of trust. Gambetta's (1990) work on trust has a profound impact in the areas of Computer Science and has been widely applied within areas such as multiagent systems, computer security and distributed computing (Abdul-Rahman & Hailes, 2000).

According to Gambetta (1990) trust (or similarly distrust) is a particular level of subjective probability with which a person or an agent can use to assess the action of another agent or group of other agents or people to perform a particular task. In this regard, when people trust others, they implicitly imply that the probability that the person will carry out a task that is beneficial or at least not detrimental is high enough for them to consider co-operating. In other words, when someone is untrustworthy, the probability is low enough for people to refrain from co-operating. Gambetta's definition of trust is computed using values ranging from 0 to 1, with 0 implying total distrust and 1 meaning complete trust. Fukuyama (1995) who approach trust from an economist point of perspective, treated trust as "the expectation that arises within a community of regular, honest, and cooperative behaviour, based on commonly shared norms, on the part of other members of the community (p. 27)." From the multidisciplinary analysis of trust, it is possible that trust is variously defined resulting to many types recorded in the literature.

Types of Trust

The various theoretical contributions to the trust literature can be understood in terms of different types of trust. Generally trust can be categorized into interpersonal trust and systems trust. These categories can further be subdivided into three different levels, generalized trust (trust in human nature), rational trust (related to specific known persons), and network trust (related to social networks including family). Interpersonal trust is the direct trust an agent has in another agent, and it is context-specific (McKnight & Chervany, 1996). For instance, a person **P** will trust another person **Q** based on his/her current calculations of **Q**'s past experience. This is similar to the analysis of the concept of trust based on opportunity cost calculations (Deutsch, 1958).

In Economics, as discussed in chapter II, an opportunity cost is the cost (sacrifice) incurred by choosing one option over an alternative one that may be equally desired. Thus, when applied to trust, an opportunity cost is the cost of pursuing one choice and using it as a basis for building trust instead of another. It is the cost of an alternative decision that must be forgone in order to pursue a certain action to arrive at the most desirable decision to trust someone. Put another way, the benefits one could acquire by taking an alternative action in trusting someone are all based on personal choices and the conditions under which one is facing at a certain period of time. For example, when lost in a desert one can trust anybody regardless of what they look like, whether or not one has confidence in the person, where as trusting the same person an alternative place say in the city and where they are numerous alternatives, might not be obvious, unless under rare circumstances. In other words, when people make any trusting decision, every action has an opportunity cost, and so, in building trusting relationships, people must make certain decisions to determine whether someone is trusty worthy or not. This can be driven by several factors such as age, appearance, perceived competence and availability of alternative actions.

Interpersonal trust is generalized to many different contexts. For example, researchers at International Business Machines (IBM) Institute for Knowledge-Based Organizations (IKO) investigated different types of trust as they related to knowledge sharing in organizations. They used interaction and connection among individuals as key determinants of trust and knowledge sharing. They pointed out that trust evolves through interaction and that trust or distrust between two or more people can emerge regardless of the frequency of interactions. Two types of interpersonal trusts are analysed in this regard, competence-based trust and benevolence trust. Competence-based trust relates to a person **A** having confidence in another person **C**'s abilities. And so in a case where person **A** is faced with any kind of problem, he/she is likely to request help from person **C** because they trust their abilities in a particular context.

Benevolence trust on the other hand implies that when person **C** trusts that another person **A** will not inflict any form of harm at any time even if person **A** has a chance to do so. Situations involving competence-based trust and benevolence trusts can be both mutually inclusive and exclusive depending on a particular situation at hand. For example, person **A** will trust that another person **C** knows certain information or work procedures (competence-based trust), but person **A** can also believe that another person **C** may not release any information related to how to do a specific kind of job (benevolence trust).

A third type of trust is what can be regarded as system trust. This kind of trust is not based on any property or state of the trustee but rather on the perceived properties or reliance on the system itself. An example is a civil institution such as policing within which people have vested trust in its operation and its ability to safeguard people. The institutional view of trust often suggest that trust needs to be embodied in social institutions and cannot be fully understood and studied without examining how institutions relate to the people they serve and people's general attitudes toward their institutions.

A system type of trust extends to over-simplification of interactions in a society. For example, when a person uses her/his credit card in the supermarket machine and something goes wrong, the person is normally suspected to be the source of the problem, not the machine nor the credit card company. Even though there might be possibilities that supermarket staff might be mistaken, or something wrong with the computer or the credit card company. This over simplification of thinking happens because people tend to have a general view that the supermarket machines used for handling and processing information are reliable and trustworthy.

Trust and Related Concepts

In relation to social capital, trust is connected to other concepts. These include cooperation, reputation and recommendation. In any discussion of trust, it is critically important to make a clear distinction among these concepts and their ultimate relationship to trust. According to Gambetta (1990), trust relates to co-operation because co-operation can make demands on the level of trust. For example, in order for two people to co-operate, they should have bilateral trust in each other in relation to a specific situation. That is if person **A** trusts person **B**, and person **B** wants to co-operate with person **A**, then person **B** should trust person **A** at least to some degree within which a co-operative behaviour is expected. If there is only partial trust between **A** and **B** then co-operation between them will be partial (i.e., if only one person has trust in the other and the other does not have any trust). By the same token, if there is a complete distrust, then there will be no co-operation between the two agents or people.

Similarly, trust is closely related to the notion of recommendation. Recommendation relates to trust in a situation of uncertainty where there is a need to acquire information that is trustworthy Recommendation is critical when person **A** needs to trust person **P** but does not have sufficient information about person **A**. Typically, person **A** can contacts another person **Q** who **A** trusts, and who has known person **P**, or to some degree trusts person **P**.

Trust and Reputation

Reputation is another third concept closely associated with trust. In day-to-day interactions, many people maintain a set of reputations for the people they know and interact with. Reputation is an important input into the decisions people make about trusting others and it influences the choices to trust others on daily basis. For instance, when working with a new and unknown person, people normally ask people with whom they already have relationships with for information about the new person. It is most likely that they can obtain some information about the new person where they can base their sense of judgement and trust. As time goes by, the new person accumulates their reputation based on the way they interact with other people.

Formally, defined, a reputation is the amount of trust a person has in another person or object of interest. This definition suggests a person's level of confidence in another person is based on their previous experience acquired through interaction or simply acquired through word of mouth or gossip. In other words, a person's reputation is a function of their experiences and the perception of others. For example, the reputation of an information source not only serves as a means of belief revision in a situation of uncertainty, but also serves as a basis for making trusting relationships among people.

Additionally, a good reputation may also be used as a direct source of social capital, as a person with good reputation is most likely to be liked by many people and therefore, might be well connected to other people within the same community circle. Similarly, a person with a poor reputation might not be trusted and might have a low level of social capital within the community in which he/she has earned the reputation leading to the distrust. People with a consistently low reputation and high level of distrust will eventually be isolated from the community they belong or associate with, since others will rarely accept their justifications or arguments and will limit their interaction with them, sanctioning them socially and to some extent, putting on the permanent state of depression and self-hatred.

Exploring computer security systems and multi-agent software systems, Abdul-Rahman and Hailes (2000) came up with unconventional ways to build reputation. They suggested that "reputation is an expectation about a person's behaviour based on the information about or observation about its past behaviour". These authors further proposed that reputation should not just be based on the opinion of others but instead it should include reputational information based on the agent's/person's experience. Inference of reputation based on an agent's experience enables an agent to gather sufficient information about a subject from others and decide whether or not such information is valid. Hence reputation is calculated as a cumulative function of both positive and negative information about an agent.

According to this model, once reputation is established and associated with a particular individual, it is hard to change. This basically the reason why some people can likely explain away untrustworthy behaviour of other people whom they have known their reputation over a period of time. For example person **X** has a reputation of being a good student in subject **M**. Person **X** has failed subject **M** of exam **K** in a semester **T**. Their failure might be attributed to circumstances such as lack of preparation, or other personal problems, even though failure was in fact due to lack of understanding of material. Similarly, a person might have a bad reputation of failing a particular subject but his recent outstanding performance in same particular subject might cast doubt even though people have the ability of underperforming in the past due to personal circumstances which might be temporary reticent. These examples indicate how reputation can be used to suppress other possible outcomes of individual's performance. In real life, it is not uncommon to engage in purposeful refusal to believe that a person with good or bad reputation can perform differently due to one or more factors. Reputation acts as a powerful mechanism to determine whether or not to trust a person. In fact Jarvenpaa & Leidner (1998) suggested that swift trust (another type of trust that exists in virtual environments) is primarily based on professional reputation.

TRUST AND AWARENESS

Research on the concept of awareness has been explored extensively in Computer Supported Collaborative Work (CSCW). Awareness in CSCW generally refers to an understanding of the overall state of the system (Dourish & Bellotti, 1992). Dourish and Bellotti (1992) further suggested that: "awareness is an understanding of the activities of others to provide a context for one's own activities." In the CSCW community, most studies on awareness are geared toward the design and development of multi-user interfaces. For example, awareness in multi-user interface environments is cited to be important because it enables users to co-ordinate and structure their work. It can also allow them to perceive what others are working on (Solhlenkemp, 1999; Gutwin & Greenberg, 1998). Solhlenkemp (1999) then concludes that without awareness, coordinated and co-operative work is almost impossible. Gutwin and Greenberg (1998) suggest four types of awareness: social awareness, task awareness, concept awareness, and workspace awareness. Social awareness is the awareness that people have about the social connections within the group. Task awareness is the awareness of how a shared task will be completed. Concept awareness refers to the awareness of how a particular activity or piece of knowledge fits into an individual's existing knowledge and workspace awareness.

There are also other types of awareness mentioned in the CSCW literature: causal awareness of others in a group, which refers to the sense of who is around, what they are up to and whether people are available (Borning & Travers, 1991); and situation awareness, a phenomenon of experts interacting with complex systems (i.e., ability to adjust performance according to the situation) (Gibson 1995). Conversational awareness refers to the ability of two or more people to adjust their conversation based on cues picked up from their conversation partners (Clark 1996) (i.e., people can easily understand facial expressions, gestures, language intonation, and eye contact) Such an understanding provides them with the sense of what is going on in a conversation and is essential for establishing shared understanding or social grounding.

Daniel, McCalla, and Schwier (2002) suggested that social awareness and concept awareness provide a starting point for the conceptualization of cultural awareness and knowledge awareness in virtual communities. They defined cultural awareness as current information on every individual's social background in the community; this includes country of origin, gender, first language, known reputation, language(s), beliefs (culture) as well as information about the community, such as goals, culture, and group identity. They pointed out that cultural awareness is related to social awareness because it seeks to understand the demographic and social profile of individuals in a community. Moreover knowledge awareness refers to an individual's knowledge capabilities such as information on level of skills or, knowledge and experiences in a particular domain within a community. Similarly, knowledge awareness is related to concept awareness, since both of them attempt to provide information that is useful for learning or acquisition of knowledge in a particular domain.

These two categories of awareness can be used as secondary variables to manipulate trust as a dependent variable. As Gutwin & Greenberg (1998) noted that awareness normally comes as a secondary goal. The main goal is for individuals to be able to connect and interact with each other and particularly, the ability of individuals to form social bonds which acts as a catalyst for development of trust essential for building social capital. In certain types of communities (e.g. computer mediated communities/virtual communities); awareness is critical but intermediary to building trust. Trust depends on the development of social relationships and these relationships require social connection. Moreover, social connection requires people to become aware of who they are connecting to (cultural awareness), and under what circumstances they can obtain peer-support, collaborate, learn, and work with others who are knowledgeable in certain things (knowledge awareness).

SOURCES OF TRUST

Trust is a rather difficult human sentiment to produce intentionally in rather a more rapid way. In most circumstances, people take time to build trusting relationships. Paradoxically, trust tends to happen quickly in very informal settings, where people interact with each other freely, revealing more information about themselves, consciously or unconsciously exposing their past and present level of reputation. In many cultures, to trust someone requires asking some out for dinner, a drink, a cup of coffee or simply hanging out in free and sometimes public spaces, such encounters often are frequented long enough to understand a person, to examine their reputation and to build trust. These observations are supported by research. For example, Coleman (1998) revealed that as a rational account of human behaviour, trust can only be produced in informal, small, closed and homogeneous communities which are able to enforce normative sanctions. It is often unclear however, how people can create trust within communities, but this has not stopped researchers from researching germane conditions necessary for people to create and nurture trusting relationships.

Regardless of any kind of social relationship among individuals and how these relationships are initiated and developed, trust remains a central lubricant for continuous engagement and for maintaining healthy relationship in any community. It is a mechanism embodied in all spheres of social relations and community activities. Some contemporary writers have continuously emphasized the importance of trust not in communities but in almost all aspects of modern life. Granovetter (1985) for example, stressed that social relations create trust and that trust can help boost higher economic life. He noted that trust is generated when agreements are "embedded" within a larger structure of personal relations and social networks. The social structure of social network therefore, is an important aspect of trust not only for the creation of social capital but also for the generation of trust itself.

Putnam (1993) has argued that social trust or trust that matter can arise from norms of reciprocity, which is similar to the creation of social capital. Fukuyama (1995) argued that trust is a characteristic of systems. He proposed that a nation's well-being, as well as its ability to compete, is conditioned by the level of trust inherent in the society (Fukuyama, 1995). Communication is another mechanism fostering the development of trust. Communication improves the flow of information about the trustworthiness of individuals. They allow reputations to develop and to be spread over time. All other things being equal, it is likely that the greater the communication among participants, the greater their mutual trust and the easier they will find it to cooperate among each other.

MEASURING TRUST

Like social capital, measurement of trust is problematic at best, among other things due to divergences of thoughts and various underlying theories. However, there are at least two scales for measuring trust—partner trust (trust in a specific known person) (Lundasen, 2001) and generalized trust (trust in people in general) (Couch & Jones, 1997). Trust in people in general (generalized trust) which essentially corresponds to "thick and thin" trust (Putnam, 1993; Fukuyama, 1995). In order to understand trust the complexity associated with defining and measuring trust, the following assumptions are offered:

- Trust is a measurable construct but its measurement is based on a number of factors such as people's attitudes, perceptions, evidence, and experiences.
- Trust evolves and changes over time (i.e. person **A** may not trust person **D** for the same reason **R** within a certain period of time **T**).
- Trust is directed and relative; for example, person **D** may trust person **F** to respond quickly to certain kinds of information but not for all kinds of information.
- Trust in individuals does not necessarily translate into trust in a system or a group and vice versa. For instance, person **A** can trust a community **C**, but it might not trust person **H** who is a member of that community.
- Trust can be transferable from one context to another but not from one individual to another. For example, consumer **N** can trust grocery store **P** in selling products **K** and if the owner of **P** changes to a different owner **I**, **N** will still trust **P** but not necessarily **I**.
- Trust is not transitive, i.e. if agent **A** trusts agent **B** and person **B** trusts person **C**, this does not automatically translate that person **A** will trust person **C**.
- Trusting others can be a cultural attitude. If this is the case, then trust can be strongly influenced by individual characteristics. For instance agent **X** trusts person **Q** because both come from village **F** and share in belief **M**.
- Trust can be based on individual competence i.e. trust based on the level and type of education received. That is, agent T trusts agent **F** because agent **F** is in expert in task **M**.
- People can trust other people with whom they have a long history of interaction; for example, person **X** trusts person **Y** because person **X** has known person **Y** for a period of time **T**. This means that trust increases in an expectation of repetitive or future interaction.
- Trust can be based on personal experiences, for instance a person can trust others if they are used to being treated fairly by his/her group. A person, who

had frequent interaction in the past with untrustworthy agents, develops a built-in suspicion that could easily be held in a personal belief system.

- People can trust a legal institution more than the individual agents that belong to it—institutional or group trust.
- A person will choose to trust another person whom he/she does not know in a situation where there is not much choice in whom to trust and in which it is essential to trust somebody. This is similar to blind trust (Lampsal 2001).

MEASURING SOCIAL CAPITAL IN TERMS OF TRUST

Trust is treated as a central variable in almost any discussion of social capital. In fact, most approaches for measuring social capital tend to ask questions that are directly aimed at measuring the level of trust rather than social capital itself. Based on the analysis of past and current work on social capital, researchers treat trust as if it can directly produce social capital. The World Bank (1999) further suggested that the basic premise of social capital rests on productive interaction which enables people to build trust necessary to building communities and committing themselves to each other.

Coleman (1988) contended that a system of mutual trust is an important form of social capital on which future obligations and expectations may be based. Putnam (1993) regarded trust as a source of social capital that sustains economic dynamism and governmental performance. Nahapiet and Ghoshal (1998) treated trust as a key facet in the relational dimension of social capital. These different but related perceptions of the relationship between trust and social capital are partially the result of the close relationship between the sources of trust and the sources of social capital (Adler & Kwon, 2000).

While there can be a causal relationship between social capital and trust, such a relationship cannot be reduced to simple cause and effect interpretations. Rather, the relationship is reciprocal and complex one, involving different intermediate variables. For instance, trust can generate shared understanding and social protocols can guide and maintain trust which might then evolve into social capital. In addition, the relationship between trust and social capital can be cyclical, trust can generate social capital and more social capital can generate more trusting relationships.

Furthermore, various forms of trust influence social capital differently. For instance, individuals might trust a particular community but they might not necessarily trust some members of that community. Referring to the discussion of the shortcomings of social capital discussed in chapter II, communities that manifest strong internal cohesion might exhibit strong social capital at that level, but such a community might develop a strong resistance to outsiders and the entire society in which it belongs. In other words any community that has a strong in-group trust (trust in specific people) and lacks generalized trust (general trust in human nature) might manifest negative social capital at the societal level.

MAIN CHALLENGES OF BUILDING TRUST IN VIRTUAL COMMUNITIES

Studies on trusting behavior emphasize building relationships through interactions in face-to-face settings. However, it is still unknown what mechanisms can promote trust in a community where face-to-face interaction is very limited and in situations where individuals hardly know each other or simply lack awareness about themselves or those vital aspects of individuals necessary for building trust. In these situations, social capital can be at risk. This is further complicated by the fact that the notion of trust, especially in virtual communities, consists of other variables such as reputation and recommendation.

A number of researchers offer different arguments on the relationship between trust and social capital. One school of thought considers trust as a precondition for building social capital while a second one regards trust as a product or a benefit of social capital. For many researchers, social capital depends on trust. Therefore, the social relationships, communities, cooperation, and mutual commitment that characterize social capital could not exist without a reasonable level of trust. In addition, many writers tend to think that the relationship between trust and social capital is inevitable to an extent that without some foundation of trust, social capital cannot develop. For example though Bourdieu (1983) did not specifically mentioned trust in his work, it was clearly implicit in his argument concerning the link between social capital and trust. He stated that "the reproduction of social capital presupposes an unceasing effort of sociability, a continuous series of exchanges in which recognition is endlessly affirmed and reaffirmed (pp. 250)". An interpretation of this suggests that people must base their commitments on trust to expand their useful connections.

A number of other researchers, however, doubt whether trust should be treated as an integral component of social capital. They argue that trust itself is a complex and varied phenomenon as discussed in this Chapter. And so the integration of trust, network, and norms make the concept of social capital an extremely complicated one. Misztal criticized Putnam of adopting a "rather circular" definition of social capital and lacking theoretical precision by incorporating the concept of trust into his definition of social capital (Misztal 2000, pp. 121).

According to Putnam (2000) trusting relationships among economic actors evolve from shared cultures and become embedded within a localized economy which then forms the possibilities and result in the fact of networks of civic engagement. This thought "takes for granted" the "causal link that connects trust and a rich network of associations (Sztompka 1999). For example, in the case of the Silicon Valley, the building block of their particular brand of social capital was a performance-generalized trust based on frequent commercial contacts rather than based on civic engagement that makes for economic success. Cohen and Fields (1999) have argued that this form of trust might be a superior form and can be extended to people from other places and other cultures, and even to people with different ideas. Cohen and Fields (1999) further argued that Putnam's concept of social capital obscures the specific nature of the social capital on which the Silicon Valley was built and through which it continues to construct itself.

Unlike Coleman, Putnam and Fukuyama, Woolcock (1998) argued that the measure of social capital should focus primarily on resources rather than consequences. For example, trust and norms of reciprocity, fairness, and cooperation are 'benefits' that are nurtured in and by particular combinations of social relationships; they are undeniably important for facilitating and reinforcing efficient institutional performance, but they do not exist independently of social relationships. Woolcock (2001) later proposed that trust may better be seen as "a consequence of social capital rather than as an integral component of social capital (p.13)." Field (2003) takes similar line of argument and pointed out that trust may not be treated as an only component variable in social because many relationships can operate perfectly well with a minimum of trust, including many of those which rest on institutional sanction (pp. 64). In his view, trust is best treated as an independent factor which is generally a consequence rather than an integral component, of social capital (pp. 65).

While recognizing that defining and comprehending trust is complex and problematic, Lazaric and Lorenz (1998) argued that three conditions are common in definitions of trust and together they provide a basis for a general definition. First, trust is identified with an agent's belief rather than with his or her behavior or action. Second, trust refers to beliefs about the likely behavior of another, or others, which influence decision-making. Finally, trust pertains to situations where the complexity of the relationship, or the fact that it is marked by unanticipated contingencies, precludes having recourse to complete contingent contracts with third party enforcement.

CONCLUSION

Reconciling the different views on trust and its relationship to social capital is important in arriving at solid indicators of social capital and the role of trust itself. Current analysis revealed that the ability to achieve trusting relationships and good outcomes within a community is influenced by several factors. For example, the ability to trust institutions of law and order, which for most part are culturally embedded. For example, in countries with corrupt civic institutions, people have little trust on government, especially those responsible for enforcing law and order. In other words, the capacity to trust someone is based on deeply rooted cultural traditions as Fukuyama (1995) suggested. This can also be influenced by the kinds of institutions that can be socially constructed and nurtured.

Though conditions necessary for breeding trusting relationships in any community are essential for building social capital, it seems trust is not the only indicator of social capital. And therefore studies that over rely on trust or one aspect of it might be subjective to wrong general interpretation of what constitute social capital and the yardsticks necessary for measuring it. For instance, trusting relationships might be developed under specific circumstances.

Trust can be based on similarity—trust in other people who are like you or trust in other people who are not like you. It can be based on traditional confidence in institutions at various levels. In addition, trust and context are inextricably related. For example, we can experience trust in numerous contexts, such as within family, between and among friends, and colleagues, with organizations and institutions. Further, trust we have in our civil institutions is not the same as the kinds of trust we invest on our neighbours, co-workers, and passersby. Even within institutional settings, people tend to demonstrate various levels of trusting behaviour. For instance, we can differently trust a big name super market than a smaller one with our credits card numbers or policeman in uniform rather than one without.

Any discussion of trust must be contextualized to have meaning and relevance. Trust within the context of family differs from the trust we experience within civil society. Due to the complexity of trust as a concept and as an ingredient for stimulating social capital, it is necessary to ask the right questions when investigating social capital through trust. It is perhaps essential to ask questions such as; what kind of trust generates more social capital and under what conditions? If trust is viewed different does it make more sense to reduce it to a single indicator of social capital?

This chapter described the notion of trust and its relationship to social capital. From overall analysis, the chapter concludes that trust is not the only indicator of social capital. It is suggested that in the context of virtual communities, researchers should be concerned with analysis of variables such as shared understanding different forms of awareness and how they relate to our theoretical description and measurement of social capital. Nonetheless, awareness which is central to the notion of trust in virtual communities is mediated differently by various kinds of technologies. Section II is devoted to the discussion of virtual communities and social computing. More specifically, chapter VI discusses various kinds of technologies that support virtual communities.

REFERENCES

Adler, P. S., & Kwon, S. (2002). Social capital: Prospects for a new concept. Academy of management. *The Academy of Management Review, 27*, 17-40.

Abdul-Rahman, A., & Hailes, S. (2000). Supporting trust in virtual communities. *IEEE Proceedings of the Hawaii International Conference on Systems Sciences.* Jan. 4-7, Maui. Hawaii. Retrieved November 23rd 2008 from http://www.cs.ucl. ac.uk/staff/F.AbdulRahman/docs/

Barber, B. (1983). *Logic and limits of trust*. New Jersey: Rutgers University Press.

Borning, A., & Travers, M. (1991). Two approaches to casual interaction over computer and video networks. *Proceedings of the conference on Human Factors in Computing Systems* (pp. 13-19). New Orleans, LA.

Bourdieu, P. (1983). Forms of social capital. In J. C. Richards (Ed.), *Handbook of theory and research for sociology of education* (pp. 241-258). New York: Greenwood Press.

Clark, H. (1996). *Using language*. Cambridge: Cambridge University Press.

Cohen, D., & Prusak, L. (2001). *In good company: How social capital makes organizations work*. Massachusetts: Harvard Business School Press.

Cohen, S., & Fields, G. (1999). Social capital and capital gains in Silicon Valley. *California Management Review, 41*(2).

Coleman, J. S. (1988). Social capital in the creation of human capital. *American Journal of Sociology, 94*, 95-120.

Couch, L., & Jones, W. (1997). Measuring levels of trust. *Journal of Research in Personality, 31*, 317-336.

Daniel, B., McCalla, G., & Schwier, R. (2002). A process model for building social capital in virtual learning communities. *Proceedings of the International Conference on Computers in Education (ICCE)* (pp, 574-577). Auckland, New Zealand.

Deutch, M. (1958). Trust and Suspicion. *Journal of Conflict Resolution, 2*, 265-279.

Dourish, P., & Bellotti, V. (1992). Awareness and coordination in shared workspace. *Proceedings of CSCW 1992* (pp. 107-114). Toronto: ACM Press.

Field, J. (2003). Civic engagement and lifelong learning: Survey findings on social capital and attitudes towards learning. *Studies in the Education of Adults, 35*(2), 142-156(15).

Fukuyama, F. (1995). *Trust: The social virtues and the creation of prosperity.* New York: Free Press.

Fukuyama, F. (1999, November). *Social capital and civil society.* Paper presented at the Conference on Second Generation Reforms IMF Headquarters, Washington, D.C.

Gambetta, D. (1990). Can We Trust Trust? In D. Gambetta (Ed.), *Trust: Making and breaking cooperative relations.* Oxford: Basil Blackwell.

Gibson, R. D. (1995). Introduction to the special issue on situation awareness. *Human Factors, 37*(1), 3-4.

Granovetter, M. S. (1973). The strength of weak ties. *American Journal of Sociology, 78*(6), 1360-1380.

Gutwin, C., & Greenberg, S. (1998). Design for individuals, design for groups: Tradeoffs between power and workspace awareness. *Proceedings of the ACM Conference on Computer Supported Cooperative Work* (pp. 207-216), ACM Press.

Jarvenpaa, S. L., & Leidner, D. E. (1998). Communication and trust in global teams. *Journal of Computer-Mediated Communications, 3*(4), Retrieved November 23rd 2008 from http://jcmc.huji.ac.il/vol3/issue4/jarvenpaa.html

Lamsal, P. (2001). *Understanding trust and security.* Retrieved Novemeber 23rd 2008 from http://www.cs.helsinki.fi/u/lamsal/asgn/TrustUnderstandingTrustAnd-Security.pdf

Lazaric, N., & Lorenz, E. (1998). The learning dynamics of trust reputation and confidence. In Lazaric and Lorenz (Eds.), *Trust and Economic Learning* (pp. 1-20). London: Edward Elgar.

Luhmann, N. (2000). Familiarity, confidence, trust: Problems and alternatives. In D. Gambetta (Ed.), *Trust: Making and breaking cooperative relations* (pp. 94-107), Electronic Edition, Department of Sociology, University of Oxford. Retrieved November 23rd 2008 from http://www.sociology.ox.ac.uk/papers/luhmann94-107.pdf

Lundasen, S. (2001, September). *Can we trust the measurements of trust?* Paper presented to the Annual Meeting of the American Political Science Association, San Francisco, CA.

McKnight D. H., & Chervany, N. L. (1996). The meanings of trust. *Technical Report MISRC Working Paper Series 96-04,* University of Minnesota, Management In-formation Systems Research Center.

Misztal, B. A. (2000). *Informality: social theory and contemporary practice.* Routledge, London.

Nahapiet, J., & Ghoshal, S. (1998). Social capital, intellectual capital and the organizational advantage. *Academy of Management Review, 23*(2), 242- 266.

Putnam, R. D. (1993). *Making democracy work: Civic traditions in modern Italy.* Princeton, NJ: Princeton University Press.

Putnam R. (2000). *Bowling alone: the collapse and revival of American community.* New York: Simon and Schuster.

Sohlenkemp, M. (1999). Supporting group awareness in multi-user environments through perceptualization. *The GMD Research Series.* Berlin: Forschungszentum Informationstechnik-Germany.

Sztompka, P. (1999). *Trust: A Sociological theory.* Cambridge: Cambridge University Press.

Woolcock, M. (1998). Social capital and economic development: Toward a theoretical. synthesis and policy framework. *Theory and Society, 27*(2), 151-208.

World Bank (1999). *Social capital research group.* Retrieved November 23rd 2008 from http://www.worldbank.org/poverty/scapital/

Section II
Social Computing and Virtual Communities

Virtual communities serve various purposes to their members based on the type and focus. They can serve as knowledge sharing systems or simply a place for socialisation. With the increasing growth of social software supporting virtual communities, there is concomitant surge of interests among researchers in many disciplines raises many interesting research groups. Some researchers are interested in investigating various social structures influenced by technological development; others look at ways for designing robust technologies that can support emerging social structures in online settings. Subsequently various technologies have been built supporting various kinds of virtual communities.

This section builds on where section I left. It gently introduces the reader to topics that are technology related but focuses on technologies there are frequently employed to support virtual communities. The section describes various types of Web technologies and discusses their relationships to social capital. Two types of virtual communities presented in the section are; distributed communities of practice, mainly comprising of professionals and virtual learning communities supporting people who learn online.

Section II covers chapter VI, chapter VII and chapter VIII. Chapter VI describes the nature of communication primarily in the two types of virtual communities. It provides examples of tools currently used for supporting these communities. More specifically chapter VI includes extensive discussion of the evolution of the Web and various associated technologies. Chapter VII provides detail description of virtual communities—virtual learning communities and distributed communities of practice. It describes the main characteristics of these communities, identifying the differences between the two communities and presents the context in which the discussion of social capital is situated in the book. Chapter VIII introduces the reader to the topic of knowledge management and its relevance to social capital.

Chapter VI
Social Computing and Social Software

INTRODUCTION

The World Wide Web or simply the Web is one of the most profound technological inventions of our time and is the core to the development of social computing. The initial purpose of the Web was to use networked hypertext system to facilitate communication among its scientists and researchers, who were located in several countries. When Sir Tim Berners-Lee invented the World Wide Web in 1989, he envisioned it as a mass collaborative authoring environment intended to facilitate information sharing among scientists and researchers. He predicted that when fully deployed, the Web would evolve into an information system capable of fostering unfathomable interaction; effective engagement and efficient document sharing. However, in 1991 when the first Web browser (Mosaic) was released, the Web still remained largely a plane information system for only passively distributing information over the Internet instead of an engaging medium.

Within the few years that followed the release of the first Web browser, Berners-Lee (1996) projected three long term goals for the Web. The first was aimed at ensuring the availability of different technologies to improve communication and engagement. The second goal was to make the Web an interactive medium that can engage individuals as well as enrich communities' activities. Berners-Lee's third goal for the Web was to create a more intelligent Web, in addition to being a space browseable by humans. He planned to develop a Web rich in data, promoting community engagement, and encouraging mass participation and information sharing.

Within this third goal, he envisioned a Web that fosters application sharing and understandable by both human and machines.

These three key goals for the Web characteristically describe the natural evolution of Web technologies. More specifically, the outcomes of the first goal were accompanied by the appearance of a plethora of authoring tools for Web. Current Web 2.0 technologies provide examples of the outcomes of the second goal. And the third goal is represented by the Semantic Web—which also marks the third and the future generation of Web technologies including intelligent software agents.

This chapter describes general trends linked to the development of the World Wide Web and discusses its related technologies within the milieu of virtual communities. The goal is to provide the reader with a quick, concise and easy way to understand the development of the Web and its related terminologies. The chapter does not account for a more comprehensive analysis of historical trends associated with the development of the Web; neither does it go into a more detailed technical discussion of Web technologies. Nonetheless, it is anticipated that the materials presented in the chapter are sufficient to provide the reader with a better understanding of the past, present and future accounts of the Web and its core related technologies.

HISTORICAL DEVELOPMENT OF THE NETWORK COMMUNICATION MEDIA

Communication plays a vital role in creating, developing, integrating and sustaining communities. It helps members of a community to support and maintain their community ties promote social cohesion, build trust and stimulate social connection necessary for building social capital. Communication serves as a critical ingredient necessary for establishing different types of social capital–bridging, bonding and linking. More specifically, communication facilitates diffusion of information, reinforces social protocols, mobilizes people for collective action and creates social support thus providing the necessary foundation for understanding how social capital operates in communities and its overall impact on community affairs.

The art of communication is engrained in all aspects of human societies. History divulges that people have constantly developed various ways to communicate with each other, even long before the establishment of postal services, newspapers, telegraph, and telephone and network communication media. In primal societies for example, communication was only possible through "word of the mouth"—person to person communication system (e.g. through a messenger). In smaller communities people relied on a "crier" (an individual employed normally by a community or town council who made most of the public announcements in the streets and other places where people gathered), to communicate important issues affecting people in the neighbourhood or in an entire village.

In those times, using the "crier" as means of communication was appropriate since only few people were literate and the size of the population was not big enough to warrant any sophisticated means of communication system. Criers used different tools for communication ranging from bullhorns in some communities to "talking drums". "Talking drums" were developed and used by cultures living in forested areas, chiefly in some African countries (e.g. West Africa). These special types of drums served as an early form of long distance communication instruments and were used in many day-to-day occasions but were more heavily used during ceremonial and religious functions (e.g. death, birth of a child marriage and other sociological events of significance to a community).

Over time, some of these old systems of communications these days are either used less or completely abandoned because they are highly impractical and unreliable for long distance communication. As a result, other systems were established such as the postal system. During the epoch of the mailing system, people started communicating by sending letters or parcels. Though still in use today, the postal system is awash with human errors.

In the dotcom era, it is undeniable that people's lives, especially in the modern world, are thoroughly imbued with a variety of network communication media and multi-information channels, enabling them to access a variety of information on anything at anytime and from anywhere. The Internet predominately plays a major role in this massive, unprecedented and sweeping technological development in mass communication systems in addition to many other communication systems that preceded the Internet (e.g. telephone and telegraph).

Before the advent of computer networks, communication between calculating machines and early computers were performed by humans by performing instructions between them or programming them to perform desirable tasks. Many of the functionalities in today's Internet were demonstrably present in nineteenth-century telegraph networks, and arguably in even earlier networks using visual signals. When the Internet was invented in the 1960s, electronic mail (e-mail) was the main dominant communication media.

THE INTERMISSION OF THE WORLD WIDE WEB

Today more and more people use computers and related technologies as primary communication tools. The Internet and particularly the World Wide Web (WWW) has drastically revolutionized computer networks and global communications systems. Perhaps the invention of the telegraph, telephone, radio, and computer set the stage for unprecedented integration of capabilities into many spheres of society. The World Wide Web, a collection of electronic documents linked together like a spider web, has evolved into a global electronic publishing medium and a medium for conducting electronic commerce, education, socialization and many other day to day activities.

Perhaps for the majority of people, the electronic mailing system or simply e-mail was the first encounter with the Internet. Later in 1980, Usenet was introduced as a group communication system. Usenet is still in use today but it is one of the oldest computer network communications systems ever used primarily for connecting people globally. Within five years, following the invention of the World Wide Web (WWW), network communication technologies spread into all the aspects of society, changing the shape of modern life, altering the way people learn, play, do business, associate with each other and build communities. For almost 18 years now, the Web has evolved from a simple group (groupware) tool for a selected number of scientists, into a global information space with more than a billion users in 2008 to date. Over the years, with the increasing transformation of individuals' tools to support communities and ability to easily integrate systems and resources, the Web is transformed into a social and participatory medium, serving as an instrument of social change by supporting individuals and communities in the way they communicate, share information and knowledge.

Communicating through the Web seems to be more convenient especially for people who find it easier and comfortable to express themselves in the absence of others. For example, it is far easier to provide honest ideas and thoughts through a computer than in face-to-face setting, virtual communications tend to be less intimidating than meeting people face-to-face. In online environments it is easier to share thoughts because one cannot see other people's reaction to what one says. Communication in virtual communities helps people to carefully organize their thoughts before sharing them with others. Through means of asynchronous communication, people can reflect more on what others have written because of the nature of the meduim and the fact that it is capable of leaving a permanent transcripts of discourse. Communication in environments supported by asynchronous tools allows people time to think about what they want to say first and revise things before they speak.

Further, people who are too shy to speak in face-to-face settings normally find it easier to express themselves in virtual communities. For them the online environment provides a conducive environment for discussion of issues that they might not be comfortably discussed in face-to-face settings. They might be shy of what others might think or what reaction they might get from others. There is also a tendency to freely and openly communicate in virtual environments such as chartrooms since one might easialy masks one's identity if need be. In other words, the anonymity afforded to individuals by various technologies provides to people some sense of privacy which one might not get in a face-to-face environment.

There are other factors that contributed to the rapid growth and success of the Web. Space does not permit to discuss these factors in more detail in the book, but few of these factors are technical, while others are more social and economic in nature. The technical factors include the exponential increase in computational power, advances in software architecture including scalability of software system and the development of robust software methodologies and workflow systems; moreover the social factors are ignited by falling prices of hardware and software, the ease of use and productivity of using software for business and day to day operations, and increase in accessibility. But perhaps the introduction of participatory social software and community building is one of the most important factor contributing enormously is the permeation of software usage into many social spheres.

In addition, individuals and organisations willing to give away software packages for free (Open Source) also contributed to the adoption and growth in usage of the Web. One way to gain more understanding in the development of the Web technologies is to trace its trace the evolution of technologies associated with its growth. This is further presented in the form of historical versioning. Figure 6-1 captures the most important technological development and the metaphors used for describing each generation of the Web technologies (Spivack, 2008).

Figure 6-1. Versioning of the Web technologies: Spivack (2008) (radarnetworks. com) used with permission

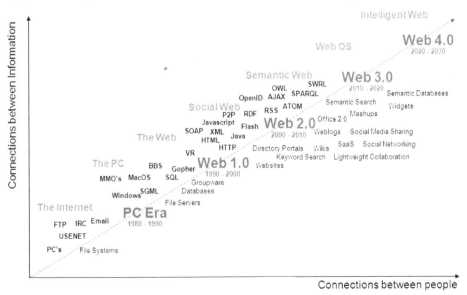

THE FIRST GENERATION OF THE WEB

Early stages in the development of the Web demonstrated increasing release of various browsers, followed by an intense competition over market dominance. Perhaps the most well-known competition occurred between Netscape Navigator, Internet Explorer and Opera. Advances in Web browsers were also accompanied by the development of more robust and versatile graphic programs and scripting languages as well as authoring environments—"what you see is what you get" (WYSWYG), and a variety of other technologies, all of which constituted the first generation of web-based tools (Web 1.0). This first generation of the Web also manifested a sporadic development in personal Web pages aimed at displaying personal information as well as organisations.

Web 1.0 was a highly specialised Web-Based software industry, distinguishing between developers and users. At best the operational model of Web 1.0 can be equated to "production—consumer model" similar to models available within economic systems, where content producers where those who possessed specialised knowledge and skills in Web development. In order to develop WebPages, one has to be proficient in Mark-up languages—the Hypertext Mark-up Language (HTML) or some scripting language (e.g. JavaScript). People who were interested in building WebPages but lacked the required Web programming skills remained mostly content consumers. In addition, those who were able to produce content for the Internet had to look for companies that can host web space. Once WebPages were put on the Website, the owner had to find ways to promote the website to the entire world; this was done through registering the webpage address to popular web engines.

Furthermore, in the early days of the Web 1.0, Web developers were concerned with finding ways to effectively utilize the Web. The impetus was delivering information to users at any cost. Most of the WebPages in the version of Web 1.0 contained information about individuals or organisations that might be useful, but few people returned to a site once they visit a site and got all that they need because content of websites never rapidly changed. For example, a personal Web page that gives information about the site's owner, but never changes was likely to be visited only once. Most technologies in Web 1.0 applications were proprietary and companies develop software applications that users can download, but they can't see how the application works or changes it. During those days, various content management systems were developed and many people use them to develop personal Web sites as a way not only to establish their personal presence on the Web but also to demonstrate their Web design skills and to prove to others, what the Web was capable of doing or what they could do with the Web.

THE SECOND GENERATION OF THE WEB

The beginning of the new millennium marked another new and important landscape in the historical development of the Web. In 2000 a number of online software companies intended to simplify the process of content creation; distribution and sharing became publicly available, with some of them free of charge (freeware) meaning available to users with no cost or little costs. Recently, as Open Source—free software with full access to program source code and permission to modify program under Open Source Licensing agreement. The usability (ease of use) and usefulness (productivity) of online technologies radically transformed the way content is produced and used and how people interact with the Web. This was the genesis of a new generation of Web technologies—Web 2.0.

Technically speaking, Web 2.0 is loosely used to describe almost any Web site, service, or technology that encourages community building, data, information and knowledge sharing and collaboration. Core technologies constituting Web 2.0 include software systems such as wikis, blogs, Really Simple Syndication (RSS), Asynchronous JavaScript (Ajax) and extensible mark-up language (XML). Unlike its antecedent, Web 2.0 technologies allow people to focus more on ideas and creativity rather than acquisition of hardcore programming and scripting skills, necessary for developing Web applications and for creating high quality content. Web 2.0 is also a collection of server-based technologies enabling the web to become a publishing platform. Instead of the traditional one-way form of web authoring, these solutions invite all Internet users to share, collaborate, and contribute in the process of website development.

Further, Web 2.0 is more participatory in nature, capable of fostering more democratic mode of operation, where people can create, edit, and distribute Web content. Due to its increasing ability to promote engagement and interactivity, these technologies witnessed more proliferation of online groups, social networks and virtual communities. Web 2.0 technologies also signify innovation in the growth of the Web, enabling a more writable and recombinant Web experience for non-technical users. In addition, Web 2.0 technologies allow people to easily publish new, rich multimedia content to the Web with little or no technical skills. Several technologies associated with Web 2.0 provide people with increased ability to contribute text, bookmarks, photos, audio, videos and more to many different websites. This ease of access to the Web content alters the way users interact with the new World Wide Web. Users can now build online social network platforms where community others can join and contribute content, share resources, collaborate on the agenda and determine the direction of the website.

In another technical level, most of Web 2.0 applications are open source program, which means the source code for the program are freely available for modification or reprogramming. Users can see how the software application works and if necessary they can make or directly suggests modifications or even build new applications based on earlier programs. Firefox is an example of Web 2.0. It provides developers with all the tools they need to create new Firefox applications. The ability to easily publish within this new generation of the Web makes Web 2.0 drastically unique from Web 1.0 days. Furthermore, fundamental to Web 2.0 is social computing and social software; emerging technologies that are entirely dedicated to supporting groups and communities. Web 2.0 is an umbrella term describing the trend in the use of World Wide Web technologies to enhance creativity, information sharing, and most notably, collaboration among users.

Web 2.0 is also a platform independent, meaning that it is not only an environment for developers to create Web applications but also provide a collaborative environment for users to create updates and share content (e.g. video or document sharing tools). Unlike its predecessors, Web 2.0 technologies represent an important shift in the way digital information is created, shared, stored, distributed, and manipulated. They make it easier for software architects to create online applications that are highly social in nature encouraging users to manipulate and interact with content in various new ways, fostering community engagement, encourage relationships building and stimulating the development of social capital, through collaborative discourse.

The technologies of Web 2.0 are evolving. A few examples of Web 2.0 applications include: Blogs, Wikis, Really Simple Syndication (RSS), Twitter, generally Social Networks and Web Services (Facebook, Myspace, Youtube etc.). This section describes few of these technologies. The goal is to highlights the importance of these technologies in supporting virtual communities.

Blogs

Blogs are online journals or online diaries hosted on a Web site. They represent personal thoughts, reflections, and links to resources such as documents, music and websites. They can also be linked to other blogs. Blogs are often distributed to other sites or readers using Really Simple Syndication (RSS) technologies. Blogs can also be considered as websites with entries updated on a regular basis and displayed in reverse chronological order. Precisely, blogs run on specialized software, making them easy to implement, use and manage without knowledge of hypertext mark-up language or technical know-how of scripting languages.

There are currently several blog search engines available. They are used to search blog contents, such as Bloglines, BlogScope, and Technorati. Technorati, which is among the most popular blog search engines, provides current information on both popular searches and tags used to categorize blog postings. Work is underway to develop more robust and efficient algorithms for searching and navigating through blogosphere systems.

Since they are easy to implement, there are tens of thousands of blogs in existence today. Most of the blogs in existence today are written and maintained by a wide range of people—individuals and groups, covering every possible topic, technical, social, economic, personal and educational. The collections of blogs that are linked to each other constitute blogospheres. Before blogs were invented, personal homepages were the main spaces for people to establish their presence on the Web. However, as noted in the previous discussion on Web 1.0 in this chapter, personal Web pages are cumbersome to update and manage. They required a great deal of time especially for larger websites.

Further, compared to traditional websites where content might be static, content of blogs are dynamic in nature and since they are more personal reflections of the authors, blogs tend to convey messages in a very honest and powerful way and are more likely to be updated on a regular basis. With blogs normally being written in a first-person format, the voice of the author comes through clearly, thereby supporting the message being narrated.

Furthermore, the first generation of the Internet reflected in the version of Web 1.0 offered one way communication. People got online, found the information they were looking for, which, was often provided by another individual or a company. They had limited choices in filtering or altering the information they got online. Web 2.0, offers two way communication channels. Blogs, for example, offer readers the opportunity to communicate with others through feedback, and social networks create communities which offer people the opportunity to express themselves whether in words, music, documents, or drawings or some combinations of the above.

Though primarily used for documenting personal stories, blogs can be used to promote community engagement. When people blog; they are exposing their ideas, sometimes sharing with others their personal information. They are blogging primarily because they require readership. Bloggers (people who blog), often share their thoughts, insights, concerns, issues, feelings and stories with others. For some, blogging means sharing their life experiences and lessons with the hope of making the world a better place or making themselves heard by others who might care. For other people, blogging is an avenue for sharing their interests with the hope of attracting other like-minded folks or connecting to their communities.

Depending on topics of interest, comments in blogs can trigger further discussions that can ultimately lead to useful aggregation of knowledge and social networking connections. Further, as people link to each other's blogs, they share contents and links but also implicitly create some social networks (latent relationships). For example, **Y** maintains a blog on complex systems thinking, **X** has a blog on organisational development but is interested in complex thinking theory as well.

X discovers that **Y** writes and maintains a blog on this topic and is always on top of issues relating to complex system thinking. **X** occasionally adds comments to **Y**'s blogs and **Y** suddenly discovers new insights that help him/her reflect better as a result of **X**'s comments. **Y** links to **X**'s blog and discovers other issues on organisational development that are relevant to complex system's theory. They contacted each other and got connected and suddenly started exchanging information, sharing resources on organisational development and complex systems theory. As the number of **Xs** and the **Ys** increase, so are their social network and ultimately the feeling of the sense of a community is created. This scenario illustrates how blogs can evolve from a personal reflective tool to a community platform for sharing experiences and personal views.

Really Simple Syndication

Briefly, Really Simple Syndication or sometimes referred to as Rich Site Summary (RSS) is software for distributing headlines and article summaries for news systems and announcements. RSS makes it possible for people to keep up with their favorite web sites in an automated manner. RSS technologies can be considered as one-stop-shop place for links to news articles, blogs and websites of interests that are updated on regular basis.

A major utility of RSS technologies is that they allow people to subscribe to online distributions of news, blogs, podcasts, or other information. In addition, they help people who are interested in keeping up to date with content from many websites. RSS technologies also make it easy to deliver content to community members. The members of a community to connect to those communities they are interested in linking to. This suit of Web 2.0 challenges its predecessor in that in the past it was challenging to build a virtual community with personalised content relevant to diverse individual interests. However, with the advancement in Really Simple Syndication (RSS) technologies, this issue is becoming less critical, since RSS technologies enable community architectures, to easily and quickly link members to content already created by others. By using tools such as bloglines, which aggregate content of interest and place them in a one-stop-shop, people can now remain connected to content that interest them, without having to worry about surfing through thousands of web sites to retrieve content.

Wiki

Ward Cunningham created the first Wiki (WikiWikiWeb) in 1995. The term "Wiki" was named after Hawaiian bus service, Wiki Wiki, essentially meaning "quick". According to its founder, a Wiki was initially meant to be the "simplest online database that could possibly work with minimum technical requirement. It was intended for users to generate and edit content in collaborative manner. The goal was to facilitate the process of co-creation of meaningful content through democratic participation and consensus building. In more simple terms, a wiki is a software program that allows users to create, edit, and link web pages easily without learning HTML or web design. Like blogs, a wiki can be a website. However, unlike blogs, it is mostly created and maintained by a group rather than by an individual. Wikipedia is one of the best known and perhaps intensively used Wiki.

A Wiki tool fosters community around content development and sharing. Due to its co-editing features, a wiki is an excellent tool for collaboration and for building a virtual community. A wiki can serve as an online document management and document sharing systems, allowing a group or community members to contribute to a knowledge repository. Since it is a community authoring tool, a wiki imposes minimum or no control over who can create or edit web pages, making it very simple to update and an ideal tool for virtual communities to share knowledge.

In addition, its affordance to easily upload, edit, share modify content with others is an important strategy for building shared understanding among people with diverse views. Wiki systems can also be used essentially to create various forms of awareness, whether it is determining "who knows what" in community, or simply visualising others professional backgrounds, as members coalesce as a community.

Further, the joint collaborative nature of wikis and their ability to display what others are doing enables community members to review each other's work and allow those revisions to benefit all community members. Moreover, knowledge collaboratively developed in wikis can serve as collective community memory. This in turn helps people to effectively participate in extending conversations, with more detail.

Twitter

Twitter is another example of Web 2.0 technology. Twitter is a free online service intended to foster connections among people through quick, short and succinct messages, which are normally up to 140 characters or less. People type these brief updates, known as "tweets," into Twitter's site or send them to Twitter as text messages. Friends and colleagues can then check the site to monitor each other's activities (whereabouts and events updates). It is a service intended to help friends, family, and co–workers to communicate and stay connected to each other, through instant and condensed exchange of messages. People normally utilize Twitter to ask quick questions such as "where are you?" And get quick answers like "I am on my way to work, running little late for the meeting." Twitter also is increasingly being described as personal news-wire—shared world events like there was an earth earthquake this morning near Los Angeles or it is raining here.

The ability to twit over mobile and handheld devices adds more possibility to extend connections to ubiquitous circumstances. Vascellaro (2008) reported a critical life saving use of twitter. She indicated that doctors are increasingly using Twitter to update their patients about office hours and Fire Department personnel have also started using Twitter to share details about service calls with interested residents, occasionally with graphic descriptions of the victims' conditions. Twitter is already spreading quickly at several companies, employees in many companies are using the service to communicate with one another on topics ranging from politics, help to marketing plans and to keep abreast of fellow employee's activities. Moreover, technology companies such as Dell Inc. use twitter to share deals and product news with people who sign up for the service.

Within educational settings, University and College professors use Twitter to connect with their colleagues and students. They also use it in large academic conferences, to find out what's going on around them, what presentations their colleagues are attending and who might be in other presentation venues. Due to its compactness, portability and ubiquity, other professionals are finding it increasingly valuable to use twitter to connect to their community and build up their professional reputation by sharing updates about their work in a less time-intensive way than starting a blog.

These case scenarios of twitter suggest its growing popularity as a tool for community building and nurturing of social capital under distributed circumstance. Due to its increasing usage, the Wall Street Journal reported that Twitter developers are looking at ways to allow people to indicate that they are attending a particular event, so they can more easily share updates with others who are there. Within virtual communities, twitter serves as quick, brief and up to date awareness fostering tool. Twitting facilitates succinct information sharing and the kinds of updates necessary for maintaining the most needed connections within community members and creating tighter connections.

Web Radio

Web radio or simply e-radio is an audio broadcasting service transmitted via the Internet or webcasting since it is not transmitted broadly through wireless means. Web radio involves a streaming medium that presents listeners with a continuous "stream" of audio over which they have no control, much like traditional broadcast media. Web radio is perhaps an example of a Web 2.0 technology that is rarely discussed, though it presents some interesting community connections. This service evolved from simple distribution of audio files to complex multicast streaming of audio files over networks. In 1994, The Rolling Stones offered a concert online marking the first cyberspace multicast concert. Currently, there are numerous web radio stations featuring community issues. As of the year this book went to press, the CanadianWebRadio.com, a web radio directory lists over 600 radio stations from across Canada streaming radio programs live over the Internet, connecting various communities with a variety of entertainment programs, ranging from music, politics, culture to folklore and language learning..

Web radio also provides individuals with current international news, entertainments and educational programs one can usually get on local or international radio. The British Broadcasting Corporation (BBC) for example provides many of its international news programs online. An important aspect of the Web radio is its ability to inculcate the sense of a community to individuals beyond what traditional radio stations usually offer. Some of the current Web radios broadcast live programs, which enables individuals who are now used to digital technology to stay connected to their communities regardless of where they are located and listen to news over networks channelled through different forms of technologies.

Besides, because of its ubiquitous nature, Web radio is accessible to many people with Internet connections. Participation in Web radio can strengthen, deepen and widen social connections among a community of listeners. In small communities radio has been influential in helping people lubricate community activities by spurring dialogue, debate and decision making on issues of local concern. For those who are interested in staying closely connected to their communities and who might find themselves far away from their communities, Web radio provide them with the alternatives and opportunities to stay updated on local issues in their communities.

Social TV

Social TV is another example of emergent technologies for supporting virtual communities. They are driven by the recent rise of social networks, and based on the seemingly paradoxical trend of individualized viewing on personal devices, or simply one's "own" TV, and the customization of the user experience with "widgets." Social TV describes a new breed of video services that integrate other communication services like voice, chat, context awareness and peer rating systems to support a shared TV experience with one's peer groups (Klym & Montpetit, 2008). Social TV stems from two trends intrinsically linked to the TV individual and group social experiences. The individual experience relates to particular viewing preferences, tastes and favourites. Moreover, individuals' experiences can be transmitted to others who share similar tastes, and interests. It is when an individual meets with others experiences, where community experience is created and a key motivation for creating tools for the social TV.

Microsoft Corp. primarily instigated Social TV technologies to connect hard-core gamers for competitive matches. Since 2002, when Microsoft launched Xbox Live, the gaming and entertainment service that allows Xbox-console owners to connect to the Internet and compete against each other in multiplayer games. Through these technologies, gamers are able to establish new connections with other gamers and maintain existing relationship with each other through television channels. Since its popularity within the online gaming communities, social TV technologies have made their way to other virtual communities. Subsequently, companies have started to seek various ways to entice a broader audience to chat with friends, share photos and recommend movies and music over their television screens.

Some key software applications of Web 2.0 such as MySpace and Facebook are now being incorporated into WebTV, but the shared TV experience is now returning in a new form. The typical family room of the 1950s is being replaced by online virtual communities accessed through personal devices. These communities extend far beyond the home to span entire neighborhoods, cities, countries, and hemispheres. And like the traditional living room, these communities are increasingly organized around video, connecting families, friends, and some strangers alike in a shared video space defined by interactions, common interest, or location.

The majority of the Social TV applications are geared primarily at real-time interactivity with peer groups (shared viewing) and peer. This new community experience can be contrasted to Putnam (1995) observation that the family-room TV experience itself was an instance of the "individualization" of news and entertainment since it constrained people to watch it in the privacy of their own homes—and is therefore, considered to be anti-social. Putnam's (1995) analysis came at a time when Web 2.0 technologies were just being developed and people's sociability were limited to engagement in entertainment activities in public spaces, e.g., the baseball park, bowling clubs, the dance hall and the movie theater and so solitude watching of television was considered detrimental to health of a community and subsequently leading to the decline of social capital. However, it should be noted that when television appeared in the 1950s, it was a social object where typically family, friends and neighbors gathered to have a shared viewing experience. In this regard, television viewing was considered to be a communal activity involving people gathering in the living room around the TV, choosing what to watch, sharing reactions to the same program, and exchanging comments. As television technologies became more affordable, more and more family started to own their own TV set and therefore, decrease communal social viewing.

Even in the 21st century, it is not uncommon to find a group of friends gathering in a living room to collectively view TV and share experiences, especially during important events such as football, political debates, boxing and other mutually shared activities. Further, going out to the movies is still considered, in many societies, a social phenomenon intended to initiate or maintain an innermost feeling of connection or friendship. The social nature of the interaction involved during these activities or the collective viewing experience is the cornerstone for building social capital. In addition, there are countries in some parts of Africa and other continents, where television or video cassette recoding systems or digital video disc players viewing event still bring people together, whether it is to watch movies or sporting events.

Based on these observations, it can be concluded that television technologies themselves do not deter the social interaction necessary for community building. Instead, when fully developed; they are capable of fostering sophisticated kinds of social interaction necessary for building complex social relationships. The communal gathering facilitated by maturing and converging television technologies is creating the kinds of social connections necessary for building not only local but global social capital. Thus far, the typical family room of the 1950s is being replaced by an increasing feeling of virtual communities, which extend far beyond the home to other countries, connecting not only gamers but families, friends, and also strangers.

THE THIRD GENERATION OF THE WEB

Tim Berners-Lee extended his vision of the Web as a participatory medium to the next level. He coined the term "Semantic Web" to mean the third generation of Web technologies with set of artificial intelligent tools. He pointed that the Semantic Web is a place where machines can read Web pages much as people read them, a place where search engines and software agents can better troll the Net and find what people are looking for and interested in. Fundamental to the Semantic Web are deliberation of content as microformats, use of natural language search, deployment of data-mining, machine learning, emphasizing machine-facilitated understanding of information in order to provide a more productive and intuitive user experience.

The Semantic Web is an attempt to make computers act smarter, be independent and productive and for the most part, act on behalf of their users. The Semantic Web is a vision of information that is understandable by computers, so that they can perform more of the tedious work involved in finding, sharing and combining information on the web. In addition, the Semantic Web aims at making Web sites interoperable, intelligent, context relevant. It focuses on creating a network of interlinked and semantically rich knowledge.

According to Nova Spivack (radarnetwork.com), the Semantic Web is the next generation of web technology. The focal point of the Semantic Web is to make data on web pages and in online databases better able to be read and understood by computers and used and shared by different software applications, making the Web universally searchable and sharable. Another important motivation for the development of the Semantic Web is driven by the belief that current search engines are not adequate because they are unable to provide the epistemological and historical context of a question which gives query results more meaning. Search engines are designed as tools for information aggregation instead of knowledge integration. In addition, the vast majority of current documents on the web have little or no semantic information associated with them and the ability to automatically add semantic annotations would be a huge benefit to users.

The Semantic Web will become one gigantic world-wide database, which relies on machine-readable information and metadata expressed in Resource Description Framework. RDF is a family of The World Wide Web Consortium (The W3C) specifications originally designed as a metadata data model, but which has come to be used as a general method of modeling information through a variety of syntax formats. The core feature of RDF is that it is a mesh of information linked up in such a way to enable machines to easily process it a massive and global scale. In the Semantic Web, data itself becomes part of the Web and is able to be processed independently of application, platform, or domain. This is in contrast to the World Wide Web as of today, which contains virtually boundless information in the form of documents, links, audio, video and graphic files. Fundamental to all kinds of information on the Web, is that we can use computers to search for information, but they still have to be read and interpreted by humans before any useful information can be extrapolated.

In terms of a virtual community building, the Semantic Web enables people to search, filter, find and retrieve information in an intelligent and friendly way. It also enhance data and information sharing based on users attributes such as context, preference, tasks and etc, making social connectivity among people with similar interests, and similar content faster and easier. The realization of the full potential of the Semantic Web involves developing programs that collect Web content from diverse sources, process the information and exchange the results with other programs leading to the future generation of the Web technologies (Web 4.0).

THE FOURTH GENERATION OF THE WEB

Web 4.0 involves interaction of people with personal software agents and their massive deployment on the Web. The initiative of using agents to act on behalf of humans originated from human agents that provide useful and sometimes indispensable services to others. Human agents include those working within the real estate industry, insurance and travel. Human agents often have specialised skills and knowledge to access relevant information, as well as contacts for obtaining information and are focused on a particular task. In the same vein personal software agents are autonomous systems that work on behalf of their users (Bradshaw 1997). In Computer Science, a software agent is a piece of software that acts for a user or other program. Personal software agents exhibit the ability to recognise what their users need to accomplish and reacts to other users input. Personal software agents may continuously operate in the background on behalf of their users and they might act autonomously to suggest ways in which the learner might improve performance.

Personal software agent research is not new. It is an area which has been considerably investigated within the artificial intelligence community. This research for the most part has generated many tangibles systems and procedures. Intelligent tutoring systems that provide support to students are examples systems built out of personal agents' research. The iHelp system, developed by the Laboratory for Advanced Research in Intelligent Educational Systems, at the University of Saskatchewan, is a long standing example of an intelligent educational system, built entirely on the idea of personal agents. The iHelp system is a suite of tools made up of a number of web based applications designed to support both learners and instructors throughout the learning process. There are many other examples of deployment of personal software agents within commercial systems.

The integration of personal software agents to inhabit the Web is likely to change the face of virtual communities. Personal software agents are built with capacity to decide for the users and sometimes autonomously act on their behalf. Fundamental to this line of autonomous personal agents in the Web is based on the expectation that personal software agents are not strictly invoked for a task, but activate themselves. In the future, the effectiveness of such personal software agents will increase exponentially as more machine-readable Web content and automated services (including other agents) become available. The Semantic Web promotes this synergy: even agents that were not expressly designed to work together can transfer data among themselves when the data come with semantics.

In terms of their application to Web 4.0, personal software agents are capable of predicting people's behaviour. They can track and register people's purchases, surfing behaviour on the Web, as well as your professional, commercial and recreational activities. The future seems to promise a truly brave new world of targeted and meaningful information. People's past behaviors and activities will be considered predictors of future behaviors, and information collected from individual past behavior be used in personalised software to the needs of an individual. For example, when a person is interested in looking up for information, a personal software agent learns to suggest appropriate links by analyzing previous traces, tastes, looking up others with shared interests and making appropriate recommendations.

SOCIAL COMPUTING AND SOCIAL SOFTWARE

Social computing is an emergent area of applied Computer Science concerned with the analysis, understanding and supporting of social behaviour and accompanying interaction patterns within computational systems. For systems designers, the idea of social computing involves creation of social software, together with the social conventions. It is also to ensure that the ultimate tangible social software technologies are socially aware and that their design is socially informed and is human-centred. Social computing emerged due to easy affordability of connections brought about by cheap devices, modular content, and shared computing resources. These technologies have profoundly impinged on our global economy and social structure. Social computing is also concerned with the creation of software packages that are either dynamically personalised or provide individuals with possibilities of customisation which is timely, relevant and useful.

Social software is one example of social computing systems. According to Shirky (2003) social software is simply a piece of software that can support group interaction. This definition covers all forms of synchronous and asynchronous communication systems. In a common usage, social software describes group software that fall within the category of Web 2.0 and beyond. Social software can also be regarded as a particular sub-class of software dedicated to the augmentation of human social and or collaborative abilities through structured mediation (Coates, 2003). Owen, Grant, Sayers and Facer (2006) mentioned a number of benefits associated with social software including, removing the real world limitations placed on social and collaborative behaviours by factors such as language, geography and background.

Further, social software has the ability to compensate for human inadequacies in processing, maintaining or developing social and or collaborative mechanisms. This is achieved through ease of information overload and generating appropriate filtering mechanisms. The proceeding section presents some of the key technologies associated with social computing in general and social software in particular.

Peer-to-Peer Networking Systems

Peer-to-peer networking (sometimes called P2P) are social oriented systems that are often used for efficiently sharing files (music, videos, or text) either over the

Internet or within a closed set of people. Peer-to peer systems enable any unit within a network to communicate with and provide services to another unit within the network. All participants in peer-to-peer networks are of the same importance to the system; no single peer is critical to the functionality of the system and the application functions without the control or authorization of an external entity. Peers can be assumed to be of variable connectivity and can join and leave the system at their own discretion.

Peer-to-Peer music sharing demonstrates one of the core technologies that enable virtual communities to actively engage in sharing music and other files online, creating a sense of community online among their members around the kinds of music people are interested in. This practice had also put a negative effect on the music industry revenue, leading to legal actions against systems such as Napster. Previous P2P systems such as Napster allowed people to easily copy and distribute music files among each other, bypassing the established market for such songs and thus leading to the music industry's accusations of massive copyright violations. Although Napster was shut down by court order, its lead in the field paved the way for decentralized peer-to-peer file-sharing programs, which are much harder to control. Subsequently, they have increasingly propagated growth in those types of virtual communities dedicated to sharing various kinds of resources from music to electronic books, videos and other valuable materials.

Social Network Systems

Social network systems predate online social networks. Some trace the roots of social network analysis to the work of Georg Simmel, a German sociologist and philosopher who is known for his work on studies of urban Sociology, social conflict theory, and small-group relationships. According to Simmel, a society consists of a web of patterned interactions, and that it is the task of Sociology to study the forms of these interactions as they occur and reoccur in their diverse historical periods and cultural settings. This approach is thought of as a natural departure from August Comte and Herbert Spencer organic view of progression of society and the survival of fittest theory.

Though Simmel's views were considered antagonistic by most of his contemporary Sociology scholars and for most part, rejected, he pioneered the concept of social structure, a key precursor of social network analysis. In the 1950s, the theory of social network gained pre-eminence as a sociological and mathematical approach to understanding patterns of relationships among people, objects and systems. In the epoch of computing and an increasing availability of network communication systems, the study of social network has now become more germane than before. More specifically, the Internet provides a technological network infrastructure to support various social networks, with millions of people who are related to each other in various ways. In recent times, with the help of various generations of Web technologies, notably Web 2.0, the development of social networking has become a norm across age groups, transcending geography, culture, language and discipline.

Social network systems operate as an identity management tool, helping people to manage vast amount of ties with friends, acquaintances, colleagues at work or relatives. For many years, many people managed their social and professional networks manually, either in a paper or electronic based address book. Moreover social network systems enable people to articulate a list of other members in the systems with which they share some connections. In addition, social networking systems have created new ways for people to connect, expand and exchange personal contact information, but what makes these systems even more powerful than a personal address book is their ability to provide users with easy, fast and more organised access to friends and other social networks (e.g., Facebook). In addition, they provide easy ways to find people within immediate and extended network that have particular interests, skills, relationships, etc.

Furthermore, social network systems serve as community websites whose goals are normally to enable people to expand their group of friends by introducing them to each other or inviting new ones. These systems are mechanisms to support simple creation/sharing of contents and communications information or mechanisms for visualizing the group identities to maintain some form of online awareness. Social networking systems are powerful mechanisms for creating and maintaining social connection and community building.

In the corporate sector, companies use social network systems to reach out to passive candidates and to look for hard to fill positions within their jurisdiction. Social network systems also allow companies, especially their human resource departments to build a large and more diverse talent pool that can be tapped into in times of need. For example, LinkedIn, one of the biggest and active professional social network systems available today, and the system is basically used a recruitment hub for new employees. Through similar systems, social networking systems serve as a great way to find candidates for niche and hard-to fill positions. In some social networking systems, companies can now search for candidates, research their past experience and education, and even view recommendations.

There is a close connection between social capital and the act of social networking. Referring to the discussion on structural dimensions of social capital presented in chapter II, social capital can be an outcome of a positive effect of interaction between participants in a social network. For individuals, social capital allows individuals to benefit in a variety of ways in that participation in a social network allows a person to draw on resources from other members of the network and to leverage connections from multiple social contexts. These resources can take the form of important information, employment opportunities, personal relationships, or the capacity to organize groups (Paxton, 1999).

Access to individuals outside one's close circle provides access to non-redundant information, resulting in benefits such as employment connections (Granovetter, 1973). ScienceDaily (May 12, 2008) reported that online networking sites, such as Facebook and MySpace are increasingly helping new students settle into university social and academic life and minimising the chance of them withdrawing from their courses. Social networking technologies are also changing the average number of friends people have, with some users befriending literally thousands of others. Additionally, online social networks tend to be far larger than their real-life counterparts. These loose connections are often referred to as "weak ties" (Granovetter, 1973). Within social networks, the existence of gaps – i.e. the absence of direct links among all participants and between connected individuals can actually increase the efficiency of information flows within the larger network. Members of the social network who act as hubs tie together sub-networks and act as brokering agents. Burt (2000) refers to these gaps in social networks as "structural holes" and argues that networks operate more efficiently when structural holes exist, often by supporting the importing and exporting of new information and ideas between sub-groups. Such a process allows information to flow from one group in which it is common knowledge or mundane, to another where it is new and may be more valuable.

Facebook, is perhaps the most versatile social networking of our time. The system is widely used social networking system and perhaps the most currently utilized, connects friends and family members. Facebook was originally designed for University and College students as a way of communication and connecting students to each other. It is now used by all kinds of users and it has both synchronous and asynchronous communications systems. Facebook enables people to locate their friends, college, high school colleagues and even colleagues at work place.

A key feature of Facebook and perhaps its limitation is that it can only enable engagement among close friends or acquaintance but does not extend the networking to new horizons. This is also the main weakness of the tool, it can also be considered as advantage as it can individual privacy and trust. For individuals, social capital allows a person to draw on resources from other members of the networks to which he or she belongs. These resources can take the form of useful information, personal relationships, or the capacity to organize groups (Paxton, 1999). Access to individuals outside one's close circle provides access to non-redundant information, resulting in benefits such as employment connections (Granovetter, 1973).

Recommender Systems

A recommender system is a social software system capable of creating implicit or explicit social connections among users online, which can lead into community building. A recommender system works through user profiling, by asking a user a series of questions about things a particular user likes and compares findings to other people who have similar opinions or interests. Recommendation systems are widely used for sharing information or solving problems in virtual communities. A recommendation system is capable of analyzing previous usage behaviour in order to make informed recommendations for solving new cases or making new connection. A typical example is book recommendation systems used by Amazon.com. Other applications such as online news recommendation and targeted at marketing are also becoming increasingly popular forms of recommendation systems. The innovative keyword-based advertisement adopted by Google.com is one of the many successful stories of online recommendation systems.

In current wave of technological discussions, at least within artificial intelligence, a recommender system is seen as an important technology for building a healthy community. Its major utility come from the inspiration that people would naturally rather take recommendations from friends and family because they are more trusted than others. Part of that trust is often built within recommendation systems is driven by factors such as awareness. In other words, people can make recommendations to people they know better and people take recommendations from those they trust more and are aware of their credibility.

Further, most recommender systems are modelled along the ways people in real life would normally make or take recommendations from people surrounding them. Though, currently recommender systems are mostly used for finding things, one promising way to use these systems is to find people with particular competence and capability in doing particular task and building communities along those lines. Three common approaches studied in the operation of recommendation systems include demographic-based filtering, collaborative filtering and content-based filtering. Demographic-based filtering analyzes user preference and makes recommendations based on the demographic information of the user (e.g., age, sex, income level, etc.). Collaborative filtering determines user preference and recommends based on found stereotypes of the user. That is, a user's behaviour is predicted based on evidence that has shown similarity to other users. Content-based (or attribute-based) filtering on the other hand makes recommendation based on certain attributes of an individual, for a movie, they might take into account type of the movie, the director, actors, producer, and so on.

Online Reputation Systems

An online reputation system is a type of collaborative filtering system which determines ratings for a collection of entities, given a collection of opinions that those entities hold about each other. Online reputation systems are similar to recommendation systems in many aspects. But the primary purpose of recommendation systems is to recommend objects or things used by individuals to other individuals—things range from books, movies and music while reputation system rate the credibility of those individuals using the objects in order to make informed recommendations.

The basic idea underlying any online reputation system is to let parties rate each other, for example, after the completion of a transaction, and use the aggregated ratings about a given party to derive a trust or reputation score, which can assist other parties in deciding whether or not to transact with that party in the future. Online reputation systems emerged as viable alternatives to the more established institutions for building trust (such as formal contracts) in virtual communities. These systems are intended to serve business and in situations where contractual guarantees cannot be efficiently enforced due to lack of physical cues.

Online reputation systems encourage visible history of prior interactions. They offer objective and subjective measures (ratings and comments) about an individual's past interactions. Online reputation system allow individual to decide who to trust and in general encourages trustworthy behaviour and discourage untrustworthy from prevailing in the environment. Online reputation systems are increasingly used in large scale virtual communities in which users may frequently have the opportunity to interact with other users with whom they have no prior experience or in communities where user generated content is posted like eBay.com, YouTube.com or Flickr.com. In such a situation, it is often helpful to base the decision about the quality of objects or items and whether or not to interact with that user on the prior experiences of other users.

In a typical business setting, where there is an increasing use of reputation systems, a reputation system works by collecting, distributing, and aggregating feedback and presenting it to others about a user's past behaviour. Though few of the producers or consumers of the ratings know each other, these systems help people decide whom to trust, encourage trustworthy behaviour, and deter participation by those who are unskilled or dishonest.

Others have used online reputation systems as community moderating mechanism for filtering content based on the trustworthy or the reputation of users. Slashdot.com is an example of such system, currently hosting thousands of community discussions, all of which are self-moderated on the basis of "reputation points." Users earn a reputation based on how highly other users rank their comments. Reputation systems are also crucial to the blogging community. Within these communities members' reputation is measured by Web site traffic and how many blogs are linked together.

Overall, in virtual communities, reputation systems support trust building, which is a critical variable of social capital. In addition, in online settings, there are environments characterised by partial or full anonymity and in situations where informal transactions are involved, and face-to-face interaction is lacking, reputation systems can help people make informed business decisions on users' trusting behaviour based on user traces data and interaction history

Online Introducer Systems

For many people, the complexity of the world today comes with a number of penalties and brutalities, the main one being isolation. Isolation often creates frustration and a feeling of rejection by people around ones community or neighborhood. Perhaps, those living in big cities might experience more negative effects of isolation than those in small towns—due to the nature and size of population distribution and the fact most people in big cities seem busy all throughout the day and have little time for socialization with their communities. In big cities for example, it is not uncommon to notice that people who live two doors from each other and who though, have basically everything in common, still find it hard to approach each other to create some connections. And so, the neighborhood in which some people live might have very little to do with the geographical communities they relate to or even willing to socialize.

Online introducer systems are the types of social software systems intended to help introduce people to other people, extending their social connections beyond their immediate geographical communities and neighborhoods. These systems are now widespread and extensively used within the online dating industry. Certainly, one of the greatest advantages of online introducer systems is their ability to introduce and match users to similar others and to connect them to already existing communities. For example, an online dating system such as "Desi" was established to connect people within the same culture (South Asian Culture), who would perhaps otherwise never meet. The system is focused on building a network via introductions, from friends, family and extended networks, to build relationships around the world, bringing together the "Desi" culture for example, in the largest contemporary online space for South Asians and encouraging them to meet, chat and play cupid online.

Unique in its market approach, systems such as "Desi" encourage friends to introduce, and vouch for each other, in a bid to connect people that are genuinely suited. These kinds of systems are more appealing to groups where the heritage of arranged marriages is still predominant. For many years, online introducer system, especially within the online dating industry have helped many people, find wives and husbands online, and like all kinds of marriages and relationships people form today, they have either been successful or less successful in sustainability.

Given their prevalence, it seems online introducer systems; especially dating systems have begun to influence the notion of social connection and challenging the traditional ways of dating. Though there are many social factors that can easily deter the sustainability of marriage relationships established online, it is beyond the scope this book to elaborate upon these factors. The most important thing is that the online introducer systems are essential for virtual communities and social capital.

Online Games and SecondLife

ScienceDaily (Oct. 22, 2007) indicated that online video games such as "World of Warcraft" attract thousands of simultaneous players making them the most popular online entertainment systems in the last two decades. For this reason, the online video game industry has earned tremendous financial success and is now a multibillion dollar industry. Online video games have entered many facets of many people's lives and they are becoming increasingly known for their abilities to make social connection among their players. These games provide people with environments where they socially interact and build relationship beyond the workplace/school and home.

Recent research cited in ScienceDaily (2007) suggested that while both multi-player and traditional single player video games present a double-edged sword such as greater negative consequences (decreased health, deprived from sleep, socialization and academic work), multiplayer online video game garner far greater positive results (greater enjoyment in playing, increased interest in continuing play and a rise in the acquisition of new friendships) than do single-player games. Within educational contexts, researchers have found immense advantages of online video games including collaborative problem solving, reading and writing practices that use highly specialized language, scientific habits of mind such as hypothesis testing and revision, skills in information and communication technology and argumentation.

In addition to their educational value, online games are fun and they provide a neutral environment where people get to know each other, play together and socialise without barriers of age, race, profession, and sex. A good example of online video games is A Massively Multiplayer Online Game (MMOG or MMO) is a computer game which is capable of supporting hundreds or thousands of players simultaneously, regularly played on the Internet. MMOs can enable players to compete with and against each other on a grand scale, and sometimes they interact meaningfully with people around the world. They require players to invest large amounts of their time into the game.

ScienceDaily (July 21, 2008) — Social interaction is enhanced rather than diminished by online games, according to new research on SecondLife (a computer mediated environment where users can buy their own plots of land to build pubs, schools or anything else they can imagine). SecondLife is a vast "digital continent" (as the creators called it), filled up with people, entertainment, experiences and opportunities for inhabiting in a new or SecondLife similar to actual life people live or it can also be capable of altering one's life style. Similar to many online computer games, SecondLife is a virtual world—an animated three-dimensional world created with computer graphics imagining and other rendering software. One of the hallmarks of this virtual world is that a user can interact within the environment by virtue of an avatar, or a computerized character that represents the user. The avatar manipulates and interacts with objects in the virtual world by mouse movements and keystrokes issued by the user. In SecondLife, users create three-dimensional representation of themselves and they explore a virtual earth and in the process they socialise and make connections with other individuals in real time. People are increasingly joining this "digital continent" each day, creating avatars and exploring the environment to meet up with other people and discover many ways to engage and socialise in online settings. Users in SecondLife use various technologies for communication. An important aspect of SecondLife is that people can simulate the real world and engage in communities, share resources and build social capital.

Most recently, business organizations have started to reach out to customers in Second Life, exploring the benefits associated with the environment—sharing information, holding meetings and allow employees to learn new skills and to provide an interactive multimedia online environment to reach out to customers. CIGNA, a US based health service organisation is one of that provides a wide range of healthcare products and services to individuals inhabited in SecondLife. Through SecondLife, the organisation attempts to better engage with this new generation of users educating them to gain more connections to health care and live better life. The organisation is providing interactive content, including virtual seminars and workshops during which participants can interact with the presenter or their peers, and interactive information displays to help individuals build out their knowledge of nutrition and healthy eating.

CONCLUSION

Progress in human societies, for most part can be attributed to development of all forms of communications, language, symbols, signs, and other communication instruments. Perhaps computers make the most profound impact on the field of communication since human beings invented a consistent way to communicate with each other through space and time. Core to all forms of networked communication, the World Wide Web has radically transformed the field of communication much more than any other technology of our modern time and has generated vast amount of effects on community engagement.

There are varieties of Web technologies in existence today, one way to understand the Web is to look at its different versions and their associated technologies. The first generation of the Web did not have much escalating impact on the notion of a community as much as the second generation of the Web. The second generation of the Web is distinguished from other Web technologies in that the concept, although it suggests a new version of the World Wide Web, does not refer to any technical specifications, but rather describes current changes in the ways software developers and end-users use the Web. Key features of Web 2.0 include; rich user experience, user participation, dynamic content, metadata, web standards, scalability, openness, freedom of use and collective intelligence by way of user participation. These are the key attributes of Web 2.0 that support its capability in supporting virtual communities.

The Semantic Web or Web 3.0 is a framework for describing the latest technologies of the Web. This framework seems to hold vast potentials for supporting virtual communities and transforming the way people search for information locate, connect and engage with each other. Perhaps what would make the Semantic Web vision enticing and interesting is the incorporation of intelligent software agents' technologies. These technologies are capable of acting autonomously or with some minimal directions from their owners, to look up information, synthesize and manage information and make recommendations. Personal software agents though for many years have drawn the attention of artificial intelligence research, they seem to have found new ways of transforming the future of the Web.

In concluding this chapter, it should be noted that the various stages in the development of the World Wide Web in particular helped create social structures and extend the notion of communities far beyond its traditional frontiers. Further, the Web is foremost one of the most important inventions of our time, initiating and enabling many ways we interact with each other, gather, share, disseminate information, and learn individually and in group. As Web technologies continue to entice millions of people online, helping them initiate profound social connection, critical to the development of communities, understanding how these technologies can be used to harness social capital within virtual communities is important. Chapter VII presents research in virtual communities, focusing on two types of virtual communities as two contexts for exploring social capital.

REFERENCES

Burt, R. (2000). The network structure of social capital. *Research in organisational behaviour, 22*, 345-423.

Broder, A. K., Maghoul, F., Raghavan, P., Rajagopalan, S., Stata, R., Tomkins, A., & Andwiener, J. (2000). *Graph structure in the Web. Comput. Netw.: Int. J. Comput. Telecomm. Netw. 33*(1)6, 309–320.

Granovetter, M. S. (1973). The strength of weak ties. *American Journal of Sociology, 78*(6), 1360-1380.

Vascellaro, J.E. (2008). Twitter goes mainstream. A lot more people and businesses are finding new ways to tweet. *The Wall Street Journal*. Retrieved November 17th 2008 from http://online.wsj.com/article/SB122461906719455335.html

Paxton, P. (1999). Is social capital declining in the United States? A multiple indicator assessment. *The American Journal of Sociology, 105*, 88.

Coates, T. (2003). *My working definition of social software*. Plasticbag.org. Retrieved November 17th 2008 from http://www.plasticbag.org/archives/2003/05/my_working_definition_of_social_software/

Klym, N., & Montepetit, M. J. (2008). *Innovation at the Edge: Social TV and beyond. Value Chain Dynamics Working Group (VCDWG)*. Retrieved November 17th 2008 from http://cfp.mit.edu/publications/CFP_Papers/Social_TV_Final_2008.08.01.pdf

Hinchcliffe, D. (2008). *Ten leading platforms for creating online communities*. ZDNet Artcile. Retrieved from http://blogs.zdnet.com/Hinchcliffe/?p=195

Berners-Lee, T. (1996). *The World Wide Web: Past, present and future*. Retrieved November 17th 2008 from http://www.w3.org/People/Berners-Lee/1996/ppf.html

Owen, M. Grant, L. Sayers, S. & Facer, K. (2006). *Social software and learning*. Retrieved November 17th, 2008 from http://www.futurelab.org.uk/resources/documents/opening_education/Social_Software_report.pdf

Putnam, R. (1995). 1995. Bowling alone: America's declining social capital. *Journal of Democracy, 6*, 65-78.

Shirky, C. (2005). *Ontology is Overrated: Categories, Links and Tags*. Retrieved Nomvember 17th 2008 from www.shirky.com

Syracuse University (2007, October 22). *Online Multiplayer Video Games Create Greater Negative Consequences, Elicit Greater*: Retrieved 30th July, 2008 from http://www.sciencedaily.com/releases/2007/10/071019174410.htm

Web Links Used in this Chapter

http://www.dell.com

http://www.canadianwebradio.com

http://www.cigna.com

http://www.kazaa.com

http://www.mmorpg.com

http://www.microsoft.com

http://www.napster.ca

http://www.doyoudesi.com

http:// radarnetwork.com

http://secondlife.com

http://www.sciencedaily.com

http://www.worldofwarcraft.com

http://www.w3c.org

http://www.wikipedia.org

http://www.xbox.com

Chapter VII
Virtual Communities

INTRODUCTION

The growth of virtual communities and their continuous impact on social, economic and technological structures of societies has attracted a great deal of interest among researchers, systems designers and policy makers to examine the formation, development, sustainability and utility of these communities. For examples, researchers are interested in analysing and understanding how these communities foster social interaction, influence various technological design and implementation, enhance information and knowledge sharing, support business and act as catalytic environments to support human learning. Over the last two decades, the growth in research into virtual communities, though fairly diverse, can be broadly categorized into two dominant perspectives—technological determinism and social constructivism. The basic tenet of the technology determinism research is that technology shapes cultural values, social structure, and knowledge.

In technology-related fields, such as Computer Science and Information Systems, significant attention has been given to understanding technological developments and how these changes influence social structures. The social constructivism perspective, on the other hand, posits that knowledge and world views are created through social interaction. These theories assert that a society's practical knowledge is situated in relations among practitioners, their practice, and the social organization and political economy of communities.

Irrespective of social or technological determinism, virtual communities are communities built around relationships among people. They breed different kinds of relationships anchored by unique social connections other than cultural, ethnic, racial, tribal or geographical (place-based) communities. The intensity and types of social connectivity in virtual communities vary from one community to another but they also share common features in that they might be based on common interests, passion to learn new trade or language or keeping abreast on development in a particular area of interest.

This chapter provides a general overview of research on virtual communities. It describes two particular types of virtual communities relevant to the analysis of social capital described in the book; virtual learning communities and distributed communities of practice. The goal of the chapter is to provide an overall context in which social capital is reported in the book. The chapter also describes other areas in which virtual communities are currently used. These include education, healthcare, business, socialization and mediating interaction among people in Diaspora.

HISTORICAL OVERVIEW OF VIRTUAL COMMUNITIES

Understanding the historical development of virtual communities requires a closer look at the history of the Internet, since these communities predates the history of the Web. The Internet came into inception in 1969, when the United States Department of Defense Advanced Projects Research Agency (DARPA) established a computer network designed to sanction the existence of information beyond a susceptible, central location as a means of defence against the possibility of nuclear war (Hartley, 2002, p. 122). Through this network, known as ARPANET, came the development of a system which would act as a channel for "democratic information and distribution (Hartley, 2002, p. 122). This system advanced during the 1970s, with hosts being connected to the ARPANET as well as the subsequent appearance of state-funded computer networks, which later became known as the Internet.

The pioneer technologies that supported virtual communities, started with the electronic mailing systems or simply email, then followed by listservs and notice boards and then discussion forums. In 2000, various forms of websites supported by a wide range of Web technologies (Illera, 2007) became the mainstream environments supporting interactions in virtual communities. Though virtual communities might seem new, in fact, there is a historical trend to their development. About four decades ago Licklider (1968) predicted the emergence of technology enhanced social systems—he referred to these systems "online communities".

Online communities or virtual communities in his view consisted of geographically separated individuals, who would naturally group themselves into small clusters to work together or work individually on some issues of interests. Virtual communities, he suggested would be communities not of common location, but of common interest. This prediction became accurate as there are now millions of virtual communities that are based on common interests and goals.

Virtual communities developed prior to the establishment of the Internet. However, they only began to mature with the development of the Web technologies. Other notable early examples of virtual communities included UseNet, with millions of users all around the world. Usenet was established in 1980, as a distributed Internet discussion system, which ultimately became one of the first recognized virtual communities. Membership in Usernet consisted mainly of voluntarily contributors and moderators. There were other two early virtual communities; Minitel in France and Whole Earth 'Lectronic Link (WELL) in the United States of America. The Minitel preceded the World Wide Web. It was in 1982 and was accessible to its members through the telephone lines. From its early days, members of Minitel could make online purchases, make train reservations, check stock prices, search the telephone directory, and chat in a similar way people do over the Internet. The WELL was established in 1985. Since its establishment many researchers have investigated its cultural manifestations and reported in several books (e.g. Reinghold, 1993). Many of the WELL's members voluntarily contribute to community building and maintenance (e.g., as conference hosts). The WELL, as described in its site "provides a literate watering hole for some articulate and unpretentious thinkers".

Slashdot, is perhaps one of the most popular virtual communities that is geared towards technological discussions. Slashdot hosts technology-related forums, with articles and readers comments. Slashdot subculture has become well-known in Internet circles, where its members accumulate a "karma score" and volunteer moderators are selected from those with high scores. Other virtual communities drawn directly from research reported in this book include a distributed communities of practice, intended to foster knowledge sharing and data among professionals working within the areas of governance and international development—within Canadian context (Daniel, Sarkar & O'Brien, 2003) and virtual learning communities for graduates students of educational technology in higher education (Schwier, 2007; Schwier & Daniel, 2007).

What is a Virtual Community?

Several definitions have been proposed, ranging from those that treat virtual communities as technological environments and those that describe the social configurations of the individuals participating in these environments. According to Rheingold (1993) "virtual communities are social aggregations that emerge from the Net when enough people carry on public discussions long enough, with sufficient human feeling to form webs of personal relationships in cyberspace" (p.5). Rheingold's definition is most frequently quoted in many discussions about virtual communities.

In a later book, Rheingold (2003) referred to virtual communities as "online social networks". He considered this as a more comprehensive term than virtual communities. Regardless, how it is defined, the concept of virtual community had received a frosty reception from some Sociologists, who argued that the debate over the validity of the term has raised doubts its existence and appropriate use. Weinreich (1997) for instance argued that "the idea of virtual communities must be wrong" because community is a collection of kinship networks which share a common geographic territory a common history, and a shared value system, usually rooted in a common religion. He went on to argue that the Utopian Promises - Net Realities[1], asserted that "anyone with even a basic knowledge of Sociology understands that information exchange in no way constitutes a community." This intense opposition to the use of virtual community is mainly theoretical and will not be discussed in the book. Instead the book treats the concept of virtual community as a placeholder for online interactions, drawing on many characteristics of physical or place-based communities.

In order to clearly understand the concept of a virtual community, a brief description of a place-based community is necessary. Physical or place-based community in a more general sense refers to a group of people interacting within a geographical space, normally in neighbourhoods, towns or cities. Such a group depicts a sense of shared identity, values, norms and shared interests. Members in a place-based community usually interact on a regular basis and to some extent, they are known to each based on either their contribution to the community or by virtue of the physical proximity of the space they share with others. Geographical communities are deeply rooted within historical and cultural contexts.

Are place-based communities similar to virtual communities? Depending on who answers the question? Virtual communities essentially differ from placed-based communities, primarily because of the space in which interaction takes place. In virtual communities, people interact through the mediation of information and communications technologies whereas in place-based communities people interact face-to-face. In addition, virtual communities have advantages over place-based communities in that people in virtual communities draw their members from all over the world, with various life experiences, diverse cultures and organizational affiliations. The diversity in experiences and other situational factors, presents members of virtual communities with enriched social environment and possibilities.

In addition, because people in virtual communities are normally culturally and professionally diverse, they tend to view situations in a different light than they would if they all were from the same place. Diversity in membership in virtual communities when properly managed, can position members at competitive advantage. Further, unlike in place-based communities where membership is defined by geographical space and neighbourhood, in virtual communities, the definition of membership and membership composition is significantly different.

For many people, the experience of joining a virtual community creates a close connection, which is necessary for improving social experience, through exposition to other cultures and environments they would otherwise normally never be exposed to. For example people from Canada can join virtual communities that draw membership around the globe, and as a result of close interaction with people from countries such as China, they can get to know about Chinese green tea, or the tradition around consumption of noodles. Similarly, Chinese would learn more about the story behind the famous Canadian Maple Leaf. Learning about other cultures in this aspect does not require any geographical travel but can take place via simple discussion forums or intense 3D interaction in Second Life.

While interactions in place-based communities are driven by specific goals—and tend to have clearly defined membership—virtual communities are task centred, and are formed as a need arises among its members (Johnson, 2001). Further, virtual communities do not experience much of the non-verbal communication as experienced by people in face-to-face or place-based communities. But rather virtual communities often cross cultural boundaries—bringing together participants from cultures which have different norms of behaviour and hence influencing their formation. Pallof and Pratt (1999) viewed the formation of virtual communities as a multi staged process, which includes; the definition of the community's purpose, and establishing norms and code of conduct, together with the establishment of member roles.

Social protocols guiding interactions in virtual communities and place-based communities differ. For example, in place-based communities the set of social protocols, goals, and values are normally predetermined; however in virtual communities they might emerge from interaction and they constantly change through negotiation and determination of community needs. In addition, in virtual communities, one can easily use an introducer system, or an online recommender system to find people to interact with or for people to join appropriate virtual community. Finding people to relate to one's need or interests in place-communities is more challenging especially when one is not a member of a community and sometimes entrance into a new community might be restrictive and determined by cultural or geographical features.

Further, there is certainly a common misconception surrounding how virtual communities form, which has led to intense and sometimes unnecessary debate about whether virtual communities can be built or whether these communities naturally emerge organically. Of course placing a set of software packages on the Internet or the Web does not automatically translate into a community of users. In fact, some virtual communities operate like place-based communities, they enforce a set of social protocols to guide and shape motivation. Social protocols also clearly demonstrate why people join or even contribute to discussions in virtual communities. Without these set of protocols—sociability, virtual communities will not flourish (Preece, 2000). And like place-based communities, virtual communities need to be nurtured and strategically supported in order to sustain them for a required period of time. In other words, virtual communities have life span and can easily disintegrate into social networks if not properly managed.

Kim (2000) provided a framework describing the evolution of membership in virtual communities. She stated that members of virtual communities begin their life in a community as visitors or lurkers. After getting acquainted with the culture of the community, expectations, social protocols whether written or not, they break through a barrier, they become novices and begin participating in the community. After contributing for a sustained period of time they become regular members. If they break through another barrier or simply gained increased recognition and respect from other members, they become leaders, and once they have contributed to the community for some time they become elders. This life cycle can be applied to many virtual communities.

Virtual communities have several advantages over geographical or place-based communities. In geographical communities people are often accustomed to meeting people, then getting to know them before they make any kind of social contract or commitment. In virtual communities people get to know people first before they can arrange to meet face-face. In some cases, people meet all kinds of people they would otherwise not be able to meet in face-to-face settings.

There are several online groups that can be misconceived as virtual communities. In this book a virtual community is not simply a discussion forum or any other kinds of computer mediated communication system, it is not just any group of people with common interest gathering online. But rather, a virtual community constitutes members who have purpose and a certain level of commitment to the community. Moreover, they use various forms of technologies to connect to each other in pursuance of common goals and that their very virtual existence are determined mainly by the existence of mediating technologies, the relevance of the community to its members, strong sense of belonging members create within the community and social capital that keep members together over a required period of time. The key features of virtual communities are described in Figure 7-1.

Virtual community is made up of people, the space where they interact, their goals, and the technologies that they use to communicate, collaborate, and work together to achieve their goals as a community (Daniel, Schwier & McCalla, 2003). The fact that a virtual community is one that is facilitated through the use of technology automatically eliminates people who are not computer literate. In a virtual community it is assumed that no matter how geographically and culturally dispersed

Figure 7-1. Core components of virtual community

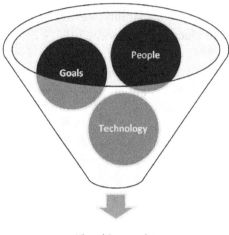

Virtual Community

members are they have to be able to effectively use the communication tools which are created through technology enable the community members to communicate and contribute to the community more effectively. Moreover, the feeling of togetherness created around the sense of a community among the members or simply the web of social relationships among people is the main engine of virtual communities. The following summarises some of the fundamental features of virtual communities as opposed to geographical communities:

- **Membership:** Membership can be drawn globally, from any culture and national, identity etc. There is a non-binding membership (retreat from communication is rather easily possible).
- **Anonymity:** Some virtual communities allow anonymity while others encourage openness.
- **Domain focused:** Virtual communities are constructed along shared interests goals and are domain specific
- **Communication:** There is continued interaction, i.e. a certain temporal continuity of online communication.
- **Social protocols:** There are formal or informal conventions of online behaviour, style, and language and modes of engagement. These are either explicitly stipulated or they are implied.
- **Space-time:** Communication is spatially disembodied and temporally synchronous or asynchronous.

- **Shared meaning:** Meaning is communicated and shared among members. New meaning is negotiated.
- **Voluntary:** Interaction in virtual communities is voluntary and people are free to lurk, contribute and withdraw as they deem fit.
- **Speed:** Relationships can become intense more quickly online.
- **Delusive behaviour:** People feel more courageous online than offline because they can more easily end a conversation, they feel that there are potentially less consequences for action in a symbolic than in a physical space, and they have more time for thinking before answering and arguing.
- **Visual Cues:** The lack of physical presence and visual context queues and the invisibility of the communication partners might lower inhibitions.
- **Deep reflection:** In a virtual community people can take their time to contribute, they can retrieve what they contributed or others contributed and synthesize things.
- **Virtualisation and actualisation of relationships:** In virtual communities, members first connect in cyberspace to initiate relationship (virtualisation) and later move the relationship to continue in physical space (actualisation). Similarly, they can move actual relationships from physical space to online setting
- **Structure:** The virtual community, like any other, has a distinct structure with well-defined responsibility and roles.
- **Identity:** In some virtual communities—such as a distributed community of practice, with limited anonymity, there is a community directory which contains a listing of all the members of the community, their expertise or what they can contribute to the community. This directory provides the ability to identify resources and access resources which will enhance the knowledge sharing process.

TYPES OF VIRTUAL COMMUNITIES

The discussion about virtual communities in this book is situated within only two types of virtual communities (virtual learning communities and distributed communities of practice). These two communities were focus of previous research (Daniel, Schwier & McCalla, 2003; Schwier & Daniel, 2007). These types of virtual communities represent solid maturity to highly focused kinds of virtual communities intended to provide interesting technological, educational and social implication to learning and knowledge sharing. A simple model of these communities is described in Figure 7-2.

Virtual Learning Communities

The term virtual learning community is an aggregate of three concepts, "virtual" "learning" and "community". Defining these three concepts independently has been a difficult challenge to researchers in technology, education and sociology. Drawing from the previous discussion on what can be considered a virtual community; one would add a learning dimension to complete the meaning of a virtual learning community. The emphasis on learning signifies the clarity of purpose of learning and the distinct task-oriented nature of the type of learning involved. Of course, like any new concept some writers use the term virtual learning community in vain. It is often quoted out of context to refer to online communities in general or other kinds of social groups online, even though some of them do not have direct and explicit learning.

The limits and the boundaries of the term virtual learning community are drawn from other related terms, and it simply refers to the kinds of learning within the contexts described in Figure 7-2. Further, before proceeding any farther with the formal definition of a virtual learning community, it is appropriate to first review the concept of learning and a learning community. The goal is not to divert the reader from the main focus of the book but to provide some details in an attempt to create a context in which the term virtual learning community can be interpreted.

Figure 7-2. Two type of virtual communities

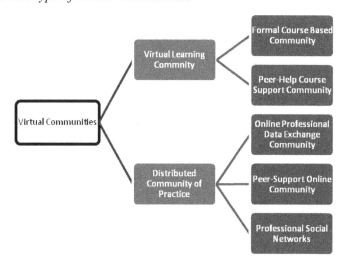

Defining Learning

For years, the term learning or the process of learning has been a subject of increased investigation by many Behavioural Scientists. They have considered learning as one of the most important mental function of humans, animals and other artificial cognitive systems. Many scientists have presented different types of learning theories, describing learning process in various ways, although some of them share common assumptions about what constitutes learning. One of the shared views among theoreticians about learning is that it is a persistence of change in performance brought about by learners' experiences and interactions with the world (Driscoll, 2000). Learning is also regarded as changes in behavioural patterns that might have implicit or explicit impact on performance outcomes, including the means to stimulate the conditions that can promote learning (the process) and the results from that process (the outcomes).

Further most of the theoreticians concur that learning or what can be considered as learning often leads to the development of new capacities, skills, values, understanding, and preferences. And that the goal of any learning environment is to increase an individual and group experience. In terms of cognitive sciences, learning functions can be performed by different brain learning processes, which depend on an individual's mental capacities of learning a subject the type of knowledge which has to be acquitted, as well as on socio-cognitive and environmental circumstances. Knowledge and learning are social phenomena embedded in human interactions.

Interest in research into learning has been significant and reported by Educational researchers, Psychologists and Social Anthropologists to mention a few. These researchers have investigated learning in an individual, a group or a community. It is the process of learning within a community context that is relevant to the discussion in this book. In a community context, individuals learn by constructing knowledge and connecting meanings to their understanding. They learn by sharing these meanings with other members of the community. It has been argued that most learning activities in communities are informal, involving the exchange of personal experiences, lessons and information (Brown & Duguid, 1991). The informal nature of learning in communities is also prominent in socio-cultural learning and constructivist theories of learning (Vygotsky, 1978) and recently constructivist's theories of learning.

According to constructivist theory (Newby, Stepich, Lehman & Russell, 1996), how people construct knowledge depend on to a larger extent what they already know, including the kinds of historical experiences that they have had and how they have come to organize these into existing knowledge structures. Over the years several versions of constructivist theories have been proposed, among them is social constructivism. Social constructivism is associated with learning in groups where members' activities are mediated by information communication technologies (Kanuka & Andersen, 1998).

Social constructivism views knowledge as grounded in the relationship between the knower and the known, which means knowledge is generated through social interaction and through this interaction individuals gradually accumulate advances in their levels of knowing. Within the social constructivist theory, there are numerous categories of interactions signifying various ways learners can learn in communities. For example Garrison and Anderson (2003) investigated different ways students interact in groups during learning processes. They stated that the type of interactions taking place in a learning community is complex and include student-student interaction, student-teacher interaction and student-content interaction.

Researchers have also explored the decisions individuals make along the way as they begin the process of learning—learning preferences (Matheos, Daniel & McCalla, 2004). Learning preferences as opposed to learning styles are the conditions in which learners prefer to work and learn. Learning preferences range from a preference to work and learn independently to working in collaboration with others as a group or as a community, and with or without the help of an instructor. All of which are important in understanding the nature of learning taking place whether within individuals or communities.

Learning and Virtual Communities

Collaboration in virtual communities can be regarded as the process and outcome involved in interactions and engagement between two or more people through computer mediated communication systems. This can encompass a variety of behaviours, including communication, information sharing, knowledge sharing, problem solving and negotiation. In virtual communities, people can collaborate via two modes of communications determined by time; collaboration can occur at the same time (synchronous) or at different times (asynchronous). Individuals can also be in one place (co-located) or in different places (distributed).

For many years researchers within the field of Human Computer-Interaction and Human Factors have investigated the impact of various collaborative technologies in virtual communities and other collaborative social systems. Two important research communities are directly involved in this endeavour; researchers from the Computer-Supported Collaborative Work (CSCW), who are often interested in examining how people interact in workplace environments in order to provide them with tools and procedures to improve productivity, and Computer-Supported Collaborative Learning (CSCL), who are preoccupied with analysis of collaborative factors and outcomes of learning resulting from the use of various media in learning environments. Researchers within this community considers collaborative learning as an instructional method in which learners at various performance levels work together in small groups or communities to achieve desirable learning outcomes.

In educational research, collaborative learning is a well developed paradigm. Piaget (1977) For instance, pointed out the importance of collaborative learning in constructive cognitive development within individuals. He regarded learning as a social process that involves the learner interacting with the object of learning whether it is a book, a computer system or another person. Learning as a social process is also reflected in the work of Vygotsky (1962; 1978), who emphasized social interaction as a means to foster an individual's cognitive development. Vygotsky's theory of socio-cultural constructivism does not negate Piaget's interpretation of social constructivism. However, socio-cultural constructivists believe that social interaction occurs among learners themselves rather than with the object of learning. Despite their different approaches, Vygotsky and Piaget have laid a solid foundation for the development of theories of learning as social processes. Examples of these theories include situated learning and distributed learning. Proponents of situated learning believe that learning is derived from a community of practice, it is social and it involves mutual engagement and shared understanding among different individuals (Wenger, 1998, Kumar, 1996).

Kumar (1996) suggests that the promise of collaborative learning is to allow learners to learn in relatively realistic, cognitively motivating, and socially enriched learning contexts. For instance, a learner might discuss different strategies to solve a given problem in a problem-solving domain. They can further discuss different issues with a group of fellow learners who can advise, motivate, criticize, compete, and direct them toward a better understanding of a particular subject matter.

There are different collaborative learning styles in groups and communities that can be used for building collaborative learning systems. Hiltz & Turoff (1993) and Hiltz (1998) proposed strategies to enhance collaborative learning. These include collaborative learning activities such as seminar-style presentations and discussions, debates, group projects, simulation and role-playing exercises, and collaborative composition of essays, exam questions, stories and research plans. There are many collaborative systems that are built upon these strategies.

Building on the theory of constructivism, individuals in a community learn by constructing knowledge and connecting meanings to their understanding, and by sharing these meanings with others in the community. Most of the learning activities in communities involve exchanging personal experiences, lessons and information and tacit knowledge. Wenger, McDermott and Snyder (2002) suggested that sharing tacit knowledge (knowledge driven from personal experiences) within a community yields higher success than in more formalized learning settings. Tacit knowledge can enable co-workers interact socially, help each other to solve problems, seek new challenges and in doing so advance the goals of the community. It is also suggested that much of the learning between and within communities occurs with boundaries rich in interactions, whether formal, informal, or through a computer based system (Wenger, 1998).

It is suggested that bounded learning communities are created across courses in higher education or corporate settings. Furthermore, bounded learning communities emerge in direct response to guidance provided by an instructor who is supported by a resource base. In virtual learning communities, where learners are often isolated from each other, and their instructor; knowledge sharing can be fundamental to effective learning. But promoting knowledge sharing requires understanding the social relationships and connections that are critical to information and knowledge sharing.

Information and communications technologies have enabled the creation of communities that are not based on a locale, what can be formally termed as virtual learning communities. Virtual learning communities are learning communities based not on actual geography, but on shared purpose of learning. In such communities, learners can be drawn together from almost anywhere, and they can construct their own formal or informal learning groups within computer mediated learning environments. Virtual learning communities are considered to be collections of individuals who are bound together by social will and a set of shared ideas and ideals (Kowch & Schwier, 1998). Schwier (2004) later on suggested that a virtual learning community is a particular type of virtual learning environment. He indicated that for a community to emerge, a learning environment must allow learners to engage each other intentionally and collectively in the transaction or transformation of knowledge. He further suggested it is necessary for individuals to take advantage of, and in some cases invent, a process for engaging ideas, negotiating meaning and learning collectively. Virtual learning communities have structural elements, which include elements of online communities include size, lifespan, situation or distribution of the community, and the relative homogeneity of its members.

In virtual learning communities, learning involves sharing knowledge, exchanging information, and these require participation and contributing to community, sharing, exploring, and deploying a collective knowledge base (Perkins, 1993; O'Neill & Gomez, 1994). Research has indicated that people in communities learn as they navigate to solve problems together (Koschmann et al., 1996). Learning in virtual learning communities also manifests itself differently depending on the context of the community in which it is created, such as whether communities are bounded or unbounded, formal, informal or non-formal. Wilson, Ludwig-Hardman, Thornam and Dunlap (2004) distinguished between bounded and unbounded learning communities.

Distributed Communities of Practice

The notion of a distributed community of practice draws from the theory of a community if practice (Lave & Wenger, 1991) but it differs from community of practice in many significant ways. A distributed community of practice describes a group of geographically dispersed professionals who share common practices and interests in a particular area of concern, and whose activities can be enriched and mediated by information and communication technology (Daniel, Schwier & McCalla, 2003). The concept of distributed communities of practice aims to move beyond connectivity to achieve new levels of community interactivity, bringing together diverse groups and encouraging knowledge and information sharing among people, organizations, and communities.

In many aspects, a distributed community of practice can be regarded as a type of a virtual community, serving as a vehicle for data and information exchange among a dispersed, multisectoral and highly distributed professionals, practitioners and scientists, who are interested in various issues within a certain field of practice. An example of a distributed community of practice is a group of researchers in Canadian Universities and Colleges, various government departments, non-governmental organizations and private consulting who are though diverse in organisational backgrounds, and distributed all over Canada, are all interested in various issues in within the field of governance and international development (Daniel, Sarkar & O'Brien, 2008).

What holds members together in a distributed community of practice is a common sense of purpose and a need to know what each other knows and to share knowledge and exchange information. A distributed community of practice is the second type of a virtual community, whose ultimate goals of learning are not formalised but rather informally binding. For a distributed community of practice to evolve, it requires individuals who are geographically distributed, organizationally and culturally diverse, but members are regularly connected through various forms of computer mediated communication tools. The key features of distributed communities of practice are listed below:

- **Shared interests:** Membership is organized around topics or domain issues that are important to them.
- **Common identity:** Members develop shared understanding and common identity.
- **Shared information and knowledge:** Members share information and knowledge, or they are willing to develop a culture of sharing, voluntarily responding to requests for help.

Figure 7-3.

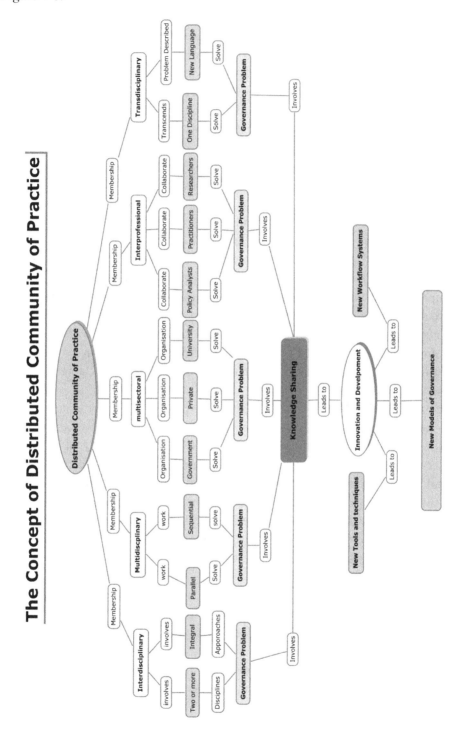

- **Voluntary participation:** Members normally voluntarily participate in the activities of the community.
- **Autonomy in setting goals:** A distributed community of practice sets its own agenda based on the needs of the members and these needs change over time as the community evolves and membership and environment changes.
- **Awareness of social protocols and goals:** Members in a distributed community of practice are normally aware of the acceptable social protocols and goals of the community.
- **Awareness of membership:** Members in a distributed community of practice are normally aware of each other in the community; that is, individuals have a reasonable knowledge of who is who and what they do in the community.
- **Effective means of communications:** Effective communication among others remains a key distinguishing factor among communities. Robust communication may include face-to-face meetings and technology-mediated communication such as email, videoconferencing, discussion forums, WebPages, intelligent agents.

Unlike a virtual learning community where membership is not necessarily professionally defined, distributed community of practice draws its members from professionals who are likely to sharing common interests and are interested in connecting to others to informally learn from each other, through the use of information and communication technologies. In addition, its life cycle of a distributed community of practice is determined by the value it creates for its members and the sustainability and the continuity of relevance of its goals to the members. Unlike in a virtual learning community, where often disband in the community when formal requirements are achieved. This stage might mark the "death" of a community but with sometimes, members continue to connect to each other after the termination of the formal requirements and thus forming a social network instead.

COMMON USE-CASES OF VIRTUAL COMMUNITIES

Brunett (2000) noted that a virtual community is one of the most significant points at which information and communication converge. Virtual communities have the potential to support a wide variety of activities related to learning, social networking, information seeking, information provision, and information sharing. These sections of the book describe some key use-cases of virtual communities. This is not an exhaustive list of what virtual communities are used for but rather handful of examples to illustrate some of the critical areas in which virtual communities are

Table 7-1. Virtual learning communities and distributed communities of practice

Virtual learning communities	Distributed communities of practice
Membership is explicit and identities are generally known	Membership may or may not be explicit
Presences of an instructor	Facilitator, coordinator or a system
Participation is often required	Participation is mainly voluntary
Explicit set of social protocols for interaction	Implicit and implied set of social protocols for interactions
Formal learning goals	Informal learning goals
Possibly diverse backgrounds	Common subject-matter
Low shared understanding of domain	High shared understanding of domain
Loose sense of professionalism	Strong sense of professional identity
Strict distribution of responsibilities	No formal distribution of responsibilities
Easily disbanded once established	Less easily disbanded once established
Low level of trust	Reasonable level of trust
Life span determined by extent in which goals are achieved	Life span determined by the instrumental/expressive value the community provides to its members
Pre-planned activities and fixed goals	A joint enterprise as understood and continually renegotiated by its members

deployed. The examples described in the sections emerged from direct involvement of the author through research observation.

Information Needs and Socialisation

Virtual communities ideally serve as information forums. Members of virtual communities often join virtual communities primarily to seek for information and to meet and interact with like-minded individuals, during which people build reciprocal relationships around the information sharing activities. As information centres virtual communities are spaces for social engagement where people meet, play, share stories with others and socialize with each other in various forms. Virtual communities act as information filters for their members, and thus helping them cope with information overload, as individual become fragmented members of virtual communities (McCalla, 2000). This is usually accomplished through information sharing, guided by social protocols requiring reciprocal relations, in that one is required to participate and contribute to the community.

Members of virtual communities come to them both to find answers to specific information needs, and to situate themselves within an affable social environment. They are environments where members can, on an ongoing basis, keep a lookout for any information related to their general interests and concerns. Once they are members, people come to virtual communities as they would come to more place-based communities for information resources, to make explicit queries with the expectation of receiving relevant answers. In addition, participation in virtual communities also allows for less formal types of human information behaviour such as browsing and information encountering (Burnett, 2000). The fact members of virtual communities often share information through a group wide broadcasting suggests they do so with expectation of exchange; rather than simply giving information away and with a hope of building a reciprocal relationship within the community.

People come to join virtual communities knowing that because other members share their interests, they are likely to be congenial information environments, places where information in which they are interested is likely to be found, even if they do not have explicit queries. And they can do so in a situation which, while it lacks the face-to-face interactions of more traditional communities, provides considerable opportunity for socializing and other types of interaction along with the exchange of information. In the context of virtual communities, announcing information to others to get informed and keep up to date on issues of mutual interests plays a significant role in the informational economics of the community.

Supporting Business

Typically in business, virtual communities are used as platforms for advertising or selling products and services. They are used as hubs to attract customers and to expand market shares to new horizons or to strengthen relationships with customers and trade partners. The hallmark of virtual communities within the business context is the ability to bring together buyers and sellers together online to engage in brand discussion or product related issues. For most businesses, virtual communities extend the proposition of the physical community, facilitate commercial discussions and help peers to find each other.

There are business organisations that use virtual communities as knowledge management infrastructure to improve collaboration and knowledge sharing among their employees. The rich interaction and knowledge sharing typical within virtual communities allows for talent development and retention within organizations. The profusion of Web technologies, such as Wikis and Blogs, provide unprecedented capabilities to generate, process, exchange and manage knowledge. Virtual communities are also used in business to identify customer needs, and enable open discussions relating to innovation.

There are many other examples of deployment of virtual communities in business. E-Bay, Google, IBM, Yahoo, and Microsoft virtual communities are some of the well-known examples of high tech companies with various kinds of virtual communities intended to facilitate exchanges and knowledge sharing between their members and address fundamental economic issues of supply and demand. For example IBM and Microsoft use virtual communities as a means of customer support by monitoring communities as an early warning system for product issues that can be expected to strike the help desk and prepares to respond accordingly.

Virtual communities in business provide many important insights into new features and opportunities. They help businesses to attract potential global customers, identify customer needs, and enable open innovation. Business also expects that the increasing deployment of virtual communities through instituting a bi-directional conversation, companies can help engage top prospects and influence purchase decisions.

Educational Systems Delivery

Virtual learning communities foster learning and for students to collaboratively solve problems. Schwier (2002) suggested that the notion of a virtual learning community enable educators to discuss richer, deeper, more complex types of interplay among learners. Since the 1990s the technologies that support the growth of virtual communities have long since infiltrated formal educational systems and corporate training. Within educational systems, technologies have been used to support face-to-face and online classes and are now entering the social spheres of students and faculty—resulting into deployment of social network systems such as Facebook and Youtube.

The growing interests in the implementation of virtual learning communities in education have been phenomenal and for many years, virtual learning communities have added important dimension to the nature of learning, teaching and research, particularly in higher institutions of learning. Essentially, virtual learning communities help learners share common interests on acquisition of knowledge on a domain or set of issues and subjects. They are used to support off-campus, distance, and blended learning programs. For on campus programs, virtual learning communities serve as peer-help support systems and supplementary instructional environments.

Connecting People in Diaspora

Current technologies of the Web have provided members of Diaspora who live in disparate countries and locations. Though this aspect of virtual communities is under researched, it is gaining global momentum. Within this usage, virtual communities provide comfortable environments where people with shared identities, nationalities, cultures, language, race, tribe and values can communicate about the cultural and social issues important to them without actually coming together at a physical location. They often yarn for connectivity and interaction with individuals from their own countries, who are either living in Diaspora or at home through virtual communities. There are numerous national and ethnic groups in Diaspora are increasingly using virtual communities to reconnect to their national, ethnic and social roots. Typical examples of such groups include nationals from countries like The Sudan, Ukraine, Serbia, Ethiopia, Eritrea, and Somalia, all which have been constantly wrecked by wars and natural disasters.

These groups formed various virtual communities to use them as social systems to meet other people from their countries, to keep themselves connected to some of their friends, families living at home and in other countries. Virtual communities for these groups also serve as political forums, social systems, information boards, and social networking environments. They used by these groups as transnational, global communication systems to draw attention not only to the history, presence and lives of particular groups but also as platforms for discussion of the social, cultural, political and economic conditions and realities under which they live in Diaspora.

Exchanging Scientific Data

There are numerous researchers and scientists who are using virtual communities to exchange scientific data, to collaborate, and build communities. A good example of a successful virtual community intended to support scientists to exchange data is the Governance Knowledge Network—an example of a distributed community of practice. The Governance Knowledge Network sought to strengthen links among communities of practitioners, researchers and policymakers. It was intended to support a knowledge repository to enable individuals to gather and gain access to policy and technical information. The project was inspired by the observation that the relationship between governance and international development is increasingly becoming interdisciplinary, drawing professionals, policymakers, researchers from a variety of disciplines, sectors, geography and culture.

Further, within the Canadian context, it was observed that those interested in policy, research or practice are diverse, dispersed and have uneven access to data, with ensuing implications for their effective participation, reflection and evidence-based decision-making and a need for co-ordination of data, information and knowledge was identified (Daniel, Sarkar, &O'Brien , 2008).

The governance knowledge network project focused on understanding the nature of collaboration on exchange of scientific data, social networking and community formation among people who are geographical distributed, professionally diverse, and situated in different sectors of government, civil society, private organization and business and to encourage organizations and people to share data and learn from each other.

Healthcare and Health Delivery

Web technologies have profound effects on healthcare and health delivery. Similar to other social systems, Web technologies are transforming most health systems by creating a new conduit not only for communication but also in the access, sharing, and exchange of information among people and machines. One of the most promising aspects of Web technologies in healthcare and health delivery is in supporting the deployment of e-Health[2] infrastructure. The promises of e-health include increasing efficiency in healthcare, thereby decreasing costs and avoiding duplicative through enhanced communication possibilities between healthcare establishments, and through patient involvement. e-Health also provides opportunities for enhancing and improving quality. It also offers further opportunities for Evidence based e-health interventions.

However, virtual communities within the e-Health systems are underutilized and to some extent underdeveloped. Despite, these communities offer a lot of opportunities to build strong partnerships between patients and clinicians and among clinicians themselves. The use of virtual communities in e-Health is grounded on availability of people with common interests to share experiences, ask questions, or provide emotional support and self help within the context of health. For a long period of time virtual communities have serve as environment for promoting, sharing information and emotional support within healthcare and health delivery. There are several virtual communities employed for discussion of health issues. WebMD [http://www.webmd.com] is perhaps one of the oldest medical virtual communities, which for many years has provided valuable health information, tools for managing health, and support to those who seek information on health related issues for more than a decade now.

WebMD is designed for anyone, who is trying to improve their life, allows users to share ideas on issues such as diets, workouts, thoughts, opinions, videos, pictures and more; thereby creating a unique training experience. By aggregating knowledge and insight of its members, this new and improved approach to healthcare is integrated with innovative tracking tools, videos and insights from experts that make training easier. In WebMD, many patients already construct narratives of their illnesses on personal home pages. The community enable patients to discuss symptoms, treatments, and get support

Virtual communities are more ideal in healthcare domain since healthcare problems are increasingly becoming more complex, requiring organisations involved to build synergies, partnerships and strategic alliance to find equally complex solutions to the healthcare crisis, whether it being national or global. In the health research front, virtual communities enable healthcare, biomedical, clinician collaborate on interdisciplinary issues of interests to solve healthcare problems. By using virtual communities, interdisciplinary healthcare professionals are able to conduct conversation at distance, share knowledge and information and have informed decisions healthcare policies. This is also likely to help increase their understanding issues important to them, spark innovation, provide decision-support, enable better problem-solving, and mobilize grass-roots efforts where necessary.

Virtual communities are increasingly used to support patients, caregivers, medical insurance companies, families and healthcare providers and facilitate information exchange, provide support and enhance communication among people who do not have to be physically present at the same time at one location. Most of the health delivery virtual communities are corporate owned has their own accessible set of protocols and credibility for their members. In addition, a number of virtual communities are developing various ways to support health living.

For example, many organisations are adding virtual communities as a supplementary strategy to their healthcare delivery modalities. They have started to help people find relevant information and support in order to make important health decisions, all in virtual communities. There are number of health, insurance companies currently implementing virtual community with 3-D video game-like interactivity that enables people to learn and interact anonymously with like-minded peers in order to positively change the way they live their lives. For example, a newly developed nutrition zone helps participants develop their nutrition knowledge, learn how to make healthier food choices, manage their weight and understand portion sizes and food labels. It was also intended to teach them acquire skills that will enable them to lead healthier, more energetic and productive lives. Stress, physical activity and sleep zones within the community are planned to be developed following an evaluation of people's experience with the nutrition zone. Such trends suggest the increasing use of virtual communities in many domains and to support various objectives.

Enhancing International Development

The use of the Internet within international development has helped the emergence of new research and practice areas such as information communication technology for development or commonly known as "ICT4D". Leading organizations within this area include the World Bank, the International Development Research Council of Canada (IDRC) and other development agencies which have launched telecenters in Africa and built databases and virtual communities that promote information exchange among researchers in developing countries.

As Internet connectivity has expanded globally to even very remote places in the developing and underdeveloped countries, virtual communities are gaining prominence in the international development community circles for several practical reasons. Fundamentally, virtual communities used in international development bring together people in a cost-effective manner. Instead of organizing expensive face-to-face conferences, workshops, and courses, an organization can achieve many of the same goals by linking participants electronically to each other and to a wealth of online resources.

There are several models of virtual communities within the international development context. For example, some of the models are designed to support think tanks and research institutes mainly in developing countries. The focus is on promoting and sharing the knowledge created by researchers in countries in the developed world with countries in the underdeveloped countries.

Similar to virtual communities' models implemented in businesses, some models within the international development are intended to promote internal knowledge sharing practices within organizations. Thematic Groups are the World Bank is a typical example of a successful use of virtual communities within and international development perspective. Thematic Groups at the World Bank consist of groups of people who are focused on a common subject. Memberships are normally drawn from the Bank's staff working in the regions and networks. The virtual community side is only one element of their work which also involves numerous face-to-face events and outreach and dissemination.

Motivation to Contribute in Virtual Communities

Virtual communities are self-organizing groups united by a shared interest, and what motivates their members is primarily a combination of the desire to contribute and the wish for recognition in a community of peers. Effective participation in virtual communities generally requires members' to volunteer their time and energy to contribute to the discourse in the community. Stimulating contributions or participating in virtual communities requires an understanding of what motivates people to join and sustain their activities in virtual communities. It is therefore, worth examining motivation in relation to the variety of reasons driving contributions in virtual communities.

Motivation is a desire to achieve a goal and a willingness to achieve the goal. According educational research, motivation refers to the process of acquiring and maintaining goal-directed behaviour. In the context of the Learning Sciences domains, two types of motivation are identified: intrinsic motivation and extrinsic motivation. These kinds of motivation are measured against individuals' directions towards rewards achievements. Intrinsic motivation occurs when individuals engage in doing tasks with no clear reciprocal expectation or value-added return attached to the activity.

In the context of virtual communities when they contribute their knowledge not because they expect others to contribute but because they are either driven by self motivations or sense of duty to contribute to others who might benefit. This kind of motivation is currently a driving factor in most voluntary activities in virtual communities as well as in physical communities. For example, there is a growing trend on the number of individuals in the open source community who develop tools and share software code with people they often do not know and have no expectation of rewards or reciprocity from them. A typical case in point is the Linux Open Source community, whose products and services have grown into a cutting edge operating system (Linux). Conversely, sometimes people contribute because they are motivated by some kinds of tangible outcomes, whether it being rewards or recognition. This kind of motivation is often referred to in the literature as extrinsic motivation. One example of an extrinsic motivation is when members in a virtual community tend to contribute and would like to be acknowledged and to get something in return.

The view that motivation is connected to goals achievement and expectations is grounded in social cognitive theory. The social cognitive perspective of motivation assumes that when individuals perform any tasks, they set goals and expectations. One aspect that can motivate individuals to participate in community is social obligation. This occurs when each individual can sense others' activities (some form of awareness) and hence they can be inclined to take part.

In virtual communities, the issue of motivation quickly gets more complicated because essentially, various levels of motivation can be identified. These include motivation to reach individual's goals and motivation to achieve collective goals. Kollock (1998) examined what motivate people to contribute to virtual communities. He outlined three motivations; anticipated reciprocity; increased recognition; and sense of efficacy. According to him these three aspects of motivation do not rely on altruistic behaviour on the part of the contributor. People who are motivated by anticipated reciprocity contribute valuable information to the community with the expectation that they will receive useful help and information in return.

In increased recognition, people are generally seeking for ways to be visible. This is also similar to Rheingold (1993) in his discussion of the WELL virtual community the desire for prestige as one of the key motivations of individuals' contributions to the group. Similar mechanisms are implemented in many social networking environments such as Facebook, MySpace, Slashshdot and Amazon which encourages members to construct their profiles to determine their contributions, often measured by their reputation increases. MySpace, for example, persuades members to describe their profiles and encourages them to share all kinds of information about themselves including what music they like.

Members' sense of efficacy is related to increased recognition but differs in that in the sense of efficacy individuals contribute to virtual communities because they might feel that their voice will be heard and that they will have effects on the community. Bandura (1995) work provides a detailed analysis of the notion of sense of efficacy. Wikipedia is a good example of a virtual community platform that provides contributors a sense of efficacy. For example, the changes one might make are instantaneous and readily available to the whole world.

Further, people in general, are fairly social beings they are likely to contribute to converse with others through direct responses what others. Most virtual communities enable this by allowing people to reply back to contributions (i.e. many Blogs allow comments from readers, one can reply back to forum posts, etc). The last motivating factor to contribute is related to a sense community and the feeling of shared identity and responsibility to contribute to the wellbeing of the community.

McMillan and Chavis (1986) defined sense of community as a feeling that members have of belonging, a feeling that members matter to one another and to the group, and a shared understanding among the members and that their needs will be met through their commitment to be together. A sense of a community emerges when people interact in a cohesive manner, continually reflecting upon the work of the group while respecting the differences individual members bring to the group (Graves, 1992). It is a result of interaction and deliberation among members of a community brought together by similar interests and common goals (Westheimer & Kahne, 1993).

Further, in addition to Kollock's framework, there is another kind of motivation, which is also likely to influence how individuals can participate in virtual communities. This kind of motivation is based mainly on an individual's competence and prior skills. For example people who are not knowledgeable in an area can feel intimidated by more knowledgeable colleagues. Given the nature of synchronous environment where the flow of conversation is unregulated, it is important for everyone to have a certain level of confidence to effectively participate in open discourse. It is also likely that some people seek social connections within virtual communities. They are enticed with the ability to make friends from all over the world, learn about their cultures, language and their country. The more people make friendship in a virtual community, the more they feel obligated to contribute and share their experiences with their friends.

Another important driving force motivating people to participate in virtual communities is emotional safety, a sense of belonging and ability to identify with the community. This particular phenomenon occurs when people become regular members of a community and stop feeling fearful and begin to feel a sense of safety in and identification with the community. In most regards, this is similar to physical communities when people get acquainted with others; they feel sense of connection and feel more comfortable with others in the community. Due to its role in motivating people to contribute, one would argue that an emotional connection is the niche most virtual communities are built upon. It tends to help people to tighten their relationships with others and develop bonded and more cohesive and experience and higher participation rate.

Further, motivation to contribute to virtual communities also is tied to the technical aspect of a system design. A system, which is prone to many errors, can frustrate individuals and hence deter them from using the system. Perhaps, feedback is another fact that encourages people to motivate in virtual communities. Feedback teases motivation among people who might be self-conscious about what they say and how others might view their personality and contribution. But in general, people are likely to participate in virtual communities, if they are encouraged to do so. For instance, if an individual post message to the discussion forum, other individuals may respond to the message, offer useful comments, ask question or suggest something. A great deal of work in the learning sciences has pointed out the importance of feedback as a learning reinforcement strategy.

Sustaining Contribution in Virtual Communities

The motivation to contribute and sustain contributions in virtual communities differs widely. But there are common elements that are critical to sustainability of participation in all forms of virtual communities. These elements include; the nature of content generated within a virtual community, the nature of connectivity and the purposes for connectivity, continuity to contribute and context in which a virtual community exist. These elements are presented in Figure 7-4 and briefly described.

Content

Virtual communities provide people with direct access to information resources, knowledge bases systems to which members can contribute their experiences to engage others in pursuing similar goals or sustaining similar interests. Ultimately, for members to engage in virtual communities there has to be relevant content. The content members contribute to the community play a role in sustaining their interests. For example, in discussion forums or in wikis, the content of discussion is what attract and retain people's interests in the community. Community goals, social protocols, the interests of its members and the technological infrastructure supporting interaction and engagement influence content.

Figure 7-4. Essential elements for sustaining virtual communities

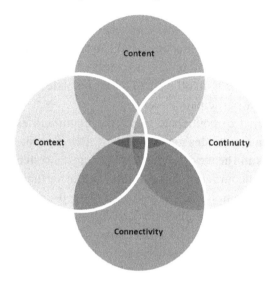

The paradoxical angle to the value of content in virtual communities is that due to increasing deployment of social software that support community engagement and where members can contribute their won content (e.g. YouTube, blogs, ubiquitous cell phones capturing photos and audio recordings and personal websites), when it is in abundance, measures of quality need to be put in place to make it relevant. In other words, sheer volume of content being created today an age where everyone and anyone can be a publisher, content is plentiful, cheaper and can quickly get irrelevant.

Virtual communities will only be valuable to their members if they deliver content that is relevant, valid, engaging and satisfactory to their members. Content of discourse sustain interests and motivate people to contribute and value others contributions. If it is a domain specific virtual communities—such as a distributed community of practice, then it is expected that content relate to people's professional life and relevant to their information needs. Content needs to be relevant and focused and consistent. They need to relate to people's realities of daily work and applicability to problem they are intending to solve. Those virtual communities that do not have relevant content are likely to discourage people from contributing or sustaining people's interests.

Context

Virtual communities provide value to their members only if content is relevant to particular context in which the virtual community operates. The value of content is determined by the community and context in which it is presented. A virtual community that does not provide content rich in context or one that does not provide meet the operational goals of the community, is not likely to thrive for long.

Providing relevant content to meet and sustain diverse needs of community's members requires an understanding of individuals' needs and goals. As McCalla (2000) indicated that every community has its own language, which determines the complexity and level of discourse and engagement among its members. Context within virtual communities influence the language of the community and the level of shared understanding. For example, the meaning of the term diagnosis depends on whether it is used in health sciences or in Artificial Intelligence which means. In Artificial Intelligence diagnosis is concerned with the development of algorithms and techniques that are able to determine whether the behaviour of a system is correct. If the system is not functioning correctly, the algorithm should be able to determine through diagnosis.

Moreover in the health sciences notably medicine, diagnosis is the process of identifying a medical condition or disease by its signs, symptoms, and from the results of various diagnostic procedures. The conclusion reached through this process is called a diagnosis. The term "diagnostic criteria" designates the combination of signs, symptoms, and test results that allows the doctor to ascertain the diagnosis of the respective disease.

Google social software technologies are perhaps the best examples of virtual community support infrastructure that are heavily driven by understanding of both content and its relevance to their users and context. Goggle's growth during its early days is attributed to its value of the role of content and context. By using innovative algorithms such as page ranking system, Google is able to leverage the web's link structure (the community) to bring the most important and relevant content to its users. By providing free content and understanding the context of users and usage Google provides some of the best virtual community services.

Continuity

A virtual community can comprise many members but numbers are meaningless if people cannot sustain their motivations to feel sense of efficacy and belonging to the community. Successful virtual communities tend to constantly devise mechanisms to encourage regular contributions and stimulating new and relevant issues. Continuity to remain vibrant contributors to community content and the willingness to remain connected to others in a community can be done through either intrinsic or extrinsic motivation mechanisms. For example, Slashdot uses "karma" to motivate and sustain its users and Amazon uses reputation mechanisms. Ultimately, communities that thrive over the Internet tend to take into account the unique needs of their members and appropriately devising ways to encourage them to continue to contribute to communities' activities.

Connectivity

Virtual communities are built on social relationships and solid connectivity. They are usually formed informally or formally due to a perceived need or a desire to relate to others. It is possible to provide an infrastructure for communities to thrive but without the desire to socially connect to others, it is unimaginable that people will participation or sustains their participation. The intensity and the types of social connections, in virtual communities emphasize building and maintaining amicable social relationships that give meaning and utility to their members.

Moreover, connectivity as a factor for sustainability participation in virtual communities entails providing a conducive and a collegiality social environment that can breed trust, which in turn stimulate people to contribute and sustain their activities in virtual communities. Connectivity also entails provision of relevant and highly robust technological infrastructure to support harmonious social relationships and generation of relevant content. In the world mobile and ubiquitous computing, connectivity also means accessibility and portability of data, content and context. People should be able to get connected to all forms of mobile devices, access their data and content and converse with members of their virtual communities in anyplace, anytime and onsite.

CONCLUSION

For many years the term community was confined within geographical location and fixed features of human culture and identity. This notion of a community had been around since the dawn of humankind and was the only accepted form of social organisation until the advent of, various computer mediated communication systems, notably the World Wide Web. These systems triggered and supported the formation of various kinds of social systems including virtual communities, radically transforming the traditional meaning of a community. Virtual communities are groups or clusters of people who gather and interact in cyberspace with explicit or implicit intention of working together to achieve or pursue common goals. People in virtual communities share common goals, interests, language, culture and common artefacts. These individuals are also held together through shared understanding, common values and social protocols.

With their increasing popularity virtual communities tend to support a wide range of human activities. Perhaps more relevant examples include their implementation to support educational systems, business, healthcare delivery and services, international development, social connections and information sharing. Virtual communities also support data sharing among researchers and Scientists. There are various reasons that motivate people to join virtual communities; among them is the need to be recognised by peers, the need to develop a reciprocal culture to share information with others and to develop sense of belonging. Regardless of particular motivations, all virtual communities service as knowledge sharing systems. In other words, a fundamental prerequisite for virtual communities to emerge is when their members identify a need for information exchange and knowledge sharing.

Virtual communities though are similar to place-based communities, sustaining them require more effort developing mechanisms to provide relevant content to members and maintain appropriate context for engagement. In addition, virtual communities thrive on the right social and technological connections, it is necessary to provide robust tools and collegial social atmosphere for productive engagement. Continuity of interactions is an important element necessary for sustaining interactions in virtual communities and for sharing knowledge. Chapter VIII is concerned with the discussion of knowledge management and knowledge sharing.

REFERENCES

Bandura, A. (1995). Exercise of personal and collective efficacy in changing societies. In A. Bandura (Ed.), *Self-efficacy in changing societies* (pp. 1-45). New York: Cambridge.

Bouton, C., & & Garth, R. Y. (1983). *Learning in gGroups*. San Francisco: Jossey-Bass, Inc.

Brown, J. S., & Duguid, P. (1991). Organisational learning and communities of practice: Towards a unified view of working, learning and innovating. *Organisational Science, 2*, 40-57.

Brunett, G. (2000). Information exchange in virtual communities: a typology. *Information Research*, 5(4). Retrieved on November 30 2008 from http://informationr.net/ir/5-4/paper82.html

Daniel, B. K., O' Brien, D., & Sarkar, A. (2003). A design aApproach for Canadian distributed community of practice on governance and international development: A preliminary report. In R. M. Verburg & J.A. De Ridder (Eds.), *Knowledge sharing under distributed circumstances* (pp.19-24). Enschede: Ipskamps.

Daniel, B. K., Schwier, R. A., & McCalla, G. I. (2003). Social capital in virtual learning communities and distributed communities of practice. *Canadian Journal of Learning and Technology, 29*(3), 113-139.

Daniel, S. & O'Brien (2008). Theory and practice of designing distributed communities of practice: Experience from the governance knowledge network in research communication. In C. Beaudet, C. P. Grant, & D. Starke-Meyerring (Eds.), *The social and human sciences: From dissemination to public engagement* (pp. 190-209). New Castle: Cambridge Scholars

Driscoll, P. (2005). *Psychology of learning for instruction* (3rd Ed.). Boston, MA: Allyn and Bacon.

Eysenbach, G. (2001). What is e-health? *Journal of Medical Internet Research, 3*(2), 20. Retrieved Nomvember 30th 2008 from [http://www.jmir.org/2001/2/e20]

Garrison, D. R. & Anderson, T. (2003). *E-Learning in the 21st Century: a framework for research and practice*. London: RoutledgeFalmer.

Graves, L. N. (1992). Cooperative learning communities: Context for a new vision of education and society. *Journal of Education, 174*(2), 57-79.

Hartley, J. (2002). *Communication, cCultural and mMedia sStudies: The key concepts*. London: Routledge.

Illera, J. L. R. (2007). *How virtual communities of practice and learning communities can change our vision of education.* Retrieved November 30th 2008 from http://sisifo.fpce.ul.pt/pdfs/sisifo03ENGconfer.pdf

Johnson, C. (2001). A Survey of current research on online communities of practice. *Internet and Higher Education, 4*, 45-60.

Kanuka, H., & Anderson, T. (1998). On-line social interchange, discord and knowledge construction. *Journal of Distance Education, 13*(1), 57-74.

Kim, A. J. (2000). *Community building on the Web: Secret strategies for successful online communities*. Berkeley, CA: Peachpit Press.

Kollock, P. (1999). *The Economies of oOnline cCooperation: Gifts and public goods in cyberspace in Communities in cyberspace.* In M. Smith & P. Kollock (Eds.), London: Routledge. Retrieved November, 30th 2008 from http://www.sscnet.ucla.edu/soc/faculty/kollock/papers/economies.htm

Koschmann, T., Kelson, A. C., Feltovich, P. J., & Barrows, H. S. (1996). Computer-supported problem-based learning: a principled approach to the use of computers in collaborative learning. In T. Koschmann, (Eds.), CSCL: *Theory & Practice in an eEmergingp Paradigm* (pp. 83-124), NJ: Lawrence Erlbaum, Mahwah.

Kowch, E., & Schwier, R.A. (1998). Considerations in the construction of technology-based virtual learning communities. *Canadian Journal of Educational Communication, 26*(1), 1-12.

Lave, J., & Wenger, E. (1991). *Situated learning: legitimate peripheral participation.* New York: Cambridge University Press.

Licklider, J. C. R. (1968). The computer as a communication device. *Science and Technology.* Reprinted in In Memoriam: J.C.R. Licklider. Systems Research Center.

Matheos, K., Daniel, B. K., & McCalla, G. I. (2005). Dimensions for blended learning technology: learners' perspectives. *Journal of Learning Design, 1*(1), 56-74.

McMillan, D. W., & Chavis, D. M. (1986). Sense of community: A definition and theory. *American Journal of Community Psychology, 14*(1), 6-23.

Newby, T. J., Stepich, D. A., Lehman, J. D., & Russell, J. D. (1996). *Instructional technology for teaching and learning.* Englewood Cliffs, NJ: Merrill.

O'Neill, D. K., & Gomez, L. M. (1994). The Collaboratory Notebook: A networked knowledge-building environment for project learning. *Proceedings of Ed-Media '94,* Vancouver, Canada.

Piaget, J. (1977). *The development of thought: Equilibration of cognitive structures.* New York: Viking Penguin.

Palloff, R., & Pratt, K. (1999). *Building learning communities in cyberspace: effective strategies for the online classroom.* San Francisco: Jossey-Bass.

Palloff, R., & Pratt, K. (2001). *Lessons from the cyberspace classroom the realities of online tTeaching.* San Francisco: Jossey-Bass.

Perkins, D. N. (1993). Creating a culture of thinking. *Educational Leadership, 51*(3), 98-99.

Preece, J. (2000). *Online communities: Designing usability and supporting sociability.* New York: John Wiley & Sons.

Rheingold, H. (1993). *The virtual community: Homesteading on the virtual frontier.* New York: Addison-Wesley.

Rheingold, H. (2003). *Smart mobs: The next social revolution. Cambridge*, MA: Perseus Publishing.

Schwier, R. A. (2007). A typology of catalysts, emphases and elements of virtual learning communities.In R. Luppicini (Ed.), *Trends in distance education: A focus on communities of learning* (pp. 17-40). Greenwich, CT: Information Age Publishing.

Schwier, R. A., & Daniel, B. K. (2007). Did we become a community? Multiple methods for identifying community and its constituent elements in formal online learning environments. In N. Lambropoulos, & P. Zaphiris (Eds.), *User- evaluation and online communities* (pp. 29-53). Hershey, PA: Idea Group Publishing.

Vygotsky, L. S. (1978). *Mind in society: The development of higher psychological processes*. Cambridge, MA: Harvard University Press.

Wenger, E. (1998). *Communities of practice. Learning meaning and identity.* Cambridge: Cambridge University Press.

Wenger, E., McDermott, R., & Snyder, W.M. (2002). *Cultivating communities of practice: A guide to managing knowledge*. Boston: Harvard Business School Press.

Weinreich, F. (1997). Establishing a point of view towards virtual communities. *Computer-Mediated Communication, 3*, (2). Retrieved November 30th 2008 from http://www.december.com/cmc/mag/1997/feb/wein.html

Westheimer, J., & Kahne, J. (1993). Building school communities: An experience-based model. *Phi Delta Kappan, 75*(4), 324-328.

Wilson, B. G., Ludwig-Hard-Hardman, S., Thorman, C. L., & Dunluap, J. C. (2004). Bounded community: Designing and facilitating learning communities in formal courses. *International Review of Research in Open and Distance Learning, 5*(3). Retrieved November, 26th 2008 from [http://cade.athabascau.ca/vo5.3/wilson].

Web Links Used in this Chapter

http://www.well.com/

http://www.facebook.com

http://www.google.com

http://www.myspace.com

http://www.slashdot.com

http://www.wikipedia.org

http://www.worldbank.org

http://www.webmd.com

http://www.idrc.ca/

http://www.minitel.fr/

http://www.youtube.com

ENDNOTES

[1]   http://www.well.com/user/hlr/texts/utopiancrit.html

[2]   "e-health is an emerging field in the intersection of medical informatics, public health and business, referring to health services and information delivered or enhanced through the Internet and related technologies. In a broader sense, the term characterizes not only a technical development, but also a state-of-mind, a way of thinking, an attitude, and a commitment for networked, global thinking, to improve healthcare locally, regionally, and worldwide by using information and communication technology." (Eysenbach, 2001)

Chapter VIII
Knowledge and Knowledge Sharing in Virtual Communities

INTRODUCTION

Knowledge management and knowledge sharing are topics best addressed in a different book. This chapter is intentionally introduced in the book to introduce the reader to knowledge management and knowledge sharing and to think about these growing areas where there are potential opportunities to apply social capital to solve real world practical problems. Though the use of social capital and knowledge management was briefly introduced in Chapter III, by reiterating these two issues here it will broaden the reader's understanding of the critical role social capital plays in enhancing knowledge management through knowledge sharing in virtual communities. In addition, this chapter discusses some of the most important challenges to knowledge sharing in virtual communities. Furthermore, this chapter describes the basic concepts often associated with knowledge management and social capital.

THE NATURE OF KNOWLEDGE

The term knowledge is subject to differing philosophical and semantic interpretations. The Webster dictionary defines knowledge as a fact or condition of knowing something with familiarity gained through experience. It is a fact or condition of being aware of something; it is also the circumstance of apprehending truth or a fact through reasoning or association. The lowest level of known facts is data. Data has no intrinsic meaning. It must be sorted, grouped, analyzed, and interpreted within some context.

When data is processed in this manner, it becomes information. Information has a substance and a purpose, however, information does not have meaning. When information is combined with experience and put into concrete context it becomes knowledge. Consequently, knowledge is a combination of information, context, and experience. Context, as far as knowledge is concerned, relates to an individual's framework for interpretations of facts and information. When knowledge is transferred from one individual to another, it is drawn into the receiver's context and experience and so the new knowledge is interpreted according to the receiver's values, context and experiences. If the receiver does not have an appropriate background or context for interpreting the new knowledge, the new knowledge will not be interpreted correctly and the knowledge will have little or no value. For example, if a person does not have experience interpreting certain procedures involved in the process of learning how to swim, they will not understand why people are able to float in water. Subsequently, they find it challenging to learn how to swim from just reading books. At the same time, if an author of a book on swim uses a poor symbolic representation of the knowledge about swimming, the reader will be misled or may even be unable to understand what is expressed in the book and the proper techniques needed to bounce and float in water.

While there is no agreed upon standard definition of what constitutes knowledge, knowledge can be conveniently classified into two broad categories; the 'silent' or tacit knowledge and explicit knowledge, one that can be deliberately shared, documented and communicated. Polanyi (1962) distinction between tacit and explicit is perhaps the most highly recognized. This distinction, which is described in Table 8-1, has major implications for virtual communities.

Knowledge Management

Knowledge management is central to the success of many organizations. In its general theoretical sense, knowledge management as a discipline helps the conceptualization and implementation of knowledge of individuals or groups or systems across organizations in ways that directly affect the production of good and services. At its best observations, the primary goal of knowledge management is to envision getting the right information within the right context to the right individual at a right time and better yet for the right business purpose.

Moreover, it has been repeatedly stressed that organisations implementing knowledge management systems have several benefits including; the ability to

Table 8-1. Comparative characteristics of tacit and explicit knowledge

Tacit Knowledge	Explicit Knowledge
Drawn from experience and is the most powerful form of knowledge	Can be articulated formally as pictures, models and documents
Difficult to articulate formally	Can become obsolete quickly - has a lag
Difficult to communicate and share	Can be duplicated and transmitted easily
Includes insights, feelings, culture and values	Can be processed and stored by automated means
Hard to steal or copy	Can be shared, copied and imitated easily
Shared only when individuals are willing to engage in social interaction	Easy to duplicate and transferable

Daniel, Schiwer and McCalla (2003)

create new value through new products or services; enhancing current value of existing products. The term knowledge management is used widely but often quite differently within the corporate sector. Over the years a number of definitions have emerged from different roots and disciplinary backgrounds. Knowledge Management (KM) refers to a range of practices used by organizations to identify, create, represent, and distribute knowledge for reuse and learning across the organization. Davenport and Prusak (1995) coined the term knowledge management in attempt to make sense of a vast number of trends that were emerging in businesses following the disruptive stage of restructuring corporations. According to them, knowledge as a new human resource includes important components such as experience, truth, judgment, and rule of thumb. In most organisations, knowledge is spread all over numerous experts, among organisational units and across national and geographical boarders.

A fundamental emphasis of knowledge management approaches in many organisations is on capturing knowledge that is highly distributed and fragmentised and consolidating it into concrete structures, capable of helping organisations advance their human and systems' competence. In more recent years emphasis on systems or technological solutions approaches to knowledge management follow the realisation that technology has a major impact in any corporate settings continuously influencing the way in which many organisations build their knowledge management systems and do business-to-business with other corporations or individuals.

More specifically, technology plays a critical role in supporting knowledge management in basically two main ways. First it can provide the means for organisations to organise, store and access explicit knowledge and information in database systems and second technologies such as social software systems can help connect individuals within organisations or outside to share ideas, experiences, or employees with information or useful documents that can help them accomplish their job. The second view of technological solutions is central to idea of social capital leading to a community driven approach to knowledge management.

Community driven knowledge management rests on simple principles. Knowledge management (or perhaps more appropriately knowledge stewardship) is a process that is best accomplished with the collective effort of multiple individuals in an organization. It is assumed that when individuals are bound by a common purpose in an organization, they can approach this stewardship as members of one community. While a community can do much to advance the knowledge that they manage, this advancement can be significantly enriched through a vetting process that recruits participants that are outside the member community. This entire process drives the community toward the formulation of competitive advantage and thereby enriching the individuals and the community, as well as the organization in which the community is situated.

Community driven knowledge management strategy uses people, processes and technology to capture and organize knowledge in ways that will enhance organizational capabilities to compete and generate value. It promotes technological ways of managing knowledge focusing on providing tools and processes for storing, indexing and retrieving knowledge.

In order to create positive effects and new knowledge, knowledge management tools that support community engagement, must truly facilitate the knowledge-based conversations within the enterprise. The technology must be adaptive to change and provide a community framework for knowledge flow and collaboration in which the broadest possible diversity of opinion can be integrated in support of organizational decisions. Community driven knowledge management approach is only as good as the activity of the members. In other words, communities must meet and evolve the conversations of their members as they work through individual topics, creating rich, stable and versatile knowledge networks.

KNOWLEDGE NETWORKS AND BASIC RELATED CONCEPTS

Though a formal knowledge network generally refers to expert groups working together to solve problems of shared concern, there is no single model to concretely describe knowledge networks (Creech & Willard, 2001). In some cases knowledge networks are simply loose associations that tend to include groups of individuals with shared interests. In knowledge networks, it is possible that members may not focus on a particular goal or collaborate on any particular projects, but instead they form a network because they share common interest. Such networks require neither strong leaders nor core members, and although they may be relatively permanent, membership itself can grow, decline or turn over as members' cycle through the network as per their interests, needs and motivations.

When knowledge networks are formalised, especially within the corporate settings, they may have operating budgets—even paid staff—and they may definitely benefit from active management and facilitation. More than just a network of interests, they may engage in goal setting, project development and collaboration. They may also act as "knowledge aggregations" or libraries capable of capturing, cataloguing, storing and providing easy access to some or all of the network's knowledge. Broadly, Creech (2001) described several kinds of knowledge networks all of which manifest the following shared characteristics:

- **Internal knowledge management networks:** Such networks are developed through identifying and mapping expertise within an organization and providing spaces for discussion, knowledge sharing and learning.
- **Strategic alliances:** Though not explicitly knowledge networks, strategic alliances are "long-term purposeful arrangements", mostly developed in the private sector, which strengthen overall ability to create and maintain competitive advantage.
- **Networks of experts:** This type is composed of individual academics or professionals. Membership is determined by an acknowledgment of expertise in a particular field.
- **Information networks:** Information networks can act as central "repositories" for a wide range of information provided by individual members or member organizations. While often comprehensive, they are basically static sites.
- **Formal knowledge networks:** These networks tend to be more focused than other networks, often concentrating on a particular goal, objective or project. Membership is often composed of formal organizations with "cross-sect oral and cross-regional" dimensions. They may, in some case, concentrate their energies on informing and influencing decision-makers.
- **Communities of practice:** Communities of practice (CoPs) are similar to information networks in that they facilitate knowledge sharing among two or more individuals. The central difference lies in the type of knowledge exchanged: explicit or codified for information networks and tacit or personalized for CoPs.

KNOWLEDGE SHARING IN VIRTUAL COMMUNITIES

The importance of knowledge sharing and management as a source of competitive advantage for organisations has been emphasized (Nonaka, 1991). More recently organisations are recognizing the benefits of tacit knowledge for developing supportive relationships across teams, departments and companies. A plethora of research has continuously stressed the importance of knowledge sharing (de Vries, van den Hooff, & de Ridder, 2006). It has been suggested that knowledge sharing improves organizational performance (Lesser & Storck, 2001), promotes competitive advantage (Argote & Ingram, 2000), enhances organizational learning (Argote, 1999) and illuminates innovation (Powell, Koput, & Smith-Doerr, 1996). This body of research has stimulated many organisations to explore ways to promote knowledge sharing amongst their employees.

In very simple terms sharing, which is not only limited to knowledge, is a process whereby a resource is given by one party and received by another. For sharing to occur, there must be an exchange; a tangible resource such as document or an individual narrating their experiences in regards to particular tasks performances or knowledge of specific things. Whether tangible or intangible, knowledge must pass between source and recipient. Knowledge sharing also implies giving and receiving of information framed within a context by the knowledge of the source. What is received is the information framed by the knowledge of the recipient. Although based on the knowledge of the source, the knowledge received cannot be identical as the process of interpretation is subjective and is framed by our existing knowledge.

Within virtual communities' contexts, knowledge sharing entails a process where individuals mutually exchange their (tacit and explicit) knowledge and jointly create new knowledge (Van den Hooff & De Ridder, 2004). For sharing to take place, there has to be a demand for knowledge, willingness to share and some social grounds binding the relationships between individuals involved in the exchange transactions. In other words, knowledge sharing consists of both the supply of new knowledge and the demand for new knowledge (Ardichvili, Page & Wentling, 2003). For people to engage in knowledge sharing in virtual communities there must be an exchange; a tangible resource such as document or an individual narrating their experiences in regards to particular tasks performances or related subject.

Knowledge sharing within distributed circumstance also implies the giving and receiving of information framed within the context by the knowledge of the source. What is received is the information framed in terms of the knowledge of the recipient. Although based on the knowledge of the source, the knowledge received cannot be identical as the process of interpretation is subjective and is interpreted by existing knowledge. Tacit and explicit knowledge are common to all kinds of virtual communities though the protocol for transmitting each one of them differs from one community to another and so is the way individuals' construction and interpretations. In virtual communities, the process involved in knowledge constructions and interpretation depends on the interaction and dependencies of data, information, knowledge and the social context in which this is embedded (see Figure 8-1).

Figure 8-1 suggests that knowledge sharing in virtual communities take a cyclical process, where, individuals share data and the data are processed into information. When information is situated within a certain particular context, it is processed into knowledge. However, this process, which is seemingly linear, depends on how the data are stored, and how information is presented, organized, communicated and received by individuals in a particular community. In addition, the way in which data is shared or information is presented to individuals and communicated depends on specific or general sets of social protocols available in a particular community. In addition, an individual's cognitive processes determine how information is processed into knowledge. The cyclical process in the model implies that knowledge is both an input and product in itself. That is to say that what constitutes knowledge for one individual might be information for another individual, and what counts as information for an individual in a specific time might become data later. Heralding knowledge sharing as a critical knowledge management strategy is as important as understanding the social and technical dynamics involved in getting people to share knowledge with other individuals. In virtual communities understanding the conditions in which people are likely to share knowledge is critical developing appropriate mechanisms to encourage culture of sharing and reciprocity. Daniel, McCalla and Schwier (2008) examined various circumstances which might negatively implicate knowledge sharing in virtual communities. These were stated in simple terms and presented here as follows:

Figure 8-1. A process model for knowledge construction in virtual communities

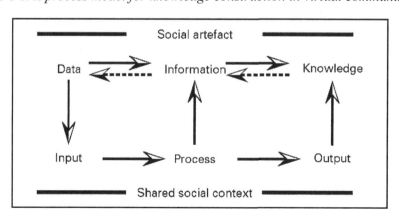

- **Awareness:** People are mostly unwilling to share knowledge with people they hardly know.
- **Trust:** People would not reveal their information if they do not trust the recipient.
- **Competition:** People would not share knowledge in an environment where competition instead of co-operation is encouraged and one in which the notion of "knowledge is power" is maintained.
- **Resistance:** People can resist new knowledge if it is not encouraged or created from within the community.
- **Doubt:** Doubt is another possible reason for not sharing, for instance, if an individual is not sure their knowledge would be used in an appropriate context, misapplied or if they suspect that others will dishonestly claim ownership.
- **Uncertainty:** People who experience information uncertainty, as well as relational uncertainty are not likely to share knowledge with others.
- **Time:** In circumstances, where knowledge sharing is voluntary and there is increasing lack of time, people are more likely to withdraw from knowledge sharing activities.
- **Technology:** In professional communities such as distributed communities of practice, if there is inadequate technology for engagement, reliability, security, and safety, people can easily and quickly withdraw from participation.
- **Incentives:** Providing monetary incentives as reward for encouraging knowledge sharing is found to be ineffective other more implicit rewards such as self-actualization and recognition seem to be more effective instead. This is also in line with previous research suggesting that non-financial incentives improve knowledge sharing across organizational boundaries (Dyer & Nobeoka, 2001).
- **Ignorance:** Ignorance and lack of self-confidence is another possibility for with-holding information that can benefit others, especially in situation where individuals are not aware that their knowledge can contribute to others.
- **Tacit knowledge:** Knowledge sharing would not occur if the technological environment can not encourage the transfer of tacit knowledge.

Some of the elements presented here signal the intricate interface of social capital and knowledge sharing in virtual communities. For instance, awareness in virtual communities is a critical social capital component of social capital. Lack of awareness in virtual communities can lead to fragile social relationships which might barely support trust, also a core component of social capital and subsequently a collapse of social capital or productive relationships.

SOCIAL CAPITAL AND KNOWLEDGE SHARING

Cohen and Prusak (2001) noted that social capital encourages better knowledge sharing due to established trusting relationships. They observed that when people develop trusting relationships within an organisation, transaction costs are significantly reduced. They also pointed out that social capital could mitigate low turnover rates, reduce severe costs as well as hiring and training expenses, which further avoid discontinuities, associated with frequent personnel changes, maintaining a valuable organisational knowledge. Further social capital enhances greater coherence of action due to organisational stability and shared understanding. Social capital has also been linked to the creation, acquisition, exchange, transfer and combination of knowledge (Adler and Kwon, 2002) positively linking to knowledge sharing. Wah et al. (2005) examined the relationship between social capital and the conditions for knowledge sharing within an organization. Subramanian and Youndt (2005) considered social capital as knowledge embedded within, available through, and utilized by interactions among individuals and their networks of interrelationships'. They observed that investment in organizational and human capital accrues high maximum returns if combined with social aspects of individual skills and inputs.

Recently, Cohen (2007) asserted that social capital is an organizational resource that can be deliberately managed and elaborated upon. He proposed four essential conditions necessary for organisations to leverage social capital, these include:

- Providing sufficient time and space for people to meet and work closely together in order to 'develop mutual understanding and trust'.
- To build trust by demonstrating trustworthiness and delegating responsibilities.
- To ensure equality in terms of opportunities and rewards and to foster 'commitment and cooperation'.
- To examine existing social networks to see where valuable relationships can be preserved and strengthened.

One of the most important variable describing learning activities in virtual communities is knowledge sharing. The importance of knowledge sharing has been extended to virtual communities. Bieber et al. (2002) indicated that virtual communities provide value to people because they induce collaboration and knowledge sharing. Daniel, Schwier and McCalla (2003) noted that increasingly, virtual communities are becoming platforms for knowledge sharing. They employed social capital as a mechanism for understanding how people exchange knowledge and information in virtual communities.

Further, drawing understanding from virtual communities' context, they regarded social capital as a collective social resource that facilitates information exchange, knowledge sharing and knowledge construction through continuous interaction, built on trust and maintained through shared understanding. The concrete operational dimensions of social capital in connection to knowledge sharing in virtual communities are at the core of value social capital provides to virtual communities, but which is certainly under investigated.

CONCLUSION

Many organisations have come to realise that knowledge or what organisations consider as knowledge, is a strategic resource that gives them sustainable competitive advantage. With this realization, they are now attempting to manage knowledge in a more systematic and effective way. The expectations are that knowledge Management encourages the creation and sharing of knowledge that, it is claimed, results in improvements in productivity, innovation, competitiveness, and better relationships among people in those organisations.

Knowledge Management is a continually evolving discipline, with a wide range of contributions and a wide range of views on what represents good practice in knowledge management. In many organisations, knowledge management programs are typically tied to organizational objectives and are intended to lead to the achievement of specific business outcomes such as shared business intelligence, improved performance, competitive advantage, or higher levels of innovation. In corporate sector, the various conceptualisations of knowledge management have lead to different ways in which performances problems are perceived.

Further, diversity in perceptions of performances problems and especially knowhow have lead to different ways in which learning is organised and different ways of interventions and performance enhancement solutions are built. Understanding the process of knowledge sharing within virtual communities is critical as more; institutions are becoming aware of the necessity to support virtual learning communities as formal learning environments. The effectiveness of virtual communities in enhancing learning depends on the ability to support the culture of knowledge sharing among its participants. Understanding the process of knowledge sharing within virtual learning is a serious concern in higher education. More and more, institutions are becoming aware of the necessity to support virtual learning communities as formal learning environments.

The effectiveness of virtual communities in enhancing learning depends on the ability to support the culture of knowledge sharing among its participants. Social capital is a vital mechanism for instituting knowledge management approaches and enhancing knowledge sharing. It is the pipeline in which knowledge can be shared and retained. If the ultimate goal of virtual communities is to encourage knowledge sharing, then social capital can play a critical role in sizing opportunities for knowledge exchange and knowledge sharing. This chapter has reviewed various ways interfacing social capital and knowledge management through understanding of knowledge sharing. The chapter has reviewed related concepts such as knowledge networks critical to knowledge sharing in virtual communities

REFERENCES

Adler, P. S., & Kwon, S. W. (2002). Social capital: propsects for a new concept. *Academy of Management Review, 27*(1), 17-40.

Argote, L. (1999). *Organizational learning: Creating, retaining, and transferring knowledge.* Boston: KluwerAcademic.

Argote, L., & Ingram, P. (2000). Knowledge transfer: A basis for competitive advantage in firms. *Organizational Behavior and Human Decision Processes, 82*(1), 150-169.

Ardichvili, A., Page, V., & Wentling, T. (2003). Motivation and barriers to participation in virtual knowledge-sharing communities of practice. *Journal of Knowledge Management, 7*(1), 64-77.

Bieber, M., Im, I., Rice, R., Goldman-Segall, R., Paul, R., Stohr, E., Hiltz, S. R., Preece, J., & Turoff, M. (2002). Towards Knowledge-Sharing and Learning in Virtual Professional Communities. *Proceedings of the 35th Hawaii International Conference on System Sciences.*

Cohen, D. (2007). Enhancing social capital for knowledge effectiveness. In K. Ichijo & I. Nanaka (Eds.), *Knowledge Creation and Management: New Challenges for Managers* (pp. 240–53). Oxford University Press, Oxford and New York.

Cohen, D., & Prusak, L. (2001). *In good company: How social capital makes organizations work.* Massachusetts: Harvard Business School Press.

Creech, H., & Willard, T. (2001). Strategic intentions: managing knowledge networks for sustainable development. *International Institute for Sustainable Development.*

Creech, H. (2001). Strategic intentions: Principles for sustainable development knowledge networks. *International Institute for Sustainable Development.*

Daniel, B. K., McCalla, G., & Schwier, R. (2003). Social Capital in Virtual Learning Communities and Distributed Communities of Practice. *The Canadian Journal of Learning Technology, 29*(3), 113-139.

Daniel, B. K., McCalla, G. I., & Schwier, R. A. (2008). Social Network Analysis techniques: implications for information and knowledge sharing in virtual learning communities. *InternationalJournal of Advanced Media and Communication (IJAMC), 2*(1), 20-34..

Davenport, T., & Prusak, L. (1998). *Working Knowledge: How Organizations Manage What They Know.* Cambridge, MA: Harvard Business School Press.

de Vries, R. E., van den Hooff, B., & de Ridder, J. A. (2006). Explaining knowledge sharing. The role of team communication styles, job satisfaction, and performance beliefs. *Journal of Communication Research, 33*(2), 115-135.

Hiltz, S. R. (1998). Collaborative learning in asynchronous learning networks: Building learning. *Proceedings of WebNet 98', World Conference of the WWW and the Internet.*

Hiltz, S. R., & Turoff, M. (1993). *The network nation.* Cambridge, MA: MIT Press.

Lesser, E., & Storck, J. (2001). Communities of practice and organizational performance. *IBM Systems Journal, 40*(4), 831-841.

Nonaka, I. (1991). The knowledge creating company. *Harvard Business Review*, (pp. 96-104).

Polanyi, M. (1962). *Personal Knowledge.* London: Routledge & Kegan Paul.

Powell, W., Koput, K., & Smith-Doerr, L. (1996). Interorganizational collaboration and the locus of innovation: Networks of learning in biotechnology. *Administrative Science Quarterly, 41*(1), 116-145.

Subramaniam, M., & Youndt, M.A. (2005) The influence of intellectual capital on the types of innovative capabilities. *Academy of Management Journal, 48*(3), 450–63.

Van den Hooff, B., & Hendrix, L. (2004, April). *Eagerness and willingness to share: The relevance of differentattitudes towards knowledge sharing.* Paper presented at the Fifth European Conference on Organizational Knowledge, Learning and Capabilities, Innsbruck, Austria.

Wah, C., Menkhoff, T., Loh, B., & Evers, H. (2005). Theorizing, measuring and predicting knowledge sharing behavior in organizations – A social capital approach. *Proceedings of the 38th Hawaii International Conference on System Sciences.*

Section III
Computational Modelling

One particular ramification of living in this new age of increased connectivity is related to increasing volume of data, especially within social sciences and humanity disciplines. For many years, social scientists have studied many social systems through traditional data gathering methods such as surveys, interviews, focus groups, or by simply placing human observers in social environments. Subsequently, a number of software tools to analyze these types of data have become increasingly sophisticated. However, within the last decade, new methods of quantifying interaction and behaviour among people have emerged that no longer require surveys or a human observer. The new resultant datasets are several orders of magnitude larger than anything before possible. Initially, this data was limited to representing people's online interactions and behaviour, typically through analysis of email or instant messaging networks.

To deal with the massive amounts of continuous human behavioural data that will be available, it will be necessary to draw on a range of fields, from traditional social network analysis to particle physics and statistical mechanics. More specifically, working with machine learning algorithms to analyse and predict social phenomenon. Today, computational modelling goes beyond simple data gathering and data analysis but rather combine these processes and use these data to build complex models that in turn use similar data to uncover and describe social reality. Some of these methods use computational modelling. The use of computational models in the social sciences has grown quickly in the past decade.

For many these models represent a bewildering and possibly intimidating approach to examining data and developing social and organizational theory. Few researchers have had courses or personal experience in the development and building of computational models and even fewer have an understanding of how to validate such models. This section represents an attempt at redressing this oversight. An overview is provided of computational modeling in the social sciences, types of validation, and some of the issues in doing model validation. The goal of section III is to provide the reader with a general technical knowledge mainly drawn from artificial intelligence and applied statistics, required for understanding and building Bayesian Belief computational models. The section includes Chapter IX, which provides overview on modelling and emphasizes social modelling approach. In Chapter X the Bayesian Belief Network as a statistical approach is presented. Chapter XI presents detailed procedures for building Bayesian Belief Network models.

Chapter IX
Foundations of Social Modelling

INTRODUCTION

A model is an abstract representation of reality. It can be an object, a system or an idea. In general terms, one could say that a model is a simplification of reality. Modeling is a fundamental and quantitative way to understand complex phenomena and systems. Modelling make up a scientific approach that can be applied to analyse a wide range of physical and social problems. Modelling of complex systems is becoming increasingly a common practice in virtually different disciplines, giving rise to active fields of studies such as mathematical modelling, econometrics, social modelling, computational physics, chemistry, mechanics, and biology, to name just a few. Through modeling one can readily cross over from one discipline to another, the basic concepts and techniques are relatively the same. Computational models are useful tools for representing abstractions and concrete realities. Computational models are intended to provide knowledge about social and technical aspect of systems and their users.

Scientists often create computational models to imitate a set of processes observed in the natural world in order to gain an understanding of these processes and to predict the outcome of natural processes given a specific set of input parameters. On the analytical level, computational models are expressed as conceptual and theoretical modeling with sets of algorithms, which are implemented as software programs. Computational models are capable of providing computer systems designers and research analysts with rich insights to build processes, procedures and tools to support systems operations in order to adapt these operations to peoples' technology needs. On the theoretical level, computational models provide researchers and scientists with the ability to investigate and develop new theoretical knowledge necessary for building systems, tools and processes.

This chapter presents an overview of computational modelling. It provides examples of computational models types and how they are currently used to inform our understanding of issues connected to users and computer systems. The goal of the chapter is to present the reader with the background knowledge necessary for understanding the Bayesian computational approach presented in this book and to draw their attention to think about ways in which modelling can be used to analyse and understand problems in other social systems.

FOUNDATION OF COMPUTATIONAL MODELLING

Modelling is a procedure for knowledge representation and sometimes with the purpose of understanding complex problems in many domains. Modelling involves a systematic and logical representation of a theoretical construct or a body of knowledge. Science or what is considered scientific knowledge is based on the notion of theories, hypothesis, deductions, inductions and predictions. To examine theory formulation in general and its relationship to computational models, a distinction between the real world and the abstract world must be clearly made. The real world in this scrutiny is represented by the knowledge of concrete things, such as people, cars, relationships and indeed all the things that we can concretely see, touch and feel. The abstract world is the concrete representations of these realities achieved through the help of scientific principles and tools. The bridge between the abstract world and the real world is a scientific model.

A computational model or a scientific model for that matter has primarily three goals to achieve, the first goal is to understand what is observed in the real world and translate these observations to abstractions. The second goal is to be able to relate and predict events of observations or abstractions and the third goal is to control the behaviour or aspects of the real world. For example, how can a meteorologist know about the conditions of the weather? How can an Economist accurately predict economic recession? How can a Neurologist study brain reasoning patterns? These are valid questions, which are frequently addressed through the help of computational models.

A computational model comes in various types, forms, sizes and representations and they are either descriptive or predictive. Descriptive models use metaphor to describe, analyze and illustrate social or natural phenomenon. Predictive models on the other hand use mathematical and statistical equations to illustrate relationships among variables or components of a system. It is convenient to think of models as lying in a continuum, with analogy and metaphor at one end and mathematical equations at the other but in reality most models lie somewhere in-between. For example, for any model to accurately make predictions, it is necessary to fully describe the object or the phenomenon in which the model represents. Similarly, descriptive models are based on some information which can be gathered from some accurate predictions of certain systems.

The process of modelling involves explicitly defining a problem and specifying modelling goals. These goals correspond to translating the problem into abstraction, or breaking down a problem into small parts and putting them all together and finally make informed and valid judgements about the situation or problem under investigation. Models help us to make informed and intelligent decisions in the designing, evaluating, or otherwise providing a basis for understanding the behaviour of a complex artefact e.g. a computer system or social theory such as social capital. By objectifying social capital, its relative components can be identified and the relationships among them explicitly defined.

The process of model building starts with observation, followed by identification of patterns and building relationships among the patterns observed. When scientific logical rules are applied to determine the interaction of data patterns within a model, we end up with scientific or computational models.

Though they are many kinds of models, the discussion here will be limited to predictive models. A mathematical model is a perfect illustration of a predictive

Figure 9-1. Process of a computational model

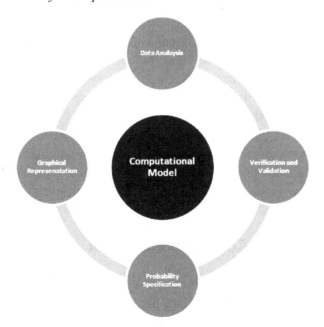

scientific model. A mathematical model is an artifact illustrating a mathematical idea and one that uses expressive mathematical language to describe it. A mathematical model, especially in the Natural Sciences and Engineering disciplines (e.g. Computer Science, Physics, Biology, and Electrical Engineering) and also more recently in the social sciences (such as Economics, Sociology and Political Science) is the basis in which most computational knowledge representation schemes are represented.

Computational Models

In Computer Science, a computational model is technically based on mathematical abstractions. It is a description of a computer system and abstractions of how the computer or a software program works or how users of such a system would possibly use a program. There are conceptual as well as theoretical models in computer science. A computational model in computer science is often expressed as sets of algorithms and implemented as software package or a procedure or a technique or workflow or even a methodology. Further, in Computer Science, a computational model is described by a set of variables and a set of equations that establish relationships between the variables. The values of the variables can be variously initiated or represented by real or integer numbers, Boolean values or strings.

The idea that computers should adapt to the characteristics of their human users has always been a major concerned of Computer Science researchers, especially within the Artificial Intelligent as well as Human Computer Interactions research communities. McTear (1993) pointed out that as computer systems become more complex and the range of users of these systems become increasingly diverse, it seems apparent then that there is a need for computer systems to adapt to various types of user. Adaptation can be achieved in many ways. In the simplest case a user can personalised a system to meet user's unique requirements and the computer stores these adaptations or user traces within the systems, and automatically or manually invoke the set of adaptation each time a computer becomes operational and when there is a need to do so.

There are more complex systems which automatically store the user's choices for future usage. In each case adaptation is concerned with providing options regarding aspects of the user and the computer interface with which the user interacts. Many widely used systems today have incorporated these basic levels of adaptation into their user interfaces.

Characteristics of a Computational Model

Above many others, there are broadly two shared characteristics of computational models. They are representation of reality and are seldom complete. In other words, computer models do not include every aspect of reality we observe or are likely to observe. And they also reflect the thinking of those individuals involved in building the models. In order to create a model, a scientist must first make some assumptions about the essential structure and relationships of objects and/or events in the real world. These assumptions are influenced by their environment, background knowledge, personality traits, ability to critically think and general view of the world. They can be based on data, intuition, experiences or all of the above.

During the modeling process, assumptions are made about what is necessary or important to explain the phenomena being modelled. For example, an Automobile Engineer might be interested in simulating safety procedures during car crash using a dummy. In creating the model the engineer needed to be knowledgeable about the domain being modelled and all the possible ways a car might crush and under what circumstances safety procedures such as air bags needed to be invoked. The knowledge engineer as they are sometimes referred to would also have to decide how these factors interact with each other when constructing the model. It would be naïve for an Engineer to totally assume that only factors included in the model are the only ones that can affect the outcome. In practice, people operate in a world that is highly uncertain, unreliable, incomplete and volatile. There are other factors that the engineer might not be able to capture such as all the possible issues that could go wrong and cause car crush. For example, when the driver neglect to put fuel or fall asleep behind the wheel after few drinks. However, the Engineer still needs to acknowledge these factors and to consider them as part of the "essential structure" of the model. It is also likely that all the factors that are not included in the model can contribute to gross error in the predictions of the model.

THE USER MODELLING APPROACH

A slightly different form of user-computer adaptation is based on the idea of user modelling. User modelling is the process of building data structures from usage or user interactions within a computer system together with the inference mechanisms involved, enabling a computer system to assess certain characteristics of a user for purposes of accurate or relative adaptation. Examples of relevant user characteristics include, user behaviour patterns, cognitive or knowledge state, preferences and goals and emotions and personality traits. User modelling taken from this perspective deals with the construction of a computational model representing its user/users, the tasks they perform or the context in which such tasks are performed. The main purpose of user modelling is to facilitate reasoning about certain properties and processes of a user. User modelling is based upon explicit assumptions about the system or user that may be justified as results of automated or human observation.

What is Inside a User Model?

User models are composed of data structures of various kinds and they store some basic or complex information about a user, tasks, context, a system or a social or a natural phenomenon. For example if we are interested in building a model that can be used to personalized a computer system to the needs of a user, we must collect some information about the user. The type of information of interest is basically of three types; the user data, the usage data and the computational environment data.

User data is the personal information about a user of a system. It is made up of various kinds of data including: name, age, gender, usage preferences, capability, demographic data, competence, attitudes, beliefs, e-mail address and any other personal information about the user. The combination of different personal information about the user constitutes the user data and their goals and purposes and intentions for using a system constitute the usage data.

The second category of user modeling data is the usage data. This is data related to the way a user uses a system. This includes user traces, navigation patterns, keyboard strokes, page view times and any other usage statistics. Usage data is often automatically generated by the system. This information is not necessarily tied to any personal information about the user, though it is possible to trace connect user information to usage information. Usage data is only limited to building models for adaptation but usage data can be used to build models that can be widely used as input for recommender systems discussed in chapter VI to predict user preferences for the purpose of facilitating and personalizing users' experiences.

The two kinds of information that can be captured about the user and their system's usage patterns are all dependent on the capabilities of the system's environment— the available of hardware and software to perform this kind of job. In some cases acquiring information about the system usage data is critical. Information of the system constitutes the third kind of data for building user models. Basically the three kinds of information are the core of the user modeling research investigation.

TWO MAIN USER MODELLING RESEARCH PERSPECTIVES

For more than a decade, user modelling continues to be an important sub-area of Artificial Intelligence and Human Computer Interaction, with both theoretical and practical implications to users and computer systems. The theoretical foundations of user modelling in Artificial Intelligence research include areas of knowledge representation and plan recognition educational systems, while its practical applications are demonstrated in the construction of intelligent user interfaces and adaptive systems in Human Computer Interactions. Examples of user modeling in

Human Computer Interaction can be seen in various Human-Centered Systems whose goals are to enable users customize and personalize systems' environments. For many Human Computer Interaction and Artificial Intelligence are the two main streams of research in the user modeling area.

User Models: Human Computer Interaction Perspectives

The goal of Human Computer Interaction research is to understand how users work with computer systems. Human Computer Interaction research builds on the systems and skills humans have acquired through evolution and experience and search for ways to apply them to communicating with a computer. Direct manipulation interfaces have attained great success, particularly with new users, largely because they draw on analogies to existing human skills (pointing, grabbing, moving objects in space), rather than trained behaviours (Shneiderman, 1983). The overarching principle of Human-Computer Interaction system is based on the fundamental assumption that a user and a computer system can fully take advantage of their intelligence to learn from each other, and cooperate to perform a task but this is only necessary when the characteristics of the users and a system are explicitly known or assumed.

The Human Computer Interaction perspectives on user modelling are therefore connected to the understanding of the user's cognitive style and personality factors. The emphasis of which is on providing a dialogue adapted to the requirements of the user and to the particular task which the user is currently engaged in. In a Human Computer Interaction system, users are described by their knowledge, cognitive and behavioral abilities. The main goal of a user model then is to capture personal characteristics of a user including their physical and cognitive factors (Zhao, Tu, & Wang, 2004) to help users efficiently navigate a system or use a system with minimal distraction or learnability(reduce time to learn how to use a system). For example, Human Computer Interaction researchers investigate physical factors as carriers for sending or receiving information, which consist of sensory modality e.g. vision, hearing, speech and response modality such as eyes, ears, mouth.

Direct manipulation is the most dominant approach for building user models within the Human Computer Interaction research. According to Schneiderman (1983) who developed this approach, direct manipulation is an interaction style which involves continuous representation of objects of interest, and rapid, reversible, incremental actions and feedback. It presents a set of objects on a screen and provides the user a repertoire of manipulations that can be performed on any of the objects. Ultimately, the goal of direct manipulation is to allow a user of a computer system to directly manipulate objects presented to them by the computer. This involves using actions that correspond at least loosely to the physical world.

Proponents of direct manipulation approaches believe that having real-world metaphors for describing objects and actions can make it easier for a computer user to learn and in anticipation naturally or intuitively use an interface. Through direct manipulation they suggested, rapid and incremental feedback could allow a user to make fewer errors and complete tasks in less time, because they can see the results of an action before completing the action.

The Artificial Intelligence perspective on user modelling differs from the Human Computer Interaction research angles but it is important to note that the two views are essentially complimentary, though there often seems to be a heated disagreement among researchers about each dimension.

User Modelling: Artificial Intelligence Perspective

Artificial intelligence (AI) is a branch of Computer Science and Information Science. It focuses on developing hardware and software systems that solve problems and accomplish tasks that—if accomplished by humans—would be considered a display of intelligence. The field of AI includes studying and developing machines such as robots, automatic pilots for airplanes and space ships, and "smart" military weapons and intelligent educational systems. The theory and practice of AI is leading to the development of a wide range of artificially intelligent tools. These tools, sometimes working under the guidance of a human and sometimes without external guidance, are able to solve or help solve a steadily increasing range of problems. The field of artificial intelligence in education is an extension of AI theoretical application to solve real world problem.

Artificial intelligence in education (AIED) involved building models of users and learning environments. AIED uses computational models to capture characteristics of learners that can themselves be used by tools to support learning (McCalla, 2000). Models are also used to represent educational systems and the thinking behind the design of these systems. There are many purposes of computational models in AIED. Baker (2000) distinguished three major purposes of models within AIED research: models as scientific tools for understanding learning problems; models as components of educational systems; and models as educational artifacts. Baker (2000) had envisioned that the future of artificial intelligence in education (AIED) would involve building models to support learners in learning communities and to help educators manage learning under distributed circumstances.

In Artificial intelligence in education, user modeling is a particular theoretical approach based on inductive or nonmonotonic reasoning. Unlike Human Computer Interaction views on user modeling emphasizing psychological relevance of a system to a user, artificial intelligent approaches to user modeling are aimed at developing systems that can automatically construct a model of a user as they interact with the system. The goal is to provide adaptive mechanism or personalization to its user. Artificial intelligent researchers believe that systems' adaptation to users need provide a prime example of intelligent behavior. Intelligent tutoring systems are the main examples of AIED and these systems have evolved into different kinds and use in many facets of individualized as well as community learning.

Intelligent Tutoring Systems

An intelligent tutoring system uses extensive amount of modeling, drawing fundamental principles and techniques from artificial intelligence. They are broadly conceived as computer systems that contains some intelligence and capable of supporting human learning (Greer & McCalla, 1994). Historically, intelligent tutoring systems are treated as more active and reactive computer-based learning programs.

A key distinguishing factor of intelligent tutoring systems from other learning systems is that ITS can carry out some sort of diagnosis of the learner before dynamically constructing a learning environment for the learner. When diagnosing a learner, the system makes inferences about the current state of knowledge of the learner as well as the right pedagogical interventions, and the kinds of feedback necessary to present knowledge to the learner. A learner's knowledge in intelligent tutoring systems is expected to change frequently during the course of a lesson or a course, so that the system has to continuously update its model of the learner.

Furthermore, it is often the case that a learner lacks knowledge or has misconceptions about what is being taught. For this reason the learner modelling has to be concerned with how a learner's represents and reasons with his or her knowledge. Explaining a learner's knowledge or behaviour ultimately requires deeper modelling, based on possibly some psychological theories of learning.

Requirements for user modeling in intelligent tutoring systems vary, but essentially most intelligent tutoring systems comprise of five or more modules, which include the learner model, the pedagogical model, the communication model, the domain knowledge model and the expert model (Beck & Haugsjaa, 2001). The learner model contains information specific to the learner's knowledge of the domain. It explicitly records the learner's understanding of the domain and possible misconceptions about the domain. In some cases it records the learner's current state of knowledge, current progress in a particular learning activity, their performance in answering the system's questions, and solving problems (Devedzic, Debenham & Popovic, 2001).

The instructional model contains information about the teaching process. This includes what the system needs to present to the learner, when to present it and which information needs to be reviewed. The domain knowledge model contains knowledge on what is to be taught to the learner. This model is usually represented using different knowledge representation techniques, modules, lessons, learning activities and assessments. The communication model controls the learner's interaction with the domain knowledge. The goal of this model is to present the material to the learner in the most effective way possible.

Finally, the expert model has similar functions to the domain model, except that the expert model is intended as an expert, who is talented in solving problems specific to the domain. The expert model compares the learner's solution to that of an expert skilled in the domain, identifying the areas where the learner has some difficulties in solving particular problems and recommending appropriate intervention strategies. Research in intelligent tutoring systems has radically moved away from more one-to-one tutoring to more social and community models of learning.

Modelling Social Issues in Virtual Communities

Unlike the kinds of modelling approaches employed in intelligent tutoring systems, in virtual communities the focus of the modelling is on the social aspects of the users. For the sake of simplicity this type of modelling of modelling is referred to as social modelling. Social modelling can be formally defined as the application of computational techniques to the analysis of complex social systems. It is more than finding the skills and knowledge gaps among learners within a given domain. But rather it extends to the analysis of learners' social characteristics and the social aspects critical to creating an amicable atmosphere conducive for people to effectively engage with each other and to support a community to emerge.

Several advantages can be attached to the social modelling approach. For example, modelling social characteristics of people in a virtual community help system designers to build systems to help people socially network with each other based on mutual interests and goals. In fact, some of the recommender systems built today use a great deal of social modelling techniques to develop computational tools to connect people-to-people and people-to-content and people-to-systems as demonstrated by most e-commerce and online dating systems.

Social modeling is becoming a mainstream modeling approach, especially within virtual community systems. Almost eight years ago, McCalla (2000) envisioned that in the future modelling approaches will go beyond traditional approaches of simply modelling knowledge and skills but rather they would involve capturing information about the learner, their context and the community in which they belong. The vision suggests that the modelling process would require the diagnosis of a learner's state of knowledge and skills, social context in which learning takes place, motivations, and attitudes of a learner and different pedagogical strategies that are well suited to particular learning environments. McCalla (2000) pointed out that the significance of modelling social characteristics of learners in virtual communities such as: groups, social and cultural issues in learning environments, help us to develop novel pedagogical approaches and computational tools to support learning in virtual communities.

As the need to understand social issues in virtual communities grow, there is an increasing need for building computational models, to simulate and analyze social issues emerging in these communities. In order to take full advantage of social models of users in virtual communities, real or authentic scenarios need to be developed. Unfortunately some of these phenomena are as complex as the notion of social capital, leading to further need to develop ways to model these phenomena using scenarios.

MODELLING SCENARIOS

The art and practice of modelling is not only limited to the user, tasks, or systems but it extend to modelling of situations or ideas. Modelling of an idea for a social construct such as social capital for example is accomplished through a scenario modelling A scenario modeling refers to a set of procedures for describing specific sequences of behaviours within a model that illustrate actual interactions of people within a community.

The goal of scenario modelling is to understand and explain the interactions of variables or set of events within a model and how these might possibly influence the direction of interaction patterns, and subsequently their influence on the level of social capital within a community. This means that a single scenario might describe a possible set of interactions as they occurred in a community, and upon its implementation possible alternative explanations can be inferred about current and future behaviours of a model.

Scenario modelling provides us with the ability to take a complex concept, deconstruct it, analyse all its constituent parts individually, and put them together, in order to draw a complete picture of the concept. Modelling scenarios has been used in many domains including business studies. For instance, they were used to reflect new business priorities and review the impact across the whole organisational settings.

When several scenarios are used to describe possible outcomes of events within a model, they can exceed the power of predictions that are only based on a single hypothesis or a set of propositions drawn from a single data set. While a hypothesis normally refers to a set of unproven ideas, beliefs, and arguments, a scenario describes proven states of events, which can be used to understand future changes within a model. Further, the outcomes of the events might be used to generate new set of hypothesis. These hypotheses can then be used to explain a specific situation within a model. Moreover, the results of a scenario and hypothesis can be combined to further refine the consistency and accuracy of a particular model representing a specific situation. However, for a scenario-based approach to be useful the scenarios created within any particular evidence or data sets must be plausible and internally consistent. Scenarios provide alternative explanations to particular changes in variables and their effects on a particular model.

Finally, modelling scenarios offers to scientists a common vocabulary and an effective way for communicating complex situations. In the context of social capital, scenario modeling provides an opportunity to analyzing social capital based on investigation of various components constituting the concept.

CONCLUSION

When a complex system can be simplified (reduced) to a tractable level that makes clear the essential properties and how the internal constituents interact with each other, provide us with immense benefits to understanding systems and deriving application from theory. Computational models are important components of scientific theories. Models have different sizes, shapes, complexities, representation and functions. Regardless of their magnitude and intended functions, computational models are not the actual representation of the things modelled rather they mirror the objects being modelled and capture the instances of the objects with some details and accuracy. The validity of the models and their usability are all depended on how accurate the modelers can capture reality and how the reality can be represented mathematical in some form of equation.

The process of creating a computational model is iterative, involving organization of data, establishing logical relationships among the data and coming up with a knowledge representation scheme. It involves making dependencies between different concepts explicit, defining some of the concepts in terms of the other concepts, or in terms of a smaller number of primitive concepts.

A fundamental assumption underlying most of the model building process is that data are available which a researcher can use to infer logical relationships and draw logical and concrete conclusions from the model. It also suggests simplifying assumptions must be made; boundary conditions or initial conditions must be identified; the range of applicability of the model should be understood.

A user modelling system has to acquire information about users, and construct and maintain user models. The techniques used are based on standard artificial intelligence techniques, including machine learning, knowledge representation, and reasoning with uncertain and inconsistent information. In addition, a user modelling system functions as a component of a larger system so that considerations of the relationship of the user-modelling component to other system components such as the dialogue manager and the back-end application are paramount.

There are modeling approaches that do not allow the introduction of prior knowledge during the modeling process. These approaches normally prevent the introduction of extraneous data to avoid skewing the experimental results. However, there are times when the use of prior knowledge would be a useful contribution to the modeling and evaluation processes and the overall observation of the behaviour of a model. In chapter X, the semantics and pragmatics of the Bayesian Computational Approach are discussed.

REFERENCES

Baker, M. (2000). The Roles of Models in Artificial Intelligence and Education Research: A Prospective View. *International Journal of Artificial Intelligence in Education, 11*(2), pp.122-143.

Beck, J., Haugsjaa, E., & Stern, M. (2001). Applications of AI in Education. *ACM Crossroads Student Magazine.*

Devedzic, V., Debenham, J., Popovic, D. (2000). Teaching formal languages by an intelligent tutoring system. *Educational Technology & Society, 3*(2), 36-49.

Greer, J., & McCalla, G. (1994). Student Modelling: Key to Individualized Knowledge-Based Instruction (pp. 36-62). *Nato ASI series F: Computer and Systems Science.* Berlin Heidelberg: Springer Verlag.

McCalla, G. (2000). The fragmentation of culture, learning, teaching and technology: Implications for artificial intelligence in education research. *International Journal of Artificial Intelligence, 11*(2),177-196.

McTear, M. F. (1993). User modelling for adaptive computer systems: a survey of recent developments. *Artificial Intelligence Review, 7*(157), 184, 1993.

Schneiderman, B. (1983). Direct Manipulation: A step beyond programming languages. *IEEE Computer, 16*(8), 57-69.

Zhao, Q. I., Tu, D. W., & Wang, R. S. (2004). Human computer interaction models. *Proceedings of the Third International Conference on Machine Learning and Cybernetics,* Shanghai, 26-29 August, 2274-2278.

Chapter X
Overview of Bayesian
Belief Network

INTRODUCTION

Statistical and probability inferences are basically dependent on two major methods of reasoning, conventional (frequentist) and Bayesian probability. Frequentists' methods are mainly based on numerous events, where Bayesian probability applies prior knowledge and subjective belief. Frequentist models of probability do not permit the introduction of prior knowledge into the calculations. This is traditionally to maintain the rigour of a scientific method and as a way to prevent the introduction of extraneous data that might skew the experimental results. However, there are times when the use of prior knowledge would be a useful contribution to the evaluation of a situation. The Bayesian approach was proposed to help us reason in situation where prior knowledge is need, and especially under highly uncertain circumstances.

This chapter provides an overview of the main principles underlying the Bayesian method and Bayesian belief networks. The ultimate goal is to provide the reader with the basic knowledge necessary for understanding the Bayesian Belief Network approach to building computational model. The chapter does not go into more technical details of probability theory and Bayesian statistics. To make it more accessible to a wide range of readers, some technical details are simplified.

Approaches to Probability Theory

Probabilistic and statistical analysis techniques and models have the longest history and strongest theoretical foundation for data analysis. Although it is not rooted in artificial intelligence research, statistical analysis achieves data analysis and knowledge discovery objectives similar to machine learning. Popular statistical techniques, such as regression analysis, discriminant analysis, time series analysis, principal component analysis, and multi-dimensional scaling, are widely used in data mining and are often considered benchmarks for comparison with other newer machine learning techniques. Frequentist and Bayesian are two broad approaches to formal statistical inference, which are concerned with the development of methods for analyzing noisy empirical data and in particular as the attaching of measures of uncertainty to conclusions. These approaches dominate probability reasoning.

In the frequentist approach probabilities are associated only with the data or the outcomes of repeatable observations. This suggests that if an experiment is repeated many times under essentially identical conditions and if an event occurs for a certain number of outcomes, then as number of experiments grows large but on the average the ratio of the same outcomes approaches a fixed limit and this is taken as the probability of **A**.

The probability of an event therefore entails the observations of the frequency of the occurrence of a given event. In other words, the probability **P** of an uncertain event **A**, written **P (A),** is defined by the frequency of that event based on previous observations. For example, in Saskatchewan, there can be a 50 % chance of snow in the spring. Suppose then that we are interested in the event **A**: 'a randomly selected spring season to predict Snow. In this case, the frequentist would provide us with a probability; **P (A) =0.50**.

The frequentist approach for defining the probability of an uncertain event is reliable providing that we have been able to record accurate information about many past instances of occurrences of an event. But this gets difficult in the situation where past occurrences of an event cannot be determined. If no such historical database exists, then we have to consider a different approach. Nevertheless, the frequentist approach to probability is considered to be more objective since it can be determined independently of the observer, even thought it restricts its application to repeatable phenomena.

Bayesian probability is the second approach to statistics and probability theory. This approach does not depend on repetitive trails but rather it naturally applies the laws of probability theory and formalism to reason about beliefs under conditions of uncertainty. The Bayesian approach is closer to everyday reasoning, where probability is interpreted as a degree of belief that something will happen, or that a parameter will have a given value. Bayesian approach uses prior knowledge to estimate values of model parameters. For example, what is the probability it will rain tonight given observed dark clouds in the sky?

Since this is a statement about a future event, nobody can state with any certainty whether or not it is true. Further different people may have different beliefs about the occurrence on an event depending on their specific knowledge of factors that might affect its likelihood. For example, consider differences in belief about the weather state of coldness conditions in Northern Saskatchewan between two friends Marlo and Emma. Marlo may have a strong belief about the stability of weather conditions in the winter based on his knowledge of the current weather and experience of the patterns of changes in weather conditions. On the other hand, Emma may have a much weaker belief in the stability of weather based on some negative experience that had affected her health in the past and that were caused by cold weather.

Thus, in general, a person's subjective belief in a statement will depend on some body of knowledge that a person's might have acquired under different circumstances. However, the value of Bayesian parameters can always be revised based on acquisition of new evidence.

Foundations of Bayesian Systems

Expert systems are computer systems developed by researchers in artificial intelligence during the 1970s. They are made up of programs built on a set of rules that analyze information (usually supplied by the user of the system) about a specific class of problems. Experts systems are also capable of analysing a set of problem(s), and often recommending a course of action in order to implement corrections.

Most expert systems are rule-based that use basic insights to turn data into information and decisions. These systems are usually limited to only the simplest forms of problems involving *"if-this-then-that rules"*. In other words, *if-clouds-then-it will rain*. When there are more than a few contributing factors for a decision such as wind, or if some factors involve uncertainty, the number of rules needed to fully define the decision making process can grow exponentially and these can lead into a computational complexity.

The Bayesian method to reasoning was proposed as alternative method to address the growing computational complexity within expert systems. Pearl (1985) coined the term "Bayesian networks" to emphasize three aspects; the often subjective nature of the input information, the reliance on Bayes's conditioning as the basis for updating information and the distinction between causal and evidential ways of reasoning. The Bayesian approach to statistics became one of the foundations for building many experts systems within the domain of artificial intelligence.

BAYESIAN STATISTIC AND PROBABLITY THEORY

Originating in pattern recognition research, this method was often used to classify different objects into predefined classes based on a set of features. A Bayesian model stores the probability of each class, the probability of each feature, and the probability of each feature given each class, based on the training data. When a new instance is encountered, it can be classified according to these probabilities (Langley et al., 1992).

A variation of the Bayesian model, called the Naive Bayesian model, assumes that all features are mutually independent within each class. Because of its simplicity, the Naive Bayesian model has been adopted in different domains (Fisher, 1987; Kononenko, 1991). Due to its mathematical rigor and modeling elegance, Bayesian learning has been widely used in disciplines such as education, data mining, and many other areas of applied research. The Bayesian interpretation of probability is based on the principles of conditional probability theory.

In Bayesian statistics, conditional probabilities are used with partial knowledge about an outcome of an experiment. For example, consider a situation where there are conditional relationships between two related events **A** and **B** such that the occurrence of one will affect the occurrence of the other. Suppose event **B** is true, i.e., it has occurred, the probability that **A** is true given the knowledge about **B** is expressed by: **P (A|B).** This notation suggests the following two assumptions:

1.   Two events **A** and **B** are independent of each other if:

$$P (A) = P (A|B) \tag{1}$$

2.   Two events **A** and **B** are conditionally independent of each other given **C** if:

$$P (A|C) = P (A|B, C) \tag{2}$$

Drawing from these two assumptions, Bayes' Theorem swaps the order of dependence between events. For instance:

$$P(A \mid B) = \frac{P(A, B)}{P(B)} \tag{3}$$

And Bayes' Theorem states that:

$$P(A \mid B) = \frac{P(B \mid A)P(A)}{P(B)} \tag{4}$$

$$P(A \mid B) = \frac{P(B \mid A)P(A)}{P(B)} = \frac{P(B \mid A)P(A)}{\sum_{j} P(B \mid A_{j})P(A_{j})} \tag{5}$$

where **j** indicates all possible states of **A**.

From the above equations, the following can be stated about BBN models relationships to conditional probability:

- **P (A|B)** is posterior probability given evidence **B**
- **P (A)** is the initial probability of **A**
- **P (B|A)** is the likelihood probability of the evidence given **A**
- **P (B)** is the initial probability of the evidence **B**

GRAPHICAL MODELS

Graphical models draw upon probability theory and graph theory. Graphical models provide a natural way of dealing with two major problems—uncertainty and complexity. They provide intuitive ways in which both humans and machine can model a highly interactive set of random variables as well as complex data structures to enable them to make logical, useful and valid inferences from data. In mathematical notation, a graph **G** is simply a collection of vertices **V** and edges **E** i.e. **G = (V, E)** and a typical graph **G** is associated with a set of variables (nodes) **N** = {X_1 X_2, X_3...X_n} and by establishing one-to-one relationships among the variables in **N**. Each edge in a graph can be either directed or undirected.

Directed graphs in particular consist only of directed edges. Acyclic directed graphs (ADGs) are special kinds of directed graphs that do not include cycles. One of the advantages of directed graphs over undirected graphs is that ADGs can be used to represent causal relationships among two or more variables, for example an arc from **A** to **B** indicates that **A** causes **B**. Such property can be used to construct a complex graph with many variables (a causal graph). In addition, directed graphs can encode deterministic as well as probabilistic relationships among variables. Bayesian Belief Network are examples of acyclic directed graphs, where nodes represent random variables and the arcs represent direct probabilistic dependences among the variables (Pearl, 1988; Pearl, 2000).

WHAT IS A BAYESIAN BELIEF NETWORK?

Bayesian networks, Bayesian models or Bayesian belief networks (BBNs) can be classified as part of the probabilistic graphical model family (Pearl 1988). It is a directed acyclic graph (DAG) that provides a compact representation or factorization of the joint probability distribution for a group of variables. Graphically, a BBN contains nodes and directed edges between those nodes. The links between nodes are qualitatively represented.

Each node is a variable that can be in one of a finite number of states. The links or arrows between the nodes represent causal relationships between those nodes. For example, all of the variables (**A, B, C, D, E**) in Figure 10-1 are Boolean variables, but there is no restriction on the number of states that a variable can have. Because the absence of an edge between two nodes implies conditional independence, the probability distribution of a node can be determined by considering the distributions of its parents. In this way, the joint probability distribution for the entire network can be specified. This relationship can be captured mathematically using the chain rule:

$$p(x) = \prod_{i=1}^{n} p(x_i \mid parents(x_i))$$

(6)

In general terms, this equation states that the joint probability distribution for node x is equal to the product of the probability of each component x_i of x given the parents of x_i. Each node has an associated conditional probability table that provides the probability of it being in a particular state, given any combination of parent states.

Serial Connections or D-Separation

Serial connection is a type of connection in Bayesian Belief Network indicating that slippery is conditionally dependent on wetness, which is conditionally dependent on rain. Suppose the certainty of rain and slipperiness is known, then the conditional probability of wetness can be updated. However, if it is known that it is wet and nothing else is known and then rain and slipperiness are conditionally independent given that it is wet. In other words, if it is known what has caused wetness, and then the principles of explaining away can be applied. Serial connections indicates that evidence can propagate from rain to slippery unless it is known what caused wetness.

Figure 10-1. A simple illustration of a Bayesian Network

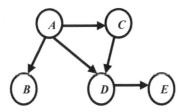

Converging Connections

In converging connections, evidence can be transmitted from two or more parents to a single child, for instance, any evidence about sprinkler and rain to wetness. This means that wetness is conditionally dependent on sprinkler and rain. However, the main concern of converging connection is whether evidence can be transmitted between sprinkler and rain. If evidence is known about rain, then it will be transmitted to wetness but it will not influence sprinkler. It also follows that if something is known about wetness, then the parents of wet in this case sprinkler and rain become conditionally dependent given evidence entered to their child (wet).

Diverging Connections

In diverging connections two variables are usually dependent upon each other and the middle variable renders them independent. Suppose the season determines whether it rains, and whether the sprinkler is on or off, then any evidence on season will affect sprinkler and rain. However, of more interest is whether information about sprinkler can be transmitted to rain and vice versa. For instance, when the season is known for certain sprinkler and rain become independent. Because the independence of sprinkler and rain is conditional on the certainty of season, we say formally that sprinkler and rain are conditionally independent (given season). Thus evidence can be transmitted from sprinkler to rain through a diverging connection of a season unless season is instantiated.

BBN models normally describe a distribution over possible observed events but they often do not indicate what will happen if a certain intervention occurs. For instance, what will happen if the sprinkler is turned on, what kinds of effects will it have to say the season or the link between wet grass and slippery (see figure 8-4). In figure 8-4 for example when the sprinkler is turned on, and the causal link between season and sprinkler is removed then all the other causal links and conditional probabilities remain intact.

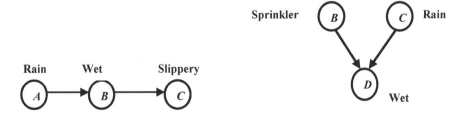

Figure 10-2. Serial connection   *Figure 10-3. Converging connections*

Figure 10-4. Diverging connections

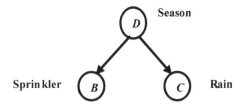

A causal network often models the environment as collections of stable components. In other words, given certain evidence the probability of certain events might change, while holding other things constant. For example, predicting that there is an 80 percent chance that it will rain tomorrow given certain weather conditions might be accurate at the time of diagnosis. But it does not guarantee that the environmental conditions remain the same tomorrow. BBN can be attuned to environmental conditions. Once a Bayesian model is built and predictions are made, the model can be revised to adapt to changing conditions through the process of network reconfiguration. Network reconfiguration enables casual nets to be used naturally to make accurate predictions.

How Does a Bayesian Network Operate?

When evidence is entered into a node in the network, the fundamental rule for probability calculus and Bayes' rule can be used to propagate this evidence through updating the network and observing the probability distributions. Evidence can be propagated from parents to children as well as from children to parents, making Bayesian network more effective for both prediction and diagnosis. The joint probabilities in Bayesian network grow exponentially given two or more states of set of variables. For instance, assuming a binary set of variables with no graphical structure specified, the number of probability values needed to determine the joint probability distribution in a BBN model is 2^n, where n = number of variables. In other words if there are **10** variables in a model, then their joint probability distribution is $2^{10} =$**2048** probability values. But sometimes it is seldom necessary that all these numbers be elicited and stored in the model.

This can be reduced through factorization and exploring independencies among variables through techniques of "explaining away". The notion of "explaining away" suggests that there are two competing causes **A** and **B** which are conditionally dependent given that their common child, **C,** is observed, even though they are marginally independent. For example, suppose the grass is wet, but that we also know that it is raining. Then the posterior probability that the sprinkler is on goes down.

The inherent structure of a Bayesian model can be defined in terms of dependency/independency assumptions between variables and it greatly simplifies the representation of the joint probability distribution capturing any dependencies, independences, conditional independences and marginal independences between variables.

APPLICATION OF BAYESIAN BELIEF NETWORKS

The Bayesian approach to uncertainty has been applied in many areas of artificial intelligence research including pattern recognition, expert systems, medical diagnosis and more recently understanding students and their learning problems in a growing area of applied artificial intelligence commonly referred to as artificial intelligence in education. Perhaps the best-known example of the application of Bayesian approach in business is Microsoft's Office Assistant, which appears as an anthropomorphic paper-clip. Microsoft Office Assistant is very popular among novice users but more advance users tend to find it irritating and annoying.

When a user calls up the assistant, Bayesian methods are used to analyze recent user's actions in order to try to work out what the user is attempting to do, with this calculation constantly being modified in the light of new actions. For example, opening up a word process sometimes triggers the Office Assistant to inquire whether the user is attempting to write a letter. In general terms Bayesian Beliefs are used in the following areas of business and social systems:

- Selecting loan opportunities with low default risk
- Understanding the stock market
- Medical diagnostic systems
- Determining whether certain marriage will last for lifetime
- Intel processor fault diagnosis.
- Generator monitoring expert system
- Troubleshooting printers
- Real-time weapons scheduling in military
- Resolving customer problems via online troubleshooting tools
- Diagnosing and troubleshooting on-site cellular networks in real-time.
- Filtering email to accurately control spam and to highlight critical messages
- Controlling autonomous vehicles and their navigation (wheeled, aquatic, aerospace, and others).
- To determine whether or not an individual qualifies for a life insurance policy

Benefits of Bayesian Belief Network Approach

Through probabilistic reasoning is possible to take rational decisions even if there is limited information. The Bayesian network is a probabilistic model that allows representing the uncertain knowledge in a given domain (of knowledge) in a graphical way.

In choosing a probabilistic approach to modeling, BBNs offer a number of advantages over other methods for the following reasons:

- Bayesian Belief Network models are powerful tools both for graphically representing the relationships among variables and for dealing with uncertainties in expert systems.
- The graphical structure of Bayesian Belief Networks provides a visual method of relating relationships among variables in a simple way.
- In BBNs, a network can be easily refined (i.e. additional variables can be easily added and mapping from the mathematics to common understanding or reference points could be quickly done).
- Overt assumptions in Bayesian models are often made clear.
- Systematic incorporation of previous knowledge
- Probability interpretation of all quantities of interest is much.
- Bayesian models are more intuitive than models based on frequentist approach.
- Ability to update as new data are received.
- Missing data is handled seamlessly as part of estimation.
- Complex models, such as hierarchical linear models, are handled easily.
- Likewise, latent variables are easily incorporated.
- Post-estimation diagnostics can be easily and flexibly conducted.
- BBNs offer an interactive graphical modeling mechanism that researchers can use to understand the behaviour of a system or situation, (e.g., it is possible to add evidence/observe variables and propagate this information throughout the whole graphical model to see/inspect the effects on particular variables of interest).
- The fact that BBN has qualitative and quantitative elements gives it many advantages over other methods.

Limitation of Bayesian Belief Network

Despite the relevance of Bayesian Belief Network, the ideas and techniques have not spread into the social sciences and humanities research communities. Daniel,

Zapata-Revera & McCalla (2007) summarized the main problems, which prevented the wider use of BBN in other domains as follows:

- Building Bayesian Belief Network requires considerable knowledge engineering effort, in which the most difficult part of it is to obtain numerical parameters for the model and apply them in complex, which are the kinds of problems social scientists are attempting to address.
- Constructing a realistic and consistent graph (i.e., the structure of the model) often requires collaboration between knowledge engineers and subject matter experts, which in most cases is hard to establish.
- Combining knowledge from various sources such as textbooks, reports, and statistical data to build models can be susceptible to gross statistical errors and by definition are subjective.
- The graphical representation of a Bayesian Belief Network is the outcome of domain specifications. However, in situations where domain knowledge is insufficient or inaccurate, the model's outcomes are prone to error.
- Acquiring knowledge from subject matter experts can be subjective.
- Finding the prior probability or a threshold weight is often complicated.
- In an event where there are many values representing belief, the nuisance parameters have to be arranged in sequence of importance, even though none of them is of intrinsic interest.
- Even if a parameter of interest changes the whole prior distribution table might change as well as the structure of the model.
- If the sampling rule or design changes in an experiment or the people involved, the prior values of variables generally will change.

Despite the problems outlined above, Bayesian Belief Network still remain a viable modelling approach in many domains, especially domains which are quite imprecise and volatile such as weather forecasting, stock market etc. The Bayesian Belief Network approach help experts and researchers build and explore initial computational models and revise and validate them as more data become available. Further, by providing appropriate tools and techniques, the process of building Bayesian models can be extended to address social issues in other domains in the social sciences and the humanities.

CONCLUSION

Bayesian Networks are directed acyclic graphs with nodes representing random variables and whose arcs represent direct probabilistic dependencies among variables. Each random variable has a set of values that it can take on, such as True or False for binary random variables. Each node in the network with predecessors has an associated Conditional

Conditional probability table (CPT), while nodes without predecessors have prior probabilities. The arcs in the networks show the dependencies amongst variables in the network, rendering nodes either dependent or independent given evidence for a good explanation of independence in Bayesian Networks). The network can be queried at any time to obtain the belief that a given node is a specified value. New evidence can be introduced into the network by setting the values of one or more of the variables in the network to a specific observed value.

A Bayesian belief network uses probability theory to manage uncertainty by explicitly representing the conditional dependencies between the different knowledge components. This provides an intuitive graphical visualization of the knowledge including the interactions among the various sources of uncertainty. A Bayesian model uses Bayesian statistical rules to calculate conditional dependencies among the variables in the network. This allows probabilistically sound propagation of evidence through the network that can be used for making inferences of various sorts about the implications and effects of various actions and events on the model. This chapter presented an overview of Bayesian approach. Those interested in learning more about the technical details of Bayesian statistics are encouraged to refer to the work of Pearl (1988).

REFERENCES

Daniel, B. K., Zapata-Rivera, J. D., & McCalla, G. I. (2007). A Bayesian Belief Network approach for modelling complex domains. In A. Mittal, A. Kassim, & T. Tan (Eds.), *Bayesian network technologies: Applications and graphical models* (pp. 13-41). Hershey, PA: IGI Publishing.

Druzdzel, M. J., & Gaag, L. C. (2000). Building probabilistic networks: Where do the numbers come from? Guest editor's introduction. *Data Engineering, 12*(4), 481-486.

Kononenko, I. (1991). Semi-naive Bayesian classiers. *Proceedings of Sixth European Working Session on Learning.* Springer-Verlag (pp. 206-219).

Fisher, D. (1987). Knowledge Acquisition Via Incremental Conceptual Clustering. *Machine Learning, 2,* 139-172.

Langley, P., Iba, W., & Thompson, K. (1992). An analysis of Bayesian classiers. In *American Asscoaition for Artificial Intelligence.*

Pearl, J. (1985). Bayesian Networks: A Model of Self-Activated Memory for Evidential Reasoning. In *Proceedings of the 7th Conference of the Cognitive Science Society*, University of California, Irvine, CA (pp. 329-334), August 15-17.

Pearl, J. (1988). *Probabilistic reasoning in intelligent systems: Networks of plausible inference.* San Mateo, CA: Morgan Kaufmann.

Pearl, J. (2000). *Causality: Models, Reasoning and Inference.* Cambridge University Press.

Chapter XI
Construction of Bayesian Models

INTRODUCTION

Bayesian Belief Networks (BBNs) are increasingly used for understanding different problems in many domains. Though BBN techniques are elegant ways of capturing uncertainties, knowledge engineering effort required to create and initialize a network has prevented many researchers from using them. Even though the structure of the network and its conditional and initial probabilities could be learned from data, data is not always available and/or too costly to obtain.

Furthermore, current algorithms used to learn relationships among variables, initial and conditional probabilities from data are often complex and cumbersome to employ. A qualitative Bayesian network approach was introduced to address some of the difficulties in building models that mainly depend on quantitative data. Building BBN models from quantitative data presupposes that relationships among variables or concepts of interests are known and can be correlated, causally related or they can relate to each other independently. The interdependency or relationships among the variables enable more reliable inferences, which in turn help in making informed decisions about results of the model.

This chapter presents qualitative techniques and algorithms for creating Bayesian belief network models. It simplifies the construction of Bayesian models in few steps. The goal of the chapter is to introduce the reader to the basic principles underlying the constructions of Bayesian Belief Network.

SIMPLIFYING THE CONSTRUCTION OF BAYESIAN MODELS

For many years the process of constructing Bayesian models remained unattractive to many scientists and researchers. This is due to the complexity of the process involved and the number of expertise required, which typically is a knowledge engineer, a domain expert, a statistician and many others. In addition, the information or knowledge necessary for building Bayesian models might not be easy to obtain, as it sometimes come from more than one source (including technical manuals, test procedures, and empirical data).

Furthermore, at a minimum level, the background needed to build Bayesian models requires expertise in applied statistic and at least a reasonable knowledge of a probability theory and its inner working. The Statistical knowledge required is for initializing or creating baseline reasoning probability numbers for a model. Most of the techniques for obtaining these numbers are quantitatively driven and for the most part quite challenging to obtain.

Most recently qualitative approaches for soliciting baseline reasoning probability numbers for Bayesian models were introduced to reduce the quantitative complexity. Qualitative-based approaches are becoming popular among researchers. For at least a decade, they have helped researchers analyze complex problems and provide guidance/support for decision-making. Using the qualitative approaches, initial Bayesian models are built and are refined once appropriate data is obtained. Wellman (1990) work perhaps is the forerunner in the employment of qualitative methods. He introduced the qualitative abstraction of Bayesian Belief Network known as qualitative Bayesian networks (QBN) to help researchers and knowledge engineers overcome the problems of building a quantitative Bayesian Belief models. In other words, instead of using numerical probability distributions, a qualitative Bayesian Network approach uses the concept of positive and negative influences between variables. It first assumes an ordering relationship between variables. For example, **X** has a positive **(+)** influence on **Z**, if choosing a high probability value of **X** produces higher probability values for **Z**. In a similar way a negative influence between two variables is defined, that is to say if **X** has a negative influence on **Z**, so similarly choosing a negative values for **X** results to negative values for **Z**.

Other researchers who have employed qualitative approach included Druzdzell and Henrion (1993), who proposed qualitative belief propagation as an efficient algorithm for reasoning in qualitative Bayesian Networks. The algorithm builds on research into the studies of verbal protocols of human subjects solving problems involving uncertainty. In qualitative propagation each variable in a network is provided a sign either positive **(+)** or negative **(-)**. The effect of an observation **e** on the **n** variables in a network propagates the sign throughout the network. The qualitative propagation algorithm is useful in situations where hard data are not available or are difficult to obtain (Druzdzell, 1996). In other words, QBN can be used as an appendage or replacement for quantitative approaches for obtaining hard data.

Unlike Frequentist school of Statistics, the Bayesian school of Statistics is based on a different view of what it means to learn Bayesian model structures from data. In the Bayesian perspective probability is used to represent uncertainty about the relationship being learned, a view that is avoided in conventional Frequentist Statistics. In Bayesian Statistics before any data is seen, prior opinions about what the true relationship might be can be expressed in a probability distribution over the network weights that define this relationship. After examining the data or after a computer program looks at the data, the revised opinions are captured by a posterior distribution over network weights. Network weights that seemed plausible before, but which do not match the data very well after data is examined, will now be seen as being much less likely, moreover, the probability for values of the weights that do fit the data well will have increased.

Researchers proposed two approaches for learning BBN models from data. The first is based on constraint-search (Pearl & Verma, 1991) and the second approach uses Bayesian search for graphs with highest posterior probability (Copper & Herskovits, 1992). Although prior probabilities can be obtained from many sources; these sources seldom offer the requirements for the quantitative aspect of the model. As a result several algorithms are required to compute the values needed, most of which are time consuming and difficult to apply in some domains in the social sciences and the humanities and to obtain them requires quantitative techniques.

In addition to QBN methods described above, researchers use simple probability distributions to initialize BNN models. e.g., NOISY-OR and NOISY-AND distributions (Conati et at. 2002), and use numerical and verbal anchors (Van der Gaal, Renooij, S., Witteman, Alema & Taal, 1999) and visualization tools available in many Bayesian network authoring tools. Eliciting probabilities from experts has its own drawbacks. It has been found that experts can exhibit problems such as overconfidence; probability estimates can be adjusted up and down based on an initial estimate (anchoring problem); there can be disagreement among experts; high probability values are often assigned to easy to remember events (availability problem) (Morgan & Henrion, 1990). All these issues can affect the quality of the probabilities elicited.

The methodology described in the book uses both a qualitative and quantitative approach for eliciting knowledge from experts (i.e., structure and initial prior and conditional probabilities) based on the descriptions of the strength of the relationship among variables in a network (Daniel, Zapata-Rivera and McCalla, 2003). This approach takes into account number of the states of a variable, the number of parents, the degree of strength (e.g., strong, medium, weak) and the kind of relationship/influence (e.g., positive or negative influence) to produce initial prior and conditional probability values. Once an initial model is developed, scenarios grounded on empirical analysis are used to refine and document the network.

In contrast to QBN methodology, which is based on particular qualitative propagation algorithms, the methodology in the book uses standard Bayesian propagation algorithms. Further, through inductive reasoning, the methodology enables us to refute, refine, or consolidate hypotheses and prior knowledge about a given situation under study, potentially filling in any missing information. In addition, the initial probabilities can be refined when data becomes available.

CONSTRUCTION PHASES OF A BAYESIAN BELIEF NETWORK

There are three fundamental phases to build Bayesian models. The first phase involves identifying and defining the problem domain, followed by the identification of the relevant variables constituting the problem being modelled. The second phase determines the relationships among the variables and establishing a graphical structure of the model. The third phase is to compute conditional probability values for each variable in the model.

The phases and associated procedures for building Bayesian belief models are graphically described in Figure 11-1. It is fairly common that the first two phases concentrate mainly on defining the problem domain with a goal of expressing the problem in its simplest form. This is often done to reduce the number of probability values in the conditional probability table, which is done in the last phase. The last phase is the most difficult one, requiring sophisticated knowledge engineering techniques to translate data obtained into initial probability values.

Defining a Problem and Purpose

The first phase of creating a Bayesian model is to identify a modeling problem and clearly defining the purpose of the model. Modelling problem come in a variety of forms, they can be embodied in one or better defined questions that we might want to ask or solve. The problems might be quite pragmatic or entirely theoretical and self-reflective or intuitive. For example, a pragmatic modelling problem might be based on what we are trying to solve or understand. A theoretical modeling problem is general intended to generate more knowledge about the hidden behaviours of an existing systems or an object works. We might be interested in understanding how certain phenomenon works and so we can establish a broad purpose (e.g. what are the fundamental components of social capital in a virtual community?).

Figure 11-1. Phases and procedures in building BBN models (Daniel, Zapata-Rivera & McCalla, 2007)

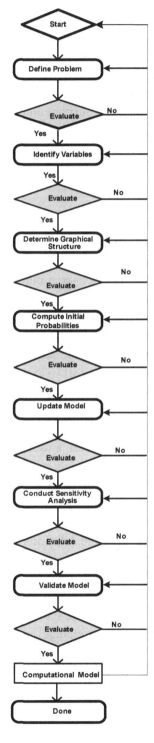

In order to come up with a well defined modeling problem, sometimes we might need to examine few books or articles that touch upon the issues they address, even if we have considerable background experience related to the general area in which they are situated. Researching related books or reports on the subject broadens our knowledge and sometimes refocusing our questions addressing the problem, in the light of issues and discussions we are not yet aware of.

Moreover, once the modelling problem is clearly defined, the next step is to state the purpose of the model. A modelling purpose aims at unleashing what the model is intended to solve. For instance, the purpose of an economic performance model is to make smart predictions about future state of our economy. A meteorology Bayesian model aims at diagnosing weather conditions. The goal of a social capital model is to understand the critical factors necessary for creating and sustaining a virtual community.

Identifying Variables

The definition of variables takes place once a modelling problem is defined and the goals of the model are well established. In a situation where the problem is ill-defined, domain experts in which a problem is situated are consulted. For example, a well defined problem within a field of homecare requires consultation with a homecare nurse, a problem with car engine requires soliciting information from a mechanic, a physician is a domain expert in examining a patient, a banker can be well proficient in analyzing an applicant income situation in order to determine whether or not to grant a loan and a network administrator can be an expert in examining network failure.

Regardless of a domain being modelled, a well defined modelling problem has a number of variables. Variables refer to measurable attributes within a problem domain, they mainly take two forms, discrete as in the number of eyes a normal human being can have and continuous, for instance in measuring a temperature of a person who is scared. In Sciences such as Statistics, Mathematics, and Computer Science, there is much controversy in the definition of a variable though these Sciences generally use variables as container for holding information.

Variables are critical building blocks of a Bayesian model. They are similar to bricks or the foundation stone to builders. The distinction between discrete and continuous variables helps us determine the stability of a model. They tell us more about how much we need to make future changes within a model. In addition, variables determine the scope of a model and limit its predictive power. For example missing an important variable within the social capital might limit its ability to accurately predict the future and consequently rander it irrelevant to the real world settings. In other words, setting wrong variables can produce wrong outcomes, and wrong outcomes are useless.

There are various kinds of variables prevalent in Bayesian models. Some these include; query variables, evidence variables, context variables and controller variables. Query variables or objective variables are those variables that are output of the model; they are what the users of the model want to know about. Evidence variables or observation variables are the variables being manipulated or the target observable variables in the model. Further, context or intermediary variables are those that link the query variables and the evidence variables within a model. The last group of variables, controllable or intervention variables could potentially be used as an intervention to insert information into the modelling process when needed.

Working with experts to elicit knowledge that can be translated into probability involves asking fundamental questions concerning the structure of the graphical model. It involves determining the variables and the causal or direction of the edge of the variables. For instance, does trust affect social capital, is awareness influenced by interactions? Since experts can be vague about their own domain knowledge, it is necessary for the knowledge engineer to verify using alternative methods the accuracy of the information they gather. Another important aspect is to determine the level of reasoning or the level of granularity of the graphical model. In other words, it is necessary to determine whether trust is the most primitive level of granularity in the model and determining how other variables are likely to influence it.

Graphical models need to be compared with competing models or views that could somehow be reconciled into one Bayesian network model. There are also decisions to make regarding conditional and unconditional dependence among variables in a model. This can be achieved through the "divide and conquer" approach to manage complexity or reusing previously encountered Bayesian patterns in different domains.

Establishing a Graphical Structure

A Bayesian Model is represented as a graph and a graph is composed of variables with explicit or implicit causal relationships or links. Determining causal relationships among variables requires in a graph, isolating the main variables and sub-variables within the problem domain using qualitative reasoning. This can be either grounded in research, personal experience or intuition.

Model builders sometimes use questions to come up with causal relationships among variables. They ask simple questions such as; does a person's appearance tell us more about his reasoning ability? Does a positive teacher's expectation of a student's performance increase student's performances? Does more education mean more money? Increasingly, causal questions similar to the indicated here are the basis of many Bayesian models. For a Bayesian Modeller, it is very important to ask valid causal questions and to clearly establish causal links among variables in the model. Other modellers depend on domain experts for developing causal relationships. These include asking experts questions such as: what can cause variable **X** to take on state **T**? For instance, what can cause communication to breakdown between two culturally diverse groups? Others involved using one's expert knowledge to analyze a particular domain and identify variables of interest. Sometimes involving reviewing existing knowledge and identifying relevant variables on domain of interest and running confirmatory studies.

Identifying variables of interest within a well defined domain and establishing causal relationships among them leads to the construction of a graphical representation of the problem being modelled. In constructing the graphical representation, it is necessary to specify the parameters of the model and keep the causal relationship between variables tractable.

Generating Initial Probabilities

Developing a conditional probability table is the most difficult part of the modelling process. It requires coming up with initial probability values for each of the state of each of the variables in the model. This means if we have more variables in a model, we need an equivalent number of initial probabilities assigned to all the various states the variables can take. For example, a variable with two states of good and bad requires two probability values representing good and bad. In other words, the more variables we have, the more we need to come up with those initial probability values—a Bayesian model depicts an exponential growth in its probability values given increase in the number of variables.

Gathering initial probability values from domain experts is the most common practice. However, others have reported a number of problems with this approach. For example, domain experts sometimes exhibit problems such as overconfidence; probability estimates can be adjusted up and down based on an initial estimate leading to what is generally referred to as "anchoring problem". There can be disagreements among experts; high probability values are often assigned to easy to remember events referred to as "availability problem" (Morgan & Henrion, 1990). All these problems affect the quality of the probabilities gathered from experts. These problems are overcome by using special probability distributions technique known as NOISY-OR and NOISY-AND distributions (Conati et al. 2002). Other researchers have used numerical and verbal and visualization tools available to refine initial probabilities provided by domain experts.

Process for Querying the Model

The mechanism for drawing conclusions in Bayesian network is based on propagation of probabilities through the network achieved through querying a network. As evidence is entered into the model through the observable variables, the effects of this evidence can be propagated using the rules of Bayesian probability through to the output variables. This is termed "querying the Bayesian network". It is sometimes the case that a Bayesian network contains many variables each of which can be relevant for some kind of reasoning but rarely are all variables relevant for all kinds of reasoning at once. Therefore, it is often necessary to identify a subset of the model that is relevant for reasoning in a particular situation. Such a decision can be made based on some qualitative inferences from real world data using scenarios to query the relevant part of the network (Daniel, McCalla & Schwier, 2005; Zapata-Rivera, 2002).

Druzdzell and Suemondt (1994) suggest that one way of querying a network is to instantiate variables to their observed values. Some evidence suggests the presence of other evidence (e.g., when a computer boots it implies it is on, which will also indicate there is electricity or the battery is filled up). Lin and Druzdzel (1998) use a reduction method through variables instantiation rendering some variables as d-separated and hence, can reduce computational complexity. Since it is necessary to construct accurate models, it is also important that the data used for training the network are reliable and that the model is stable and capable of predicting and reflecting real world situations. Further, since any measurement often has an element of imprecision associated with it, it is expected that probabilities of events obtained through measurement cannot always be precise. In such cases reliance on approximation of probabilities is important.

Process for Updating Bayesian Models

Constructing and updating a Bayesian model is a complex task since there are numerous underlying variables that are not necessarily obvious. Once a Bayesian network has been constructed and initial conditional probability tables have been generated by training on prior data, the network is ready for the introduction of external evidence based on sensor observations.

Upon the introduction of external evidence, those nodes representing sensor observations are forced to take on a specific value while the remaining nodes must adjust their own "belief" (probability of being in each of the potential states) in order to remain consistent with the new evidence. It is these updated beliefs that will be observed and relied upon as the output of the process monitoring and diagnosis system. One way to facilitate model construction and updating is to develop scenarios illustrating various events, based on either directly obtained evidence or an expert's knowledge. A scenario can generally be described as a set of written stories or synopsis of acts in stories built around carefully constructed events.

In a scientific and technical sense a scenario describes a vision of a future state of a situation, object or a system. Such a description can be based on current assessment of the system or data describing a system—the variables and assumptions, and the likely interaction between system variables in the progression from current conditions to a future state. Scenarios provide simple, intuitive, examples based upon descriptions of the patterns of interactions between two or more variables of interest. They can be developed based on observation of interactions among people in a virtual community.

CONCLUSION

Bayesian networks are directed acyclic graphs in which each node represents a random variable that can take on two or more discrete values. The arcs in the network signify the existence of direct causal influences between the linked variables, and the strengths of these influences are quantified by conditional probabilities. The directionality of the arrows is essential for displaying causality and non-transitive dependencies. The causal relationships expressed through the network structure are based on prior knowledge, experience, or statistically observed correlations.

Each variable has distinct states or levels that signify the values that the particular node can take. A Bayesian network must be an acyclic graph, although it may be multiply connected. Each node is associated with a conditional probability table that defines probabilities for the different states of the node given the states of the parents. Bayesian approach to modelling is distinct from other statistical approaches in that it explicitly uses probability theory to quantify uncertainty of inferences. It makes clear the acceptance (embrace) of subjective probability and an explicit use of prior information, beliefs, theory in specification of models. The Bayesian approach also makes an explicit rule for incorporating new data in the updating of beliefs.

The modeling process in BBNs requires capturing domain concepts, variables and their associated prior probability values, as well as building a graphical representation of the variables of the domain being modeled. The role of graphs in probabilistic modeling in BBNs provides a convenient means of expressing substantial assumptions, and graphs facilitate economical representation of a joint probability function to enhance making efficient inferences from observations.

One of the most challenging tasks of building Bayesian models is obtaining prior information or data for populating the model. A way of doing this is to consult with domain experts. When working with experts to elicit knowledge that can be translated into probability involves asking fundamental questions concerning the structure of the graphical model. It involves determining the variables and the causal or direction of the edge of the variables. For instance, does trust affect social capital, is awareness influenced by engagement? Since experts can be vague about their own domain knowledge, it is necessary for the knowledge engineer to verify knowledge elicited using alternative methods the accuracy of the information they gather.

This is normally done through surveys or consultation of documents. Another important aspect is to determine the level of reasoning or the level of granularity of the graphical model. In other words, it is necessary to determine whether trust is the most primitive level and that other variables that are likely to influence trust are least important.

Graphical models need to be compared with competing models/views that could somehow be reconciled into one BN model at all. There are also decisions to make regarding conditional and unconditional dependence among the nodes in the model. This can be achieved through the "divide and conquer" approach to manage complexity or reusing previously encountered BN patterns be reused in different domains. The qualitative Bayesian network approach was introduced to address some of the difficulties in building models that mainly depend on quantitative data. Building BBN models from quantitative data presupposes that relationships among variables or concepts of interests are known and can be correlated, causally related or they can relate to each other independently.

REFERENCES

Conati, C., Gertner, A., & VanLehn, K. (2002). Using bayesian networks to manage uncertainty in student modeling. *User Modeling and User-Adapted Interaction, 12*(4), 371–417.

Cooper, G. F., & Herskovits, E. (1992). A Bayesian Method for the Induction of Probabilistic Networks from Data. *Machine Learning, 9*(4), p.309-347.

Daniel, B. K., McCalla, G. I., & Schwier, R. A. (2005). Data mining and modeling social capital in virtual learning communities. *Proceedings of the 12th International Conference on Artificial Intelligence in Education*, Amsterdam, 18-22 July, 2000-2008.

Daniel, B. K., Zapata-Rivera, J. D. & McCalla, G. I. (in press2007). A Bayesian Belief Network Approach for Modelling Complex Domains. In A. Mittal, A. Kassim, & T. Tan (Eds.), *Bayesian Network Technologies: Applications and Graphical Models. Hershey*: Idea Group.

Druzdzel, M. (1996). Qualitative verbal explanations in bayesian belief networks. *Artificial Intelligence and Simulation of Behaviour Quarterly, 9*(4), 43-54.

Druzdzel, M. J. & Henrion, M. (1993). Efficient reasoning in qualitative probabilistic Networks. *AAAI* (pp. 548-553).

Druzdzel, M. J., & Suermondt, H. J. (1994). Relevance in probabilistic models: „backyards" in a small world. *The AAAI-94 Fall Symposium on Relevance.*

Gutwin, C., & Greenberg, S. (1998). Design for individuals, design for groups: Tradeoffs between power and workspace awareness. *Proceedings of the ACM Conference on Computer Supported Cooperative Work* (pp. 207-216), ACM Press.

Lin, Y., & Druzdzel, M. J. (1999). Relevance-based incremental belief updating in Bayesian networks. *International Journal of Pattern Recognition and Artificial Intelligence (IJPRAI), 13*(2), 285-295.

Morgan, M. G., & Henrion, M. (1990). *Uncertainty: A Guide to Dealing with Uncertainty in Quantitative Risk and Policy Analysis*. Cambridge, UK: Cambridge University Press.

Pearl, J., & Verma, T. (1991). A theory of inferred causation: Principles of knowledge representation and reasoning, in Representation and Reasoning. *Proceedings of the Second International Conference*. San Mateo, CA: Morgan Kaufmann.

Wellman, M. P. (1990). Fundamental concepts of qualitative probabilistic networks. *Artificial Intelligence, (44), 257-303.*

Zapata-Rivera. J. D. (2002). cbCPT: Knowledge engineering support for CPTs in Bayesian networks. *Canadian Conference on AI*, (pp. 368-370).

Van der Gaag, L. C., Renooij, S., Witteman, C., Aleman, B. M. P., & Taal, B. G. (1999). How to elicit many probabilities. *Proceedings of Incertainty in Artificial Intelligence* (pp.647-654), UI99.

Section IV
Computational Model of Social Capital

One of the main problems in computational social science, and the humanities, is to realistically and practically develop theoretical frameworks that explain social or human behavioural systems. Modelling social and human systems and it provides potentials for describing and understanding complex systems at a low costs and minimum risk. Currently, Artificial Intelligence researchers have done a great deal of work on building sophisticated models of social systems. Already this effort is being extended to researchers and practitioners interested in studying the dynamics of human activity via the use of computation in discussions over complex versus simple agents. Modelling social capital helps address some of the previous attempts aimed at coming with concrete indicators for measuring social capital.

Section IV presents the last 4 chapters of the book. The section mainly discusses the computational model of social capital. This involves the description of the process involved in building it and critical decisions made at each stage are discussed. Chapter XII presents the model of social capital, beginning with the identification of important components of social capitals, followed by the graphical representation of these components and the initial values assigned to the variables representing the components of social capital. Chapter XII also presents insights and procedures for conducting sensitivity analysis, of Bayesian models, illustrating example of social capital model are presented in Chapter XIII. In Chapter XIV the importance doing Bayesian model validation is discussed, this is followed by discussion on examples drawn from social capital model. Chapter XV concludes the book. In this last chapter, key issues that matter to researchers on social capital are presented. It is also here in this chapter that the main limitations of the book are outlined.

Chapter XII
A Computational Model
of Social Capital

INTRODUCTION

This chapter presents the Bayesian Belief computational model of social capital developed within the context of virtual communities discussed in chapter VII. The development of the model was based on insights drawn from research. The chapter presents the key variables constituting social capital in virtual communities and shows how the model was created and updated. The scenarios described in the chapter were authentic cases drawn from several virtual communities. The key issues predicted by the model as well as challenges encountered in building, verifying and updating the model are discussed. The ultimate goal of the chapter is to share experiences in developing a model of social capital and to encourage the reader to think about how such experiences can be extended to model similar constructs or build more scenarios to update the model. The model presented in the chapter is a proof-of-a concept and a demonstration of a procedure. Notwithstanding that some of the model's predictions are accurate while others require more substantial empirical corroboration.

FUNDAMENTAL COMPONENTS OF SOCIAL CAPITAL

In the review of current and past work on social capital as presented in previous chapters, it is evident that there are fundamentally numerous variables constituting social capital, some of which can be extended to virtual communities while others are limited to place-based communities. Examining the various definitions, it was apparent that some of definitions have shared variables. The shared variables are the loci for building the model of social capital in virtual communities, in addition to variables (e.g. different types of awareness), which are more specific to the context of virtual communities. The definitions with shared variables referred to social capital as a function of positive engagement or engagement. It suggests that when people engage in positive engagement on issues of mutual concerns, they are more likely to get to know one another and together, they can derive value from positive engagement. Typically, engagement involves sharing of personal experiences with others, endorsing positive behaviour or discouraging negative one, sharing information, recommending resources, and providing companionship and hospitality.

An attitude in Psychology simply refers to a state of mind or a feeling. It is a disposition often manifested in explicit behavioural tendencies. In other words, an attitude arises from attempts to account for observed regularities in the behaviour of individual persons. For example, one can have an impression about someone as trustworthy, warm, emotional or scary. Such an impression can used to build an attitude and the attitude externalised into observerable behaviour though some attitudes are best kept inside the individual. People can hold complex relationships with other people, the environments and the world around them based on their attitudes and their behavioural tendencies. In almost everything we do, attitude and behaviour are intertwined into the fabric of our daily life. Attitude has been a central topic of Behavioural Psychologists. Much of the work on the attitude tend revolve around two schools of thoughts. One school of thought believes that people are born into the world with certain inherited biological attitudes; emotional tendencies such as anger, patience etc. Another school of thought believes that attitudes are learned from others, the environments or experiences, they are socialized or enculturalised to individuals. For examples, religious social systems that tend to educate calmness, patience and forgiveness to their followers are typical examples in this regard. Regardless of any school of thought, people can form attitudes almost instantaneously at their first encounter with certain individuals. It follows that some of the attitudes formed in a first encounter last for a long time and in fact, they become permanently inculcated within individuals to an extent that they become basis for establishing the order of social relationships.

Irrespective of how an attitude is manifested, a person's attitude can directly affect the way they interact with other people and their ability to carry out productive engagement, which is central to building social capital. Productive engagement crucial to building social capital does not automatically happen, rather it occurs when people have a common set of expectations that are mediated by a set of shared social protocols. It also takes place when people are willing to identify with each other as members of one community.

Shared understanding is another key component of social capital. Similar to engagement, shared understand represents amicable platform for smooth interaction and engagement. It is also achieved when people are willing to interact with each other long enough to identify shared attributes, understand the language and symbolic representation of the community and effectively resolve any differences that are detrimental to communication and engagement in the community they belong.

The process involved in establishing shared understanding in any community often draws upon a set of shared beliefs, shared goals and values, experiences and knowledge. Within the context of virtual communities, shared understanding is enhanced by various forms of awareness, for example, when people become aware of each other, they identify shared interests which are basis for establishing shared understanding. In an event of possible disagreement, resolution can be achieved through effective negotiation mechanisms. This argument is substantiated by research in computer-supported collaborative learning, which asserted that meaning is constructed by social interaction until people share a common understanding (Stahl, 2000). In addition, shared understanding can be achieved from interpersonal interaction whereas individual understanding is achieved only from intrapersonal activities. In addition, for many years, researchers in Human Computer Interactions have established that awareness is critical to effective interactions and productive social relationships in virtual settings (Gutwin, at al., 1998).

Awareness can also help in enforcing productive engagement. Moreover, maintaining different forms of awareness in a virtual community can lubricate and increase the value of engagement and possibly increase shared understarding. In other words, in a virtual community, people need to be aware of the people they are interacting with. They want to know where others are located (demographic awareness) and what they are up to (activity awareness. In more professional settings or in distributed communities of practice, people are often curious of what others do for living or are interested in (professional awareness), what others know (knowledge awareness) or what they are able to do (capability awareness) (Daniel, Sarkar & O'Brien, 2003).

In addition to engagement, interaction, attitudes, shared understanding and various types of awareness, trust is another critical ingredient and component of social capital. In many instances, trust acts as an accelerating lever to almost many forms of social interactions whether online or in face-to-face settings. Trust enables people to work together, collaborate and smoothly exchange information and share knowledge without time worsted on negotiations (Cohan & Prusak, 2000). Trust can also be treated as an outcome of positive attitudes among individuals in a community. Further, in virtual communities, trust can only be created and sustained when individuals are provided with an environment that can support different forms of awareness.

Table 12-1 summarises the components of social capital in virtual communities.

These variables serve as basic components of social capital in virtual communities. In Bayesian modelling, once variables are identified, the second step is to map the variables (see Figure 12-1) into a graphical structure based on solid qualitative reasoning. In particular, the knowledge of the structure of the model and the qualitative reasoning of the causal relationships among variables were grounded in research into social capital and virtual communities (Daniel, McCalla & Schwier, 2005; Zapata-Rivera & McCalla, 2007)). For example, in previous research, Daniel, Zapata-Revera and McCalla (2007) observed that people's attitudes in virtual learning communities can strongly influence the level of their engagement with each other and consequently their ability to know various issues about themselves. Such information was viewed to be influential in building trusting relationships.

According to Bayesian Belief Network principles, causal relationships among variables (see Figure 12-1), is shown by the direction of the arrow. For example in our case attitudes influence different forms of awareness and the strength of the

Table 12-1. Social capital variables and their definitions

VARIABLE NAME	VARIABLE DEFINITION	VARIABLE STATES
Attitudes	Individuals' general perception about each other and others' actions and beliefs.	*Positive/Negative*
Shared Understanding	A mutual agreement/consensus between two or more agents about the meaning of an object or idea.	*High/Low*
Knowledge Awareness	Knowledge of people, tasks, or environment and or all of the above.	*Present/Absent*
Demographic Awareness	Knowledge of an individual: country of origin, language and location.	*Present/Absent*
Professional Awareness	Knowledge of people's background training, affiliation etc.	*Present/Absent*
Engagement	An extended period of interaction between two or more people that goes beyond exchange of words but important and meaningful social connections.	*positive/negative*
Social protocols	The mutually agreed upon, acceptable and unacceptable ways of behaviour in a community.	*Present/Absent*
Trust	A particular level of certainty or confidence with which an agent use to assess the action of another agent.	*High/Low*

influence suggest strongly positive relationship among the variables. Further, since awareness can contribute to both trust and distrust the strength of the relationships is set to medium positive, medium weak, etc. Depending on the type of the awareness, demographic awareness is set at positive influence, with a medium effect on trust, meaning that it is more likely that people will trust others regardless of their demographic backgrounds and in fact this is the case with distributed communities of practice. This type of qualitative reasoning suggests that nodes (variables) that contribute to higher nodes align themselves in "child" to "parent" relationships, where parent nodes are super-ordinate to child nodes (e.g. trust is the child of shared understanding; different forms of awareness and social protocols, which are in turn children of interaction and attitudes).

The graph (Figure 12-1) presented here relates to the context of only two kinds of virtual communities (virtual learning community and distributed community of practice as described in chapter VII). This graph topology enables one to run different forms of experiments, with results only interpreted within the evidences used and communities described. After the development of a Bayesian graph, the third stage is to obtain initial probability values to populate the graph (network). Initial probabilities can be obtained from different sources but in the Bayesian modeling practice, sometimes obtaining accurate initial numbers that can yield valid and meaningful posteriors (resulting probability values) is a difficult undertaking. Nonetheless, the approach presented in the book is intended to simplify the procedure but it entails a great deal of cross validation and tuning of the model over a period of time against various new evidences.

Figure 12-1. Graphical model of social capital

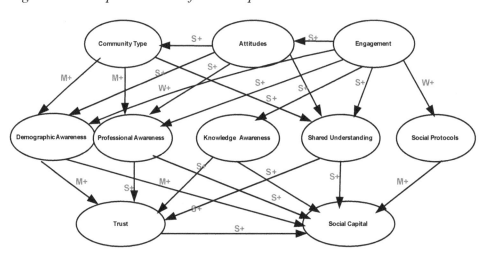

Computing Conditional Probabilities

In construction of any Bayesian network model, every stage of situation assessment requires assigning initial probabilities to the hypotheses made or the assumptions driving the construction of the model. In a typical situation, initial probabilities are obtained from knowledge of a particular situation prevailing at a particular time. However, converting a state of knowledge to probability values is a challenge facing Bayesian Modellers and if not accurately done it can result to models that are inadequate and in some cases invalid. In this book, the initial conditional probabilities for the social capital model were obtained by examining qualitative descriptions of the influence between two or more variables. Each probability value describes strength of relationships and the letters **S (strong)**, **M (medium)**, and **W (weak)** represent different degrees of influence among the variables in the model are (Daniel, Zapata-Rivera & McCalla, 2003). The signs + and - represent positive and negative relationships among the variables.

Once the initial probabilities were determined, a fully specified joint probability distribution was computed. In the process, each node, **X** (where **X** implies any variable in the graph), the probability distribution for **X** conditional upon **X**'s parents was specified. Moreover, the criterion used to obtain the conditional probability values was based on adding weights to the values of the variables depending on the number of parents and the strength of the relationship between the parents and the children. For example, Attitudes and Engagement have positive and strong **(S+)** relationships with Knowledge Awareness; the evidence of positive engagement and positive attitudes, produce a conditional probability value for Knowledge Awareness **0.98** (a threshold value for strong = **0.98**).

These weights were obtained by subtracting a base value **(1 / number of states**, **0.5** in this case) from the threshold value associated to the degree of influence and dividing the result by the number of parents **(i.e. (0.98 - 0.5) / 2 = 0.48 / 2 = 0.24)**, this follows the fact that in the graph Knowledge awareness is a child of both interactions and attitudes. Table 12-2, shows the threshold values and weights used in this example. Since it is more likely that no situation is exhaustive and perfect, i.e. a certain degree of uncertainty might exist, the value $\alpha = $ **0.02** leaves some room for uncertainty, considering evidence coming from positive and strong relationships among variables. These threshold values can be adjusted based on new evidence or expert opinion.

Using this approach it is possible to generate conditional probability tables (CPTs) for each node (variable) regardless of the number of parents and this immensely simplifies the complexity of constructing models based on partial knowledge of a domain (Zapata-Rivera, 2002). Of course the accuracy of this approach is dependent on how the consistency, coherence and validity of the initial knowledge gathered

Table 12-2. Threshold values and weights with two parents

Degree of influence	Thresholds	Weights
Strong	1-α = 1 - 0.02 = 0.98	(0.98-0.5) / 2 = 0.48 / 2 = 0.24
Medium	0.8	(0.8-0.5) / 2 =0.3 / 2 = 0.15
Weak	0.6	(0.6-0.5) / 2 =0.1 / 2 = 0.05

from experts and the decisions the knowledge engineer makes to transform the knowledge gathered into initial probabilities.

Selecting Variables for Reasoning

A Bayesian model can contain many variables each of which can be relevant for some kind of reasoning but rarely are all variables in a Bayesian model relevant for all kinds of reasoning at once. To make models practical and useful, researchers need to identify a subset of variables in a model that is relevant to their needs. In other words, it is sometimes the case that the modeller only enters evidence to few variables in order to observe changes in certain variables. In general, the mechanism for drawing conclusions in Bayesian models is based on probability propagation of evidence. Probability propagation refers to model updating based upon known set of evidence entered into the model. Probability propagation is normally carried out through querying a Bayesian model. Querying a Bayesian model refers to a process of updating the conditional probability table and making inferences based on new evidence entered into a model. There are several ways to update a model, one which is to develop a detailed number of scenarios that can be used to query the model.

A scenario can generally be described as a set of written stories or synopsis of acts in stories built around carefully constructed events. It is a written synopsis of inferences drawn from observed phenomenon or empirical data. In scientific and technical sense a scenario describes a vision of the future state of a system. Such a description can be based on current assessment of the system, of the variables and assumptions, and the likely interaction between system variables in the progression from current conditions to a future state (Collion, 1989).

Druzdzel and Henrion (993) described a scenario as an assignment of values to those variables in Bayesian network which are relevant for a certain conclusion, ordered in such a way that they form a coherent story—a causal story which is compatible with the evidence of the story. The use of scenarios as an approach in updating Bayesian network models is based on psychological research (Pennington & Hastie, 1988). This research shows that humans tend to interpret and explain any social situation by weighing the most credible stories to test and understand social phenomena.

In order to update the model presented in the book, scenarios were developed underlying various events based on either evidence or an expert's knowledge. These scenarios were intended to test and tune the model over time. The construction and presentation of the scenarios followed an approach which is at best described as "a scenario-based modelling". A scenario-based modeling in this context is essentially a set of procedures for describing specific sequences of behaviours within a model representing actual interactions within a virtual community. The goal is to understand and explain the interactions of variables or set of events within a model and how these might possible influence direction of interaction patterns, and subsequently the level of social capital within a community. A single scenario described a possible given state of interactions as were they might have happened or implied in a community, and upon its implementation possible alternative explanations are provided to describe the current and future behaviours of a model.

Scenario based modelling is a powerful approach for updating initial Bayesian Models. While a hypothesis normally refers to a set of unproven ideas, beliefs, and arguments, a scenario can describe proven states of events, which can be used to understand future changes within a model. When several scenarios are used together to describe possible outcomes of events within a model, they can exceed the power of predictions based on a single hypothesis or a set of propositions drawn from a single data set.

In scenario based modelling, the outcomes of the events might be further act as basis for generating a set of hypothesis. These hypotheses can then be used to understand a specific situation within a model. Moreover, the results of a scenario and hypothesis can be combined to further refine the consistency and accuracy of a model. However, for a scenario-based approach to be useful the scenarios created within any particular evidence or data sets must be plausible and internally consistent.

In the book, the scenario-based modeling in Bayesian Belief network model of social capital provides alternative explanations to particular changes in variables and their effects on a particular community. The use of a scenario-based approach to query a model also offers with a common vocabulary and an effective basis for communicating complex and sometimes paradoxical conditions. In the context of this book, this provides opportunity for incorporating strategies from qualitative perspectives and to avoid the potential for any sharp discontinuities between quantitative and qualitative approaches.

Case Scenarios

During the process of updating the Bayesian model, various evidences were collected and compiled as scenarios to simplify the process and to enhance clarity of the stories. Although the stories presented here are authentic and taken from real world virtual communities, these scenarios are intended only to emulate but not to replace experimental data. They were intended only to illustrate the process of updating an initial Bayesian model. However, it is assumed that likely that the results of the model predictions could change much, in the face of empirical data.

Case 1: A Virtual Learning Community of Graduate Students

Community **A** was a formal virtual learning community of graduate students learning fundamental concepts and philosophies of E-Learning. The members of this community were drawn from diverse cultural backgrounds and different professional training.

In particular, participants were practising teachers teaching in different domains at secondary and primary schools levels. Some individuals in the community had extensive experiences with educational technologies, while others were novices but had extensive experience in classroom pedagogy. These individuals were not exposed to each other before and thus were not aware of each other's talents and experiences.

Since the community was a formal one, there was a formalized discourse structure and the social protocols for interactions were explained to participants in advance. The social protocols required different forms of interactions including posting messages, critiquing others, providing feedback to others' postings, asking for clarifications etc. As the interactions progressed in this community, intense disagreements were observed in the community. Individuals began to disagree more on the issues under discussion and there was a little shared understanding among the participants in most of the discourse. Given the description of this scenario, one wonders about the faith of social capital in this community?

Case 2: A Distributed Community of Practice of Software Engineers

Community **B** was a distributed community of practice for software engineers who gathered to discuss issues around software development. The main goals of this community were to facilitate exchange of information, and knowledge and for members to provide peer-support to each other in the community. Members of this community shared common concerns. Membership skills in this community varied, ranging from highly experienced software developers to novice computer programmers. In addition, members were globally distributed and come from diverse and different organisations, including researchers at University and software support groups.

After a considerable period of interaction, individuals were exposed to each other long enough to trust each other and started exchanging personal information among themselves. It was also observed that individuals offered a lot of help to each other throughout their interactions. Though no formal social protocols were explained to the participants, members interacted as if there were social protocols guiding their interactions. Further, there were no visible roles of community leaders. In this highly professional community, with no visible social protocols and limited prior exposure, members were able to initiate useful interaction and trust each other to an extent of exchanging sensitive personal information. The most interesting question is whether or not the presence or absence of social capital played a role.

Case 3: A Distributed Community of Practice of Programmers

Community **C** consisted of a group of individuals learning fundamentals of programming in Java. It was an open community whose members were geographically distributed and had diverse demographic backgrounds and professional cultures. They did not personally know each other; they used different aliases from time to time while interacting in the community. Diverse programming experiences, skills and knowledge were also observed among the participants. It was interesting to observe that though these individuals did not know each other in advance, they were willing to offer help and to support each other in learning Java. Though there were no formal social protocols of interaction, individuals interacted as if there were clear set social protocols to be followed in the community. Can it be possible that the high spirit of community collaboration and peer-support are attributed to underlying power of social capital? How can one determine if social capital of this community is indeed high given the observed description of events?

Case 4: A Distributed Community of Practice of Biomedical and Clinicians

This case for community **D** is extracted from a recent phenomenon observed within the health system research. The continuous demand for understanding of complex human diseases, the solutions to chronic diseases and preventative measures will most likely lie within many disciplines with the biomedical sciences and clinicians, all coming together to participate in a distributed community of practice. Increasing complexity of clinical problems and the difficulty to engage all health professionals to do research, coupled with failure to rapidly move research into new clinical approaches, procedures and technologies have created a need for new approaches to clinical research, practice and policy interface. The hallmark of these new approaches is embedded in the conceptual understanding of the framework of distributed communities of practice, with members operating as an interdisciplinary unit, drawing membership from nurses, clinicians, policy analysts and academic researchers to move research findings into patient care.

Members of this community are highly distributed in terms of both epistemological stances towards addressing health problems as well as the organizations in which they work. And so for them to effectively work together, it is imperative that knowledge required for solving problems draw from theories, concepts or models that are integral of two or more disciplines. It is also required that methods of problem solving need to be developed from multiple perspectives. Throughout the collaborative process, shared understanding and awareness of what people could bring to the table were definitely some of crucial factors that could leverage collaboration in this community. Though diversity as seen in this community brings rich and diverse views, methods, approaches and procedures enriches problem solving, are difficult to enforce due to lack of shared understanding. In this unique distributed community of practice what happens to social capital?

Updating the Model

The scenarios described above all represent typical situations where the model can be applied in real world settings. In updating the initial Bayesian model of social capital, each case scenario was analysed looking for various evidence regarding the impact of individual variables in the model. Once a piece of evidence was added to the model, typically through tweaking a state of one or more variables (i.e. observing a particular state of a variable) or a process commonly known as variable initialisation, the model was updated and results were propagated to the rest of variables in the Bayesian model. This process generated a set of new marginal probabilities for the variables in the model. In the four case scenarios, the ultimate purpose was to observe changes in probability values for trust and social capital.

The outcomes of the model prediction were limited to the nature of the cases described in the chapter. It is important to note that these cases themselves represent general characteristics of virtual communities, and were not directly based on empirical evidence. However, this was an important exercise, with outcomes intended to train the model and prepare fruitful grounding for conducting empirical experiments to further validate the model. This exercise in Bayesian modelling helps experts to examine their beliefs about domain being modelled and the accuracy of the knowledge representation scheme. The whole endeavour therefore, serves as an interactive tool that enables experts to create a probabilistic model, simulate scenarios and reflect on the results of the predictions.

Community A

Community **A** is a virtual learning community (Community Type = VLC.) Based on the case description, shared understanding was set to low and professional knowledge awareness set to "does not exist". Individuals in this community were familiar with their geographical diversity and so demographic awareness was set to "exists". Further, there was well-established formal set of social protocols and so social protocols were initiated to "known". Figure 12-2 shows the Bayesian model and the posterior probabilities after the evidence from the scenario described in community A were added (see shaded nodes/variables).

The results of the predictions showed a high level of trust (P (Trust=*high*)=41.0%) and corresponding high probability level of SC (P (SC=*high*)=36.2%). These values were relatively low. Several explanations were provided for the drop in the levels of social capital and trust. First, there was an observed negative interaction in the community, which might have eventually negatively affected the level engagement. Second, there was lack of shared understanding which might have negatively skewed the level of trust and consequently social capital, since; social capital is directed influenced by trust. It was also possible that negative interactions and negative attitudes, negatively affected the levels of task knowledge awareness and individual capability awareness.

Figure 12-2. Community A showing updated probabilities

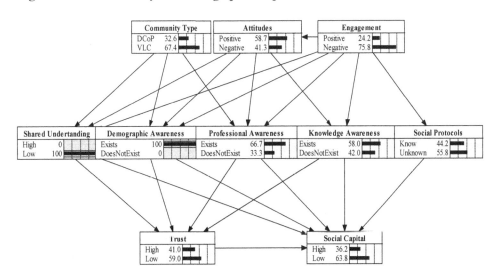

Community B

The variables observed in the scenario described in community **B** included community type that was initiated to distributed community of practice (DCoP); professional awareness set to *"exists"*. It was observed that individuals in this community became aware of their individual talents and skills after some form of interactions, so knowledge awareness was set to *"exists"*. Further, individuals in this community shared common concerns and frame of references; subsequently shared understanding was set to *high*. Figure 12-3 showed the Bayesian model after evidence was added (shaded nodes).

Propagating the evidence showed high levels of trust and SC (P (Trust=*high*) =93.1 % and P (SC=*high*) = 74%). It was also observed that interactions and attitudes had positively influenced demographic cultural awareness and social protocols. Further, the presence of shared understanding and the high degrees of different types of awareness and explicit exposition of social protocols in the community, contributed to the rise in the levels of trust and social capital.

In spite of the evidence entered, demographic cultural awareness has little influence on the level of trust in this community; as a result social capital was not significantly affected. This was attributed to the fact that professionals in most cases are likely to cherish their professional identity more than their demographic backgrounds. This is in line with a previous study, which suggested most people in distributed communities of practice mainly build and maintain social relations

Figure 12-3. Community B showing updated probabilities

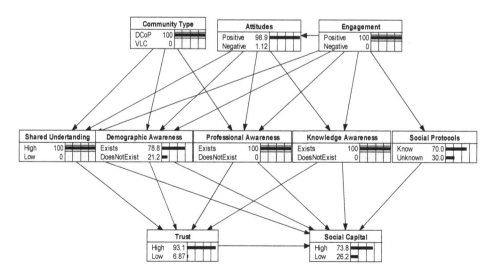

based on common concerns other than geographical distribution (Daniel, O'Brien & Sarkar, 2003).

Community C

The variables extracted from this case scenario included community type (*VLC*), shared understanding, professional awareness, demographic awareness, knowledge awareness which were all set to *exists*. Figure 12-4 shows the Bayesian model after the evidence from community C has been added (shaded nodes) and propagated through the model.

The results showed high levels of trust and SC (P (Trust=high) =92.7 % and P (SC=high) =78.4 %). The high levels of trust and social capital were attributed to the fact that the community was based on an explicit and focused domain. Though members might have participated anonymously, they were positively interacting with each other and vibrantly participated in order to learn the domain. Further the observed increase in the levels of trust and social capital was attributed to the presence of shared understanding. In other words, people in that community were able to get along well with each other, since they used the same frame of reference and have common goals of learning a domain (Java programming language).

Figure 12-4. Community C showing updated probabilities

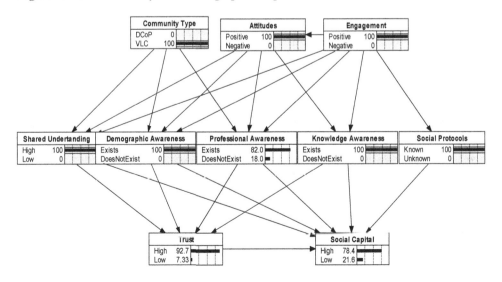

Community D

Community D showed all the features of a distributed community of practice as described in chapter VII. This community had an explicit identified need for collaboration across domains. It occurred that social capital would be a good tool to understand the platform needed to forge collaboration. However most of the variables critical to the development of social capital as identified in the beginning of the chapter were lacking. Consequently variables critical for collaboration within distributed communities of practice such as shared understanding were set to low, social protocols not observed, professional and knowledge awareness were similarly all set to low. The results are shown in Figure 12-5.

After the evidence was entered the results of the model's prediction revealed considerably low level of trust (P (Trust=high) = 59.6%) and correspondingly low level of social capital (P (SC=high) = 35%). This was expected since core the variables constituting social capital were lacking and consequently were not observed or instantiated.

CHALLENGES

In theory computational models are expected to be fully verified and valid but in practice, no computational model will ever be fully verified, guaranteeing 100%

Figure 12-5. Community D showing updated probabilities

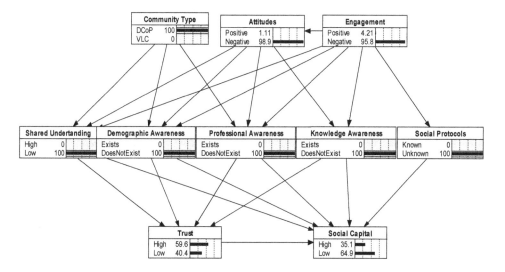

error free accuracy. But a high degree of statistical certainty is still required to demonstrate the usefulness of a model. One of greatest challenges of building a computational model is making it valid, relevant and useful, which implies in most part establishing model credibility. Establishing model credibility requires a lot of work. It involves gathering empirical data, subjecting the model to undergo several rigorous verification and validation stages and building an argument that the model has produced sound insights based on a wide range of tests comparable to data in real world settings.

The development of the social capital model did not pass rigorous model validation. In many social systems, modelling social issues is not so much about gaining 100% error free models but rather it is about gaining insights required to identify and understand a problem and address it using alternative methods. In addition, most of the approaches used for building models of social systems make use of qualitative inferences rather than quantitative predictions about the future state of systems. Besides, most social systems or constructs such as social capital cannot easily captured with one approach at single point in time since they are more dynamic.

The input variables used for building the model of social capital were extracted from the literature, which might not necessarily be empirically based, or situated within virtual communities. In addition, the assumptions made during the modelling process, might be susceptible to errors. Furthermore, research into social capital in virtual communities is still in its infancy and more is required to fully gain an understanding of the nature of the fundamental components of the model and how these interact with each other.

In terms of technical design and construction of Bayesian Belief Network models, there are two ways to construct Bayesian models. One way is to learn a graphical structure from data and the other is to initially propose a graphical structure based on some logical reasoning and train the graph to learn probability values from the structure using new evidences. The latter is the approach taken and reported in the book. It should be noted that such an approach though appealing and useful, is not necessarily consistent all the time. But validation of the structure is inevitable to demonstrate accuracy and relevance.

Validation of reasoning or assumptions is normally conducted through sensitivity analysis. The results of the sensitivity analysis conducted to validate the structure confirmed some of the assumptions made during the graphical construction of the model. But it will still be interesting to investigate the predictions of the model or formulate questions that can be pursued using an alternative method of study such as survey or Delphi technique.

CONCLUSION

The ultimate goal of this chapter was to demonstrate a working example of a computational model of social capital in virtual communities and provide guidance to researchers and practitioners interested in exploring social issues in virtual communities. Moreover issues predicted by the model were intended to open up debate about social capital in virtual communities and its technical and social implications to knowledge sharing and social networking. The model predictions revealed an increased level of trust and a corresponding increase in social capital. The predictions also suggest that professional awareness and shared understanding have an effect on the level of social capital in a community. The predictions also suggest that when people are aware of each other and are able to develop a certain level of shared understanding; they may develop better and productive relationships—social capital. The Bayesian Network technique was highly suitable for modelling social capital due to its uncertainty in definition, form and structure. By representing social capital in graphical form, researchers can isolate relevant from irrelevant variables and they can effectively communicate and share results with each other.

Summary of the model predictions, showed that where there was a high presence of shared understanding and the fact that individuals were aware of each other's capabilities (knowledge awareness), there was possible increased in trusting relationships as well high levels of social capital. Similarly, when all forms of awareness were present, there tended to be an increased level of shared understanding, the levels of trust and social capital correspondingly.

Based on the results of the predictions, it can be concluded that different forms of awareness, shared understanding and trust can variously influence to our understanding of social capital in virtual communities. Although the scenarios presented in this chapter were inadequate to fully draw final conclusions about causal links between these variables and an overall level of social capital in a community, the predictions provided a starting point for understanding and perhaps establishing grounds for serious discourse on social capital in virtual communities and possibly more thinking in terms of how to enhance social capital in virtual communities.

REFERENCES

Cohen, D., & Prusak, L. (2001). *In good company: How social capital makes organizations work*. Massachusetts: Harvard Business School Press.

Collion, M. H. (1989). Strategic planning for national agricultural research systems: An Overview. *Working Paper 26*. Retrieved November 24th 2008 from http://www.ifpri.org/divs/isnar.htm

Daniel, B. K. Zapata-Rivera, D. J., & McCalla, G. I. (2003). A Bayesian computational model of social capital. In M. Huysman, E. Wenger, & V. Wulf, (Eds.), *Communities and technologies* (pp. 287-305). London: Kluwer Publishers.

Daniel, B. K., O' Brien, D., & Sarkar, A. (2003). A design approach for canadian distributed community of practice on governance and international development: A Preliminary Report. In R. M. Verburg, & J. A. De Ridder, (Eds.), *Knowledge sharing under distributedcCircumstances* (pp. 19-24). Enschede: Ipskamps.

Daniel, B. K., Zapata-Rivera, J. D., & McCalla, G. I. (2005, November). Computational framework for constructing ayesian belief network models from incomplete, inconsistent and imprecise data in E-Learning (Poster). *The Second LORNET International Annual Conference, I2LOR-2005, November 16 to 18.* Vancouver, Canada.

Daniel, B. K., Zapata-Rivera, J. D. & McCalla, G. I. (2007). A Bayesian Belief Network approach for modelling complex domains. In A. Mittal, A. Kassim, & T. Tan (Eds.), *Bayesian Network Technologies: Applications and Graphical Models* (pp. 13-41). New York Hershey: IGI Publishing .

Druzdzel, M. J. & Henrion, M. (1993). Efficient reasoning in qualitative probabilistic networks. *Proceedings of the 11th National Conference on Artificial Intelligence,* (pp. 548-553).

Gutwin, C., & Greenberg, S. (1998). Design for individuals, design for groups: Tradeoffs between power and workspace awareness. *Proceedings of the ACM Conference on Computer Supported Cooperative Work* (pp. 207-216), ACM Press.

Pennington, N., & Hastie, R. (1988). Explanation-based decision making: effects of memory structure on judgment. *Journal of Experimental Psychology: Learning, Memory and Cognition, 14*(3), 521–533.

Stahl, G. (2000). A Model of collaborative knowledge-building. In B. Fishman, & O'Connor, S. Divelbiss (Eds.), *Fourth International Conference of the Learning Sciences* (pp. 70-77), Malwah, NJ; Erlbaum.

Zapata-Rivera. J. D. (2002). cbCPT: Knowledge engineering support for CPTs in Bayesian networks. *Proceedings of Canadian Conference on AI,* (pp. 368-370).

Chapter XIII
Sensitivity Analysis

INTRODUCTION

Sensitivity analysis is a mathematical technique for investigating the effects of inaccuracies in the parameters of a mathematical model. It analyses how variation in the output of a model (numerical or otherwise) can be apportioned qualitatively or quantitatively to different sources of data. Sensitivity analysis is an important statistical validation technique in Bayesian modelling. It is used to ascertain how a given model output depends upon or determines its input parameters. It often carried out to ensure the quality and accuracy of a model and a way of checking the robustness and reliability of assumptions built into a model.

This chapter offers an accessible introduction to sensitivity analysis of Bayesian models. The chapter could have been a section in chapter XII and presented before the scenarios sections. But because sensitivity analysis itself is a complex subject, it was deemed wise to present it as a complete chapter on its own.

OVERVIEW OF SENSITIVITY ANALYSIS

Modellers from a wide range of disciplines, including economics, educational assessment and evaluation and engineering have immensely benefited from the employment of sensitivity analysis techniques to valid their models. In a broad-spectrum sensitivity analysis within the Bayesian statistical approaches helps modellers to determine the spread of probability distribution of a particular variable or set of variables (parameters) and how they influences other variables or are influenced by values of other variables within the model. In other words, the purpose of sensitivity analysis is to know how sensitive a variable's value is to the other variables in the model. If it is very sensitive, we may want to know the state of that variable, and then invest more effort in determining the values of all the variables that substantially influences it.

Parameter sensitivity, an example of sensitivity analysis involves setting up a series of tests in where a modeller sets different parameter values to see how a change in one parameter in the model causes a change in the behaviour of one or more variables within the model. By showing how the model behaviour responds to changes in parameter values, sensitivity analysis serves as a useful tool during the process of building a model as well as in the evaluation of the model. Since modelling can be based on a lot of assumptions, some which might be less accurate, sensitivity analysis helps modellers to build confidence in the model by studying the uncertainties that are often associated with parameters in models.

Further, since some parameters in Bayesian models might represent probability values that are inaccurate, Sensitivity analysis is conducted to rectify this inaccuracy.

Sensitivity analysis allows model builders to determine what level of accuracy is needed for a parameter to make the model sufficiently useful and valid. If tests reveal that the model is insensitive, then it may be possible to use statistical estimation techniques to achieve greater precision. Within a Bayesian models, sensitivity analysis can also reveal the parameters that are reasonable or sensitive to use in the model. In practice, it might not be obvious to identify sensitive parameters but experimenting with a wide range of values can offer insights into behaviour of a model in extreme situations.

A Bayesian model is defined by a series of variables and these are treated as input parameters aimed at representing and understanding the behaviour of a system being modelled. Bayesian variables together with the assumptions made during the modelling process are often subject to many sources of uncertainty including errors of measurement, absence of information and poor or partial understanding of the driving forces and mechanisms. Such range of uncertainties can impose limitation and sometimes undermine the model's output.

Good modelling practice requires that the model builder provide an evaluation of the confidence in the model, possibly assessing the uncertainties associated with the modeling process and with the outcome of the model itself. In models involving many input variables sensitivity analysis is an essential ingredient of model building and quality assurance. It ensures that input knowledge gathered from experts is accurate and that logic used for building the structure of the model and the assumptions underlying it are valid as well.

SENSITIVITY ANALYSIS OF SOCIAL CAPITAL

It is useful to know how much our belief in a particular variable within a model is influenced by findings at other variables. For example if we want to know how sensitive our belief in shared understanding to the findings of engagement, we conduct sensitivity analysis. If we found that shared understanding was very sensitive, we might consider understanding the state of shared understanding relative to its parents or engagement.

Sensitivity analysis was applied to the analysis of social capital since the model is multivariate, with numerous states of input variables, whose influences were empirically unknown. The goal of the sensitive analysis was to help refine the model. An automated analysis (support for this type of analysis was provided in the Netica software package; https://www.norsys.com/environment) of the sensitivity of social capital to all other variables in the graph was conducted.

The results of the sensitivity analysis are presented at the end of the book (see details in Appendix 1: Sensitivity analysis results). In summary the results showed that those variables with weak level of influence to social capital manifested low mutual values. Trust, capability awareness and knowledge awareness were relatively sensitive to social capital compared to professional awareness, demographic awareness, social protocols and shared understanding. From this analysis, it can be concluded that social capital is not only sensitive to one variable, but rather it is sensitive to a number of variables and even more so to variables that were assigned strong paths (strong positive paths in the model—see Figure 12-1), demonstrated by higher values of entropy reduction. These results also supported that the qualitative reasoning used for deriving the initial probabilities presented in the social capital

Table 13-1. Sensitivity of 'Social Capital' due to a finding at another node

Node	Mutual Info	Variance of Beliefs
Social Capital	0.89607	0.2148550
Demographic Awareness	0.01716	0.0052302
Social Protocols	0.01513	0.0046189
Professional Awareness	0.01374	0.0042760
Trust	0.00879	0.0027602
Engagement	0.00383	0.0012449
Attitudes	0.00263	0.0008319
Knowledge Awareness	0.00202	0.0006326
Shared Understanding	0.00051	0.0001531
Community Type	0.00000	0.0000000

model was reasonable. In addition, the results of the sensitivity analysis can be used to improve the model by changing the threshold initial probability values presented earlier in the chapter. Further, drawing from the results, one could speculate that the individual variations in values could be caused by partial knowledge of domain experts used for building the network and early assumptions made during the development of the model, both of which are common problems inherent the development of any Bayesian model.

In addition to doing sensitivity analysis, another possible way of rectifying inconsistence in a Bayesian model is to conduct model validation. Model validation in essence is post sensitivity analysis, which is performed by altering the parameters of query variables and observing the related changes in the posterior probabilities of the target variable. This was done through help of evidence coming from empirical data and was achieved and described in chapter XII. However, in a situation, where there are N-scenarios, a straightforward analysis can be extremely time consuming and difficult to maintain, especially on larger networks. Coupe and Van der Gaag (1998) addressed this difficulty by identifying a sensitivity set of a variable given evidence and only focusing on those.

CONCLUSION

Specific parameter values can change the appearance of the graphs representing the behavior of the system. But significant changes in behavior do not occur for all parameters. System dynamics models are in general insensitive to many parameter changes. It is the structure of the system, and not the parameter values that has most influence on the behavior of the system. Sensitivity analysis is an important tool in the model building process.

By showing that the system does not react greatly to a change in a parameter value, it reduces the modeler's uncertainty in the behavior. In addition, it gives an opportunity for a better understanding of the dynamic behavior of the system. Experimenting and varying parameters will show the intensity and impact of each variable on social capital. For example, changing awareness several parameters at the same time, observe the behavior produced, and compare it to the conclusions presented in the book. Can you suggest any parameter values that would produce the "optimal or most desirable behavior? The use of sensitivity analysis in such policy analysis will be explored in a later in the book.

When building a Bayesian belief network, a huge number of probabilities will have to be assessed. To support the elicitation of these probabilities, an iteratively process is performed, which is often subject to the results of a sensitivity analysis. Sensitivity analysis of a belief network assesses the sensitivity of probabilities specified in the network and, hence, for assessing the network's robustness. Sensitivity analysis is a necessary procedure for checking the accuracy of reasoning and assessing the degree of relationships measured in entropy values between the various social capital variables. The higher the entropy value between social capital and a particular variable revealed how closely the variable was to social capital.

Sensitivity analysis conducted on social capital showed that changing the value of parameters made some difference in the behavior of the model. Some parameter changes such as shared understanding and various types of awareness affected the behavior to a larger extent than others and made those variables more closely correlated to social capital. This technique was useful in determining the more sensitive variables from the less sensitive ones but it did not add much since the results need to be further validated preferably by an alternative method of investigation.

REFERENCES

Coupe, V. M., & van der Gaag, L. C. (1998). Practicable sensitivity analysis of bayesian belief networks. *Technical report UU-CS-1998-10, Utrecht University.*

Norsys. *Netica Bayesian Network Software from Norsys.* Retrieved from https://www.norsys.com

Chapter XIV
Model Validation

INTRODUCTION

Though computational models take a lot of effort to build, a model is generally not useful unless it can help people to understand the world being modelled, or the problem the model is intended to solve. A useful model allows people to make useful predictions about how the world will behave now and possibly tomorrow. Validation is the last step required in developing a useful Bayesian model. The goal of validation is to gain confidence in a model and to demonstrate and prove that a model produces reliable results that are closely related to the problems or issues in which the model is intended to address. The goal of the Chapter is to provide the reader with a basic understanding of the validation process and to share with them key lessons learned from the model of social capital presented in the book.

While sensitivity analysis is intended to ensure that a Bayesian model is theoretically consistent with goals and assumptions of the modeller (how the modeller views the world) or the accuracy of sources of data used for building the model, the goal of validation is to demonstrate the practical application of the model in real world settings. This Chapter presents the main steps involved in the process of validating a Bayesian model. It illustrates this process by using examples drawn from the Bayesian model of social capital.

PROCEDURES FOR VALIDATING MODEL

Bayesian models are intended to predict or compare future performance of a system. Model validation is concerned with ensuring the model built is an accurate representation of a real system in a real world and that outcomes of its predictions can be applied to solve set of problems or inform us about operation of a certain phenomenon.

Model validation is achieved through the calibration of the model, which essentially compares the model to actual system behaviour and using the discrepancies between the two, and the insights gained from the process to improve or disapprove the model. This process is repeated until model accuracy is judged to be acceptable. Further, the validation process is contingent upon the model developer and people knowledgeable of how the real system works. Model validation is performed through evaluation of accuracy of the model with respect to experimental data.

There are many approaches for validating Bayesian model but it is beyond the scope of this book to elaborate on each of these approaches. One could certainly generalize that unlike mathematical models, where there are well-established procedures and to some extent concrete guidelines for validating a mathematical model, the guidelines for validating Bayesian models of social systems are inadequate and to some extent difficult to carry out.

There were two different possible ways to validate the model of social capital, one was to use an expert driven validation technique, intended to validate exploratory process involved in the model building. The second technique was an empirical driven model validation, the result of which is the highlights of some of the components of social capital discussed. The expert driven model validation involved collecting sufficient empirical data to corroborate against predictions of a model, which were based on the experts' knowledge and reflected in the initial development of the model. The validation of empirical part compared the model input-output predictions to corresponding input-output transformations for a real system and it was achieved through previous work referred to throughout the book. Figure 14-1 presents a general process of model validation; this can be applied to almost any Bayesian model.

VALIDATING A BAYESIAN MODEL

A Bayesian model is considered valid when a set of experimental conditions is performed against it to determine the model's accuracy within its intended purpose. This usually requires that the model's output variables of interest are identified and that their required amount of accuracy be specified. The amount of accuracy required is normally specified prior to starting the development of the model or at a very early in the model development process. If the variables of interest are random variables, then properties and functions of the random variables such as means and variances are usually used to determine the model validity. In practice

Figure 14-1. Validating a Bayesian model

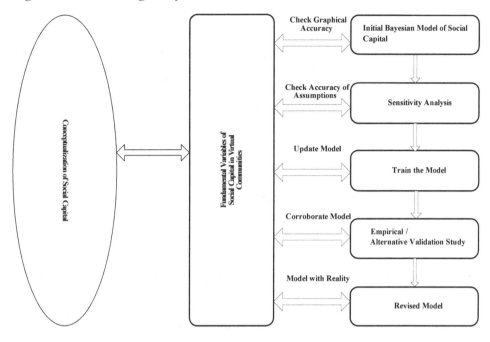

when dealing Bayesian models of social systems, several iterations of validations are required to obtain a satisfactorily valid model.

It is often too costly and time consuming to determine that a model is absolutely valid over the complete domain of its intended applicability. Instead, tests and evaluations are conducted until sufficient confidence is obtained that a model can be considered valid for its intended application (Sargent, 1999). If a test determines that a model does not have sufficient accuracy for any one of the sets of experimental conditions, then the model is invalid but not necessarily useless. It just suggests the model is not meeting the stated required standards but certainly can be improved. In a similar vein, determining that a model has sufficient accuracy for numerous experimental conditions does not guarantee that the model will remain valid all the time and in all similar contexts within its applicable domain.

VALIDATING THE MODEL OF SOCIAL CAPITAL

An expert knowledge driven approach was used to build the model of social capital as illustrated in the earlier Chapters of the book. Validating the model involved exploring the nature of those variables in the model that were sensitive to social capital revealed during the sensitivity analysis. The validation was also subjected to expert review. This was to ensure that the modelling process was fairly transparent and well documented. From the sensitivity analysis and the various scenarios testing of the model, the results revealed trust and knowledge awareness to be highly sensitive to social capital. Other less sensitivity values included professional awareness, demographic awareness, social protocols and shared understanding. The highly sensitivity issues are discussed in the proceeding sections to illustrate and shade more light into their significance to social capital within virtual community context.

TRUST AND SOCIAL CAPITAL

Trust is an important component of virtual communities; it is the main engine that sustains most social activities in virtual communities. However, it seems within virtual communities the relationship between social capital and trust is double-edged. Trust is a precondition for the development of social relationships that are at the core of social capital and more social capital in turn generates more trusting relationships. In virtual communities people develop trusting relationships among themselves over repeated transactions and act consistently in a way that is trustworthy. For instance, when they display courtesy and hospitality to others and consistently maintain collegial tone throughout interaction. The challenges facing the developing of trust in virtual communities is the ability to accept someone as a community member. However, to accept a stranger to become a community member on the basis of limited knowledge is not a trivial business and so trust tend to develop mostly based upon continuous engagement.

Trust develops when members of a virtual community get to know each other and are able to develop social relationships and maintain such relationship for a longer period of time. In virtual communities, people trust those who they can easily relate to and share certain characteristics, whether it is shared geographical proximity, gender, professional affiliation, knowledge and interest in certain domains or simply ethnic background. In a situation where individuals are complete strangers and where there is limited information for people to draw upon, trust takes much longer to build. Further, in the model presented, within the contexts of both distributed communities of practice and virtual learning communities, trust is a function of reciprocal relationships among members of these communities. It is achieved through continuous reciprocal relationships over a certain period of time. Although in these communities people can possibly develop trust on the first instance of encounter with others, it is a "quick trust", which is also fragile and it often developed in situations where people have limited information and where it is not possible to acquire further information.

AWARENESS AND SOCIAL CAPITAL

People naturally congregate around common passions, interests and goals. They tend to easily connect and interact with people who feel the same way as they do, who see the world from their own perspective and those with whom they can easily get along. As noted in chapter V, awareness is an important component of social capital within virtual communities. Awareness describes the understanding of the activities of others, which provides a context for one's own activity, whether it is monitoring others conversations (passive participation) or actively engaging in a conversation with others. In virtual communities, people tend to trust others based upon their ability to access various kinds of information about the people they interact with. For example, in virtual learning communities, people are likely to trust those they have similar demographic or professional backgrounds—"birds of the same feathers flock together". Such practices are not uncommon in geographical communities, as most people tend to believe there is safety and comfort in familiarity.

For many years researchers in Social Sciences have emphasised that similarity in individuals promote voluntary interaction. For example, it is natural for people who have similar demographic backgrounds to instantly connect to each other and have engaged conversations. Recently, Mohan, McGregor, Saunders and Archee (1997) emphasized communication as a central socially binding factor but pointed out that 'good' communication be clear, honest, democratic, sincere, logical and respectful of its audience. They viewed communication as a ttransaction model grounded in negotiation of meaning between two or more parties responding to their environment and each other.

Central to Mohan, et. al (1997), work was presentation of two models of communication, which were referred to as: transmission and transaction models. The transmission model portrays communication as a mechanistic process, essentially a transfer of messages from a source to a receiver using appropriate channel and medium. Transmission models on the other hand emphasize the construction of a message and the way it is delivered to the receiver. This model is helpful within virtual communities and helps in analysing how communication is composed, how to choose the appropriate communication tools, and prior determination of how receivers can receive and interpret the message and appropriately respond to it.

In addition, the transmission model focuses not only on the interpretation of a message but the context in which the message resides. It entails mutual awareness of the sender and the receiver, shared experience, and common language. It regards communication as the creation of negotiation of meaning in two or more parties responding to their environment and each other. Understanding is therefore more subjective in nature and it covers personal experiences and social construction of reality. This model entails that the more similar these variables are the more effective is the communication and subsequent social interaction.

Similarity in attributes such as demographic variables, beliefs and values (Touchey 1974) are more likely to enhance communication and increase engagement within a social network and ultimately social capital. Within the social network environments such as Facebook, people tend to create their personal networks based on people similarity of backgrounds, interests, goals and education. One reason individuals with similar ties predominate in social network is because demographically similar people tend to have tastes, ideas, and knowledge in common. People with shared attributes or interests associate more with each other because they find it is easier to communicate and work together. Tarde (1903) noted that social relations are generally between individuals who resemble each other in occupation and education. Professionals who share the same practice or jobs easily relate to others in the same profession. For example, artificial intelligence in education researchers can easily related to people working in the area of cognitive sciences, educational technology, and other areas of computer science.

However, the social cues essential for developing the kinds of awareness important for building trust in geographical communities are lacking in most virtual communities. This leads to difficulty in developing the kinds of awareness important for building trust. Further, even in a situation where individuals already knew each other prior to joining a virtual community, some kinds of awareness are still necessary. For example, for a productive discourse necessary for creating a rich environment for nurturing social capital, it is necessary to foster knowledge awareness.

ENGAGEMENT

It is reiterated many times in this book that virtual communities are often comprised of people with shared identity or interests who gather together for a specific purpose or goal. A shared purpose creates a common ground and forms basis for people to socially network with each other and create social connections necessary for them to carry on collaborative activities in their community. The extent to which people connect to each other and whether this was based on formal or well defined content or emergent personal interests and non-formal issues differed from one community to another. For example in virtual learning communities people tend to regularly participated in discussion of required content as well as issues around personal interests or issues outside of the required content. In distributed communities of practice where there is high professional attire and where discourse and engagement is mainly task and goal oriented, people might find focus on personal issues outside the professional lines more irrelevant than they are in virtual learning communities.

SOCIAL NETWORKING AND SHARED IDENTITY

Like geographical communities, virtual communities manifest a strong sense of community among its members. This is noticeable by the feeling of togetherness members are willing to display toward each. The feeling of togetherness in virtual communities denotes recognition of membership in a community and the feeling of friendship among peers, cohesion and bonding social capital among participants as they work, collaborate and learn together as a community, and regularly participate in community social rituals. A shared identity holds members of a virtual community together. It creates a strong feeling of a common identity. Identity plays an inherent role in defining members' participation in a community and it affects how people network with each other and with whom they choose to exchange information and share knowledge.

A community's identity is largely formed by the community's history or heritage including members' shared goals and shared values. From the validation results the feeling of togetherness in the community enables people to personally connect to each other, and to openly and respectfully challenge each other's ideas without fear of negative sanctions and exclusion from the community. The feeling of togetherness in the group is an important indicator of social capital and it is also an important element of a community identity.

Furthermore, in virtual communities when people identify with each other and the community to which they belong, they indirectly build interdependence and attachments to each other and subsequently a strong feeling of "we" versus "they" or "them" identity. The sense of belonging can be based on common geography, race, gender, language or professional affiliation. In distributed communities of practice people are more inclined to identify with those with whom they share the same experiences or who are trained in the same profession (Daniel, O'Brien & Sarkar, 2006). In other words, professionals in distributed communities of practice seem to easily associate more with those with whom they easily identify with professionally. It is also within those groups they can easily build trust and feel and identify with as a community. In addition, a group identity can influence the way individuals contribute to their community. For example, effective communication can be enhanced, if one knows the identity of those with whom one is communicating. This can also foster trust and social capital of the community.

SHARED UNDERSTANDING

Shared understanding is built upon shared knowledge and beliefs, mutually identified and agreed upon by members through a rich variety of linguistic signaling
(Clark, 1996). Shared understanding allows people in a community to communicate and cooperate easily. In most instances, shared understanding is not simply a
static assumption about shared knowledge and beliefs, but rather it is an ongoing
communication protocol maintained by members of a community. In virtual communities, shared understanding plays a critical role of supporting social capital. It
anchors and sustains discussion among people. However, in virtual communities
whose members have diverse personal goals, professional training, and various
levels of domain knowledge, achieving shared understanding can be challenging.
Shared understanding enable people to share common experiences, swap stories
and easily relate to each other and learn better as a community.

The full range of individual and/or organizational diversity and similarities,
including experience, background, opinion and lifestyle, that make each individual
member of a virtual community unique, can influence the way people connect to
each other and ultimately the social capital of these communities. The process of
leveraging the power of individual differences and similarities to achieve a shared
understanding is at the core of social capital within any virtual community. Shared
understanding reduces the possibilities of conflict to occur in the community. It
inculcates the spirit of respect among members of a community. In addition, where
there is an increased level of shared understanding, people can quickly connect to
each other and focus more on community issues rather resolving differences.

SOCIAL PROTOCOLS

A stable community is possible where there is some assumed general agreement
between its members or where a set of values can be identified which define the
limits of both the social order and of individual contributions to the community
based along the objectives or the goals. Most conventional communities exhibit a
hierarchical structure between the governed and the rules within certain constraints,
which are usually imposed by owners of the community and related to its goals. In
place-based communities, most of people are familiar with etiquette related to all
forms of social practices, such as paying respect to the deceased—do not mock the
dead, do not talk when your mouth is full of food, do not fart in public, introduce
someone using the appropriate social protocol, etc. Table manners are perhaps the
oldest etiquette shared in many cultures. Many societies enforce a need for basic
table manners. In restaurants for example when an individual violets good table

manners, it is more likely that the whole restaurant might notice. Many people are self-conscious and they often get anxious during introduction simply because making introductions correctly can be one of the more stressful aspects of good etiquette.

People often wonder, what are the guidelines? Better yet, is there even one guideline across cultures? Will it still be all right to introduce someone instead of them introducing themselves? What are people from those cultures that do not self promote they? Other cultures accept that the most important person gets introduced last and in other cultures it is vice-versa. Social protocols guided by appropriate etiquettes are central to relationship building. But they are certainly culturally diverse and carry many social implications. Regardless of their diversity, social protocols are expected to be properly adhered to and practice. This is mainly dependent upon their exposition to those who are expected to follow them. Violation is either intentional as is the case of social deviance, or accidental in circumstances people are ignorant or are deeply self induced with their own social protocols.

Engagement in most formal virtual learning communities is guided by common set of rules and protocols. However, when people do not know much about the expected norms of behaviour, they can easily engage in unacceptable behaviours and this can negatively affect the social capital of a community. Social protocols in virtual communities are essential components of social capital and they are basically the rules that guide people in the use of appropriate and inappropriate language, tone of voice, understanding and respecting community values, individuals' beliefs, attitudes and behaviours in a community. Failure to observe social protocols in most virtual communities can result to severe punishments including warning, restriction in participation (e.g. read but not write) or complete dismissal from the community. In virtual communities, social protocols can be used to set the tone for interaction and they used to fine-tune the direction of particular discussion. Just like physical communities, the policing of social protocols in virtual communities, is usually the responsibility of specific individuals.

In most formal virtual learning communities, social protocols are decent institutional standard set of policies, requirements and expectation. And the moderator/instructor of the class in the case takes the responsibility of implementing and observing adherence to the required social protocols. In distributed communities, development of social protocols often emerges or built around the interests of the members of the community or the goals of the community.

CONCLUSION

The main goal of Bayesian model validation is to remove barriers and objections to practicality and usefulness of a model. The task of a modeller is to establish an argument that the model produces sound insights and can be calibrated with a wide range of tests and criteria that "stand in" for comparing model results to data from a real world system. Bayesian models that are built on human expert knowledge, validation becomes a matter of establishing credibility in the model achieved through empirical work. In most cases, it requires collection of evidence elsewhere suggesting why the model is a valid one for its intended purposes to ensure that the actual utility of Bayesian models is accrued to its ability to make sense of the world.

But no computational model will ever be completely error-free. A high degree of statistical certainty is formally required and it is all that can be achieved for any model as long as the data collected is sufficient. Like many experimental design studies, statistical certainty is increased as relevant cases are tested on the model against more data. The end result of a Bayesian model development is technically a model that has passed all the development stages, name, identification of variables, and specification of a relevant graph structure, assigning realistic prior probability values to all variables in the graph, developing authentic scenarios to test a model, running sensitivity analysis and finally validating the model.

This chapter broadly discussed some of the procedures involved in carrying out model validation, illustrating with examples drawn from social capital. Though the chapter did not go into further details used during the validation process, the information present is considered sufficient to introduce the reader to the essence of model validation during the development of a Bayesian Belief Network model.

REFERENCES

Clark, H. (1996). *Using Language*. NY: Cambridge University Press.

Daniel, B. K., Sarkar, A., & O'Brien, D. (2006). User-Centred Design for Online Learning Communities: A Sociotechnical Approach for the Design of a Distributed Community of Practice. In N. Lambropoulos & P. Zaphiris (Eds). *User- Evaluation and Online Communities*. Hershey: Idea Group.

Daniel, B. K., Schwier, R. A., & Ross, H. (2005). Intentional and Incidental Discourse Variables in a Virtual Learning Community. *The Proceedings of E-Learn 2005--World Conference on E-Learning in Corporate, Government, Healthcare, and Higher Education*, held in Vancouver, Canada,October 24-28, 2005.

Mohan, T., McGregor, H., Saunders, S., & Archee, R. (1997). *Communicating! Theory and practice* (4th ed.). Sydney: Harcourt Brace.

Sargent, R. G. (1999). Validation and Verification of Simulation Models. *Winter Simulation Conference, IEEE, Piscataway, NJ*, (pp. 39-48).

Tarde, G. (1903). *The Laws of Imitation*. Translated by E.C. Parsons with introduction by F.Giddings, New York, Henry, Holt and Co.

Touchey, J. C. (1974). Situated identities, attitude similarity and interpersonal attraction. *Sociometry, 37,* 363-374.

Web Link Used in the Chapter

http://www.facebook.com

Chapter XV
Conclusion, Book Limitations and Future Directions

INTRODUCTION

Social capital in virtual communities offers a useful conceptual and practical tool to help us gain insights into the way people interact with each other, share information and knowledge among themselves and work together. This book has synthesized and brought together a massive volume of current and past work on social capital in geographical or place-based communities. The results of the analysis helped to extend the theory of social capital to virtual communities. It has also provided basis for e researchers, policymakers and systems designers to explore social issues that are likely to have an impact on information and knowledge sharing. The book provides useful information for people concerned with how social capital may be used to answer key questions about its fundamental components, how to study and model it within the contexts of virtual learning communities and distributed communities of practice. The main thrust of this book is the ability to identify the critical components of social capital in virtual communities and the use of modelling techniques—Bayesian Belief Network to analysis of interactions of the components of social capital. The components identified in the book serve as important proxies for examination of how social capital will operate in virtual communities.

Moreover, the conceptualization of social capital in virtual communities as a common social resource that facilitates information exchange, knowledge sharing and knowledge construction achieved through continuous interaction and engagement, built on trust and maintained through shared understanding represents an interesting and important theoretical departure, from the original role of social capital in more conventional communities. It is hoped that this fresh conceptualization of social capital in virtual communities prepares scholars to engage in useful and productive discussions on how to hone the potentials of this theory. This chapter summarises the key issues presented in the book and outlines important future directions for the discussion of social capital in virtual communities.

COMMUNITIES AND SOCIAL CAPITAL

For many years the notion of community served as a powerful but also an elusive construct for addressing social issues in many societies and is being considered as a social research pillar for understanding the operational success of many societies. For over hundred years, several scholars, especially Sociologists and Anthropologists have intense discussions around what exactly constitutes a community. Though no precise agreement is available, most writers tend to elude towards an understanding that a community is a social system composed of individuals who live in the same area, neighbourhood, city or town and who for some biological or social reasons share common values, norms, beliefs and cultural practices. As discussed in chapter I, this idea of a community based on geography and ascribed rather than achieved status and rules of socialization and engagement has been challenged by the emergence of the "information age".

Marked by rapid development in telecommunication and global communication networks, the "information age" has contributed to the mutation of an idea, that a community is limited to geographical locality. The mutation has resulted into a new definition of a community, one that takes into account human gathering and interaction and celebration in what can be described as abstract virtual spaces—virtual communities.

Virtual communities as real addition to human communities are on a rise and they have overall come to support various forms of social interaction, communication and social engagement, radically transforming the traditional structures of what we previously consider as communities. Today different forms of computer mediated communication systems are freely available to engage people in social interactions from the distance through various patterns of communication. People join virtual communities for a number of reasons. Among many others, they want to take part participation that can lead to building reciprocal relationships with likeminded peers. In other words, people are motivated to contribute to the communities they belong to in the expectation that they will receive useful help and information in return. Other factors include increased sense of recognition, the desire to obtain prestige, personal visibility to others and the powerful effects of seemingly trivial markers of recognition (e.g. stars, ranking) are overwhelming used in systems such as Slashdot. com. There is also tendency for individuals to contribute in order to increase their sense of personal efficacy. That is to say individuals contribute because the act results in a feeling that they have had some effect on the community, an example of this is Wikipedia, which is mainly built on n voluntary basis.

Many people and institutions have recognised the values of virtual communities. In business, virtual communities help improve brands, learning as in education, efficiency as in health care and health delivery. Perhaps the popularity of virtual communities is attributed to the recent technologies of Web 2.0, which enable users to generate their content and massively participate without acquiring technical skills and knowledge in Web programming and Web design. This is particular more so within the business sector and education, where these technologies are widely use to support group engagements.

For example, many companies are now exploring how to most effectively use Web technologies in order to gain brand awareness, build online relationships with their customers, receive coverage in the blogosphere, improve product development, build an online community, and enhance the user experience. In higher institutions of learning there is a new trend to integrate virtual communities to most academic course programming and to support outreach programs.

Though virtual communities continue to enter into discussions of most of our social systems, the literature is replenished with confusion on what can be the best parameters for describing the concept of virtual community. In fact, the terms virtual communities, virtual learning communities, and distributed communities of practice are wrongly used interchangeably. Furthermore, there are increasing temptations to refer to different software applications as virtual communities.

SOCIAL CAPITAL IN VIRTUAL COMMUNITIES

The increasing interest in exploring virtual communities as learning environments and knowledge hubs has been accompanied by a surge of interest among researchers in many disciplines raising many interesting issues, one that is to understand what makes some virtual communities more successful than others. Fortunately for many years, social scientists have struggled with the same problems—of understanding the performance of geographical communities. In most of the work reported in the scientific literature, social capital has always dominated the discussion of why some communities are doing better than others.

Since its discovery as an important social theory, social capital has quickly pervaded the lexicon in social science and policy circles, but clear definitions are still not available. Few of those employing the theory have elaborated a detailed description of the theory that is highly soloed and context dependent. Many contemporary scholars have begun to take a closer look and criticize under theorized and oversimplified usages of the theory of social capital, but most attack the problem by constructing their own variant conceptualization of theory and thereby increasing the inconsistency of the plethora of work on the theory.

Many scholars vary in the way they represent progress in terms of the potential the theory might offer but still the greater challenge remains to construct a theoretical explication of social capital that is not problem specific, theoretically consistent across many levels of analysis; and that extends beyond geographical communities.

For the last 8 years, the idea of extending social capital to virtual communities remained central to the research that is reported in this book. Unfortunately, the initial analysis of the previous research on social capital revealed that the theory lacks precision and consistency. It also suggested that social capital has never been explored much within the context of virtual communities. And it made much sense at this point to explore the theory in the context of virtual communities instead directly applying the theory to analysis of social issues in virtual communities. This became the hallmark of the work on social capital reported in this book—understanding the fundamental components of social capital in virtual communities.

In virtual communities, the potentials of using social capital lie in its ability to examine social issues in virtual communities are critical to the design, development and sustainability of virtual communities. But since social capital is ill defined and limited to geographical communities, this book presents a computational model of social capital, which serves as a first step in the direction of understanding, formalizing, computing and discussing social capital in virtual communities. The book employs an eclectic set of approaches and procedures to explore, analyze, understand and model social capital in two types of virtual communities: virtual learning communities and distributed communities of practice.

There is an intentional flow to the logic of issues presented in the book. The analysis first began with understanding what constitutes social capital in the literature, identifying and isolating variables that are relevant to the context of virtual communities, putting together various components of social capital within two types of virtual community: virtual learning community and distributed community of practice. Second a computational model of social capital was constructed and few authentic scenarios were selected to train the model.

In addition, a sensitivity analysis aimed at examining the statistical variability of the individual variables in the model and their effects on the overall level of social capital are conducted and a series of evidence-based scenarios are developed to test and update the model. The result of the model predictions is then used as input to construct a final empirical study aimed at verifying the model.

In the final analysis, social capital is a multi-layered, multivariate, multidimensional, imprecise and ill-defined theory that has emerged from a rather murky swamp of terminology but it is still useful for exploring and understanding social networking issues that can possibly influence our understanding of collaboration and learning in virtual communities. These results were further confirmed by the results of the model predictions and the results of the sensitivity analysis. However, the variables were narrowed to trust, different forms of awareness, social protocols and the type of the virtual community, these variables are all important in the discussion of social capital within virtual communities.

UTILITY OF BAYESIAN MODELLING IN SOCIAL SYSTEMS

Bayesian Network is a tool that helps model a situation involving uncertainty. Bayesian Belief Networks models enable reasoning when there is uncertainty. They combine the advantages of an intuitive visual representation with a solid mathematical basis in Bayesian probability. This book has shown how to build a computational framework for modeling imprecise and inconsistent data that is relevant to social software systems design. In the social sciences and indeed in many other fields, uncertainty may arise due to a variety of causes. For instance it can be the results of gaps in knowledge, complexity and imprecision of domain knowledge, ignorance, or volatility of a knowledge domain. By representing knowledge in graphical form, researchers can effectively communicate results.

A Bayesian model encodes domain knowledge, showing relationships, interdependencies and independence among variables. The qualitative part of the model is represented by links showing direction of influence or independence among variables. The information describing the details of the quantitative relationships among the variables is often stored in conditional probability tables (CPT). This enables the model to use probability theory, especially Bayesian statistics to calculate conditional dependencies among the variables in the network and resolve the uncertainties with probability inferences.

Though BBN techniques are elegant ways of capturing uncertainties, knowledge engineering effort required to create conditional probability values per each given variable in a network has prevented many researchers to use them in many domains. In addition, current algorithms that can be used to learn initial and conditional probabilities from data are often complex and cumbersome to employ and data is not always available. Even though initial probabilities can be elicited from experts, it sometimes raises the problems of accuracy in values.

In addition, translating experts' qualitative knowledge into numerical probabilistic values is a daunting and often complex task. Since Bayesian network modeling involves establishing cause and effects among variables, it is sometimes difficult to determine causal relationships or to adequately describe all the causes and effects. In such case, Bayesian networks can be described using probabilities describing what we know or believe is happening in a particular domain.

This chapter has extended the use of Bayesian Belief Network techniques to complex domains, illustrating with an example of social capital construct, it has shown different phases in which a similar model can be built. The approach described in the chapter combined both qualitative and quantitative techniques to elicit knowledge from experts without worrying about computing initial probabilities for training a model. Among the variables reported different forms of awareness, trust, shared understanding, common goals and shared values. We intend to use the results of this study to refine the initial conditional probabilities of the variables in the social capital model.

CONCLUSION AND FUTURE DIRECTIONS

At the core of social capital are productive social relationships, which are vital for virtual communities to carry on their day-to-day operations. No virtual community can thrive productively without first building social capital. The central idea behind social capital theory is that networks of relationships constitute a valuable resource for providing members with privileged access to information and to opportunities. But while having a network of individuals is a critical part of developing social capital, equally important are the key variables that contribute to structure, dimension and content of relationships. One way to understand which variables of social capital are more relevant and critical within virtual communities is to apply computational modelling approach to understand the interactions of the variables with each other, isolate the most influential from the less influential variables and possibly use alternative methodologies to further explore the causal relationships of variables and assess their overall in a community.

The idea behind modeling social issues using Bayesian approach is quite new but it is an important research innovation intended to understand the vast amount of usage and user data generated within virtual communities and other computational environments. The need to build social models of data in virtual communities and other computer-mediated systems, help us understand current critical issues in these environments and experiment with new and emergent cases. Moreover, the need to grow computational models in the social sciences is also critical to developing and testing new and old theories. These models are uniquely valuable for addressing issues of learning, knowledge sharing and information flow in virtual communities. To the researchers, the full flavored value of these models for theory building, however, will require an increased understanding of the potential of these models, and when and how they should be validated.

For researchers not trained in modeling or computational techniques such models may appear bewildering or it may be difficult to understand or hard to know when to believe their accuracy and validity. It can also be complex to interpret and use a model's results. Consequently, there are often well intentioned, but somewhat misplaced, calls for model validation without understanding what validation entails within the social systems.

This book sets the stage for discussion about social capital in virtual communities and the approach used for building the computational model. There are also other critical issues that need to be seriously discussed; these include an empirical investigation of the relationships among the constituent variables of social capital and how the model reacts to new and authentic scenarios. This requires more empirical work to help more understanding of social capital in virtual communities. The development of the Bayesian framework presented in the book was largely motivated by the need to provide a start point and a sound theoretical discourse but there are other issues that require immediate attention if social capital is to become a useful theory in virtual communities. These are summarised as follows.

First, social capital lacks clear definition and consequently, it is difficult to develop concrete measurement scales. It is a complex construct that is a mixture of more primitive variables like trust, reciprocity, cooperation, shared norms and shared understanding. There is lack of a clear, concise and consistent framework for understanding which of the contributing variables are most influential, and how they interact with each other.

Second, studies have shown that social capital emerges from interaction and it depends on the characteristics of individuals and groups. Nonetheless, it is not clear what the key characteristics of individuals and groups might be that can contribute to the development of social capital.

Third, research on social capital mainly assumes that social capital is correlated to positive, pro-social outcomes, but such research ignores the negative ways that social capital may be manifest. Social capital depends on different levels of trusting relationships. However individuals in virtual communities are geographically and culturally distributed and often have different levels of knowledge and skills. Since these individuals span space, time, and cultures, they have little knowledge of others beyond assumptions and stereotypes. A lack of sufficient information about others hinders individuals' abilities to develop trust.

Fourth, trust primarily develops through interaction in face-to-face encounters. There are limited computational tools that can augment, promote and maintain trust in virtual environments. Fifth, social capital has been applied to understand different social issues but there is no work done on the effects of social capital on learning in more traditional environments, technology based environments or "blended learning" environments.

Finally, social capital depends on other variables such as cohesion among individuals, but few studies correlate the influence of cohesion on the overall social capital in a group. Thus, research is required to develop technologies that may increase the level of social capital within communities.

BOOK LIMITATIONS

A book on any new concept or theory is not free from shortcomings; it makes sense therefore, to point out some of the limitations associated with this book. Modelling a nebulous notion such as social capital can be challenging and the methods used can impose limitations. The Bayesian belief network approach described in the book provides a novel way to understand how the various components of social capital interact with each other, though the model might be replete with assumptions (about variables, values, influences, and conditional probabilities) that may undermine the model's usefulness. In other words, the variables used for building the model and the conditional probability values assigned to the variables were done with reference to the literature, and this is possibly limited to the interpretation of the literature and the limitations of the literature itself, which might all undermine the accuracy of the model. But the main contribution of the Bayesian model is that is provides a new way to understand how variables contribute to understanding the concept. It should be tuned over time to sort out the problems.

The book has mainly struggled with two general challenges: conceptual and analytical. The conceptual challenge has to do with methodology used for analyzing social capital. The analytical challenge deals with the development and use of computational techniques to build models of a complex social phenomenon such as social capital.

In addressing these challenges the book provides a starting point for discussions on this issues and stress that much work still needs to be done to develop a deeper understanding of what constitutes social capital in virtual communities and how the key variables interact with each other and validated to ultimately provide us with useful issues to tap into the full potentials of social capital in virtual communities.

FINAL THOUGHTS

There is now a broad consensus that social capital is an important theory for addressing social issues in communities, but there is a little agreement as to what social capital actually is. Various groups of researchers frame their own definitions and incorrectly assume that others people mean the same things as they do when they use particular components and approaches for in measurement. A gradually evolving synthesis of experience leads to the expectation that there can now be rapid learning from an exchange of research findings among researchers. Unfortunately, this is not the case as the debate on the meaning of social capital is far from over. Social capital research is concerned with understanding of productive social relationships among people.

From the overall analysis, research into social capital should begin with understanding the kinds of relationships people have with others, the density of the relationships, the content as well as the purpose. Moreover the research methods employ should mirror scientific methods emphasizing reproducibility of findings, the ability to identify key measurable components including appropriate level of measurement and an understanding of causation of variables.

Social capital will continue to occupy a central position as an analytical theory in understanding social issues in virtual communities shaping the directions in which social software can be designed and research can be conducted. However, the real usefulness of social capital will depend on understanding precisely what constitutes social capital, how it operates in virtual communities and how this can be used as a decision-support tool, so that interested researchers and systems' designers can essentially use it to make informed decisions about research into information and knowledge sharing in virtual communities, system design to support virtual communities, effective engagement, learning, teaching and policy analysis within e-learning environments.

The book provides a clear exposition of its aims – to refine the concept of social capital in order to utilize it in virtual communities by constructing a formal Bayesian Belief Network model of social capital. It has also provided a comprehensive discussion of the evolution of debates surrounding the concepts of community, virtual community, social capital, trust and so on. This book aims at providing first directions to achieve these goals. In the final analysis of social capital in virtual communities, trust continues to occupy a central position within understanding of social capital but it is not the only variable. Other variables such as awareness influence trust formation in virtual communities. Nonetheless, trust by itself is confounded by other variables and its measurement continues to be challenging.

As discussed in chapter V, research studies that have used trust as proxy for measuring social capital have not properly treated its complexity. But ultimately, trust will continue to be a critical ingredient and a lubricant to almost many forms of social interactions in virtual communities. Trusting relationships enable people to work together, collaborate, and smoothly exchange information and share knowledge without time worsted on negotiation and conflict. In an event where individuals are considerably diverse, trust can help individuals create common goals and shared understanding. Without trust individuals will remain disconnected from each other and they will not get along with each other, let alone work together. In virtual communities, in trusting someone on their ability to effectively perform a task, trust depends on such instances as a person's competence level, acquired skills, self-integrity, and honesty.

There are many ways of enhancing trust in virtual communities. Trust can be generated through continuous interactions and engagement where appropriate tools and environment in which such interactions can effectively take place are provided to participants. Interactions and engagement as necessary perquisites for building trust depend on the attitudes of people involved and their levels of awareness. In other words, positive attitudes can produce high trust and the reverse is true. Building trust in virtual communities requires understanding of awareness. It also entails understanding the conditions in which people gets acquainted with each other, develops relationships, and gets to understand each other better. This is also partly dependent on how people can develop shared understanding, especially on issues of mutual concern. Shared understanding in virtual learning communities develop when people engage in productive discourse.

The idea about awareness in virtual communities cuts across many other issues in virtual communities. For example, to easily share information online, people have to be willing to share information and be aware of the information that can be shared and the people with whom they can share information. Further, there is a need to be aware of others, where they are located, what they do, the tasks and goals of interactions, shared understanding, the environment, and the available tools for interactions.

As discussed earlier in the book, different kinds of awareness have different bearings on trust and subsequently social capital. This book uncovers these issues as fundamental to our understanding of social capital in virtual communities. Finally, we are now closer to having a productive discourse on social capital in virtual communities. It is my hope that this book has provided sufficient insights and prepared the table for a theoretical and a practical discourse on how we can tap into these intangible resources and come up with useful tools and procedures to measure this immeasurable moving target.

Appendix:
Results of the Sensitivity Analysis

Probability of new finding = 2 %, of all findings = 2 %.

Sensitivity of 'SocialCapital' to findings at 'SocialCapital'				
Probability ranges	*Min*	*Current*	*Max*	*RMS Change*
High	0	0.6875	1	0.4635
Low	0	0.3125	1	0.4635
Entropy reduction = 0.8961 (100 %)				
Belief Variance = 0.2149 (100 %)				

Sensitivity of 'SocialCapital' to findings at 'DemogCultAwareness'				
Probability ranges	*Min*	*Current*	*Max*	*RMS Change*
High	0.5823	0.6875	0.7372	0.07232
Low	0.2628	0.3125	0.4177	0.07232
Entropy reduction = 0.01716 (1.91 %)				
Belief Variance = 0.00523 (2.43 %)				

Sensitivity of 'SocialCapital' to findings at 'SProtocols'				
Probability ranges	*Min*	*Current*	*Max*	*RMS Change*
High	0.5856	0.6875	0.7328	0.06796
Low	0.2672	0.3125	0.4144	0.06796
Entropy reduction = 0.01513 (1.69 %)				
Belief Variance = 0.004619 (2.15 %)				

Sensitivity of 'SocialCapital' to findings at 'ProfCultAwareness'				
Probability ranges	*Min*	*Current*	*Max*	*RMS Change*
High	0.5557	0.6875	0.7199	0.06539
Low	0.2801	0.3125	0.4443	0.06539
Entropy reduction = 0.01374 (1.53 %)				
Belief Variance = 0.004276 (1.99 %)				

Sensitivity of 'SocialCapital' to findings at 'Trust'				
Probability ranges	*Min*	*Current*	*Max*	*RMS Change*
High	0.5472	0.6875	0.7071	0.05254
Low	0.2929	0.3125	0.4528	0.05254
Entropy reduction = 0.008786 (0.98 %)				
Belief Variance = 0.00276 (1.28 %)				

Sensitivity of 'SocialCapital' to findings at 'Engagement'				
Probability ranges	*Min*	*Current*	*Max*	*RMS Change*
High	0.4405	0.6875	0.6925	0.03528
Low	0.3075	0.3125	0.5595	0.03528
Entropy reduction = 0.003828 (0.427 %)				
Belief Variance = 0.001245 (0.579 %)				

Sensitivity of 'SocialCapital' to findings at 'Attitudes'				
Probability ranges	*Min*	*Current*	*Max*	*RMS Change*
High	0.5447	0.6875	0.6933	0.02884
Low	0.3067	0.3125	0.4553	0.02884
Entropy reduction = 0.002628 (0.293 %)				
Belief Variance = 0.0008319 (0.387 %)				

Sensitivity of 'SocialCapital' to findings at 'KnowledgeAwareness'				
Probability ranges	*Min*	*Current*	*Max*	*RMS Change*
High	0.5697	0.6875	0.6928	0.02515
Low	0.3072	0.3125	0.4303	0.02515
Entropy reduction = 0.002016 (0.225 %)				
Belief Variance = 0.0006326 (0.294 %)				

Sensitivity of 'SocialCapital' to findings at 'SharedUndertanding'				
Probability ranges	*Min*	*Current*	*Max*	*RMS Change*
High	0.6663	0.6875	0.6947	0.01237
Low	0.3053	0.3125	0.3337	0.01237
Entropy reduction = 0.0005102 (0.0569 %)				
Belief Variance = 0.0001531 (0.0713 %)				

About the Author

Ben K. Daniel is a researcher and an interim manager for Research and Innovation with the Office of the Associate Vice President Research-Health (University of Saskatchewan)/Vice President Research and Innovation (Saskatoon Health Region), Saskatoon Canada. Dr. Daniel also lectures on Statistics, Research Methods and Communication Technologies at the University of Saskatchewan—Canada. Dr. Daniel is an eclectic scholar with a vast array of training and experiences drawn from many disciplines, some of which include graduate training in Computer Science, Educational and Training Systems Design, Philosophy, Statistics and Communications Technologies. Dr. Daniel has extensively published over fifty peer-reviewed conference papers, six International and National Journal articles and 10 book Chapters on variety of topics in advanced learning technologies. He reviews for half a dozen international conferences and journals on advanced learning technologies and knowledge management. His research has won two major national and international awards and was nominated for a couple of international awards. In the past, he held numerous undergraduate and graduate fellowships, awards and was a Dutch NUFFIC University Fellow at the University of Twente, Enschede, the Netherlands. Dr. Daniel has recently developed curiosity in eHealth Systems. He is interested in exploring new techniques and opportunities for extending virtual communities and social networking systems to the domain of eHealth.

Index